VEGETABLE GARDENING

This book includes: The bible to Build an Organic, Greenhouse or Raised Bed Garden and the innovation Hydroponic System that You Can Use Even in Your Backyard to Grow Vegetables, Fruits, and Herbs

© Copyright 2021 - All rights reserved.

The content contained within this book may not be reproduced, duplicated or transmitted without direct written permission from the author or the publisher.
Under no circumstances will any blame or legal responsibility be held against the publisher, or author, for any damages, reparation, or monetary loss due to the information contained within this book. Either directly or indirectly.

Legal Notice:

This book is copyright protected. This book is only for personal use. You cannot amend, distribute, sell, use, quote or paraphrase any part, or the content within this book, without the consent of the author or publisher.

Disclaimer Notice:

Please note the information contained within this document is for educational and entertainment purposes only. All effort has been executed to present accurate, up to date, and reliable, complete information. No warranties of any kind are declared or implied.

Readers acknowledge that the author is not engaging in the rendering of legal, financial, medical or professional advice. The content within this book has been derived from various sources. Please consult a licensed professional before attempting any techniques outlined in this book.

By reading this document, the reader agrees that under no circumstances is the author responsible for any losses, direct or indirect, which are incurred as a result of the use of information contained within this document, including, but not limited to, errors, omissions, or inaccuracies.

VEGETABLE GARDENING

- INTRODUCTION 8
- • A NEW WAY TO GARDEN: WIDE, DEEP, RAISED BED GARDEN 18
- • WHY PEOPLE SHOULD CHOOSE RAISED BED GARDENING 32
- • PLANNING YOUR GARDEN, GROWING YOUR PLANT 43
- • STEP BY STEP GUIDE TO STARTING AND SUSTAINING A VEGETABLE GARDEN 52
- • GROWING A SELF-SUFFICIENT GARDEN 62
- • GET TO KNOW ORGANIC GARDENING 71
- • NURTURING VEGETABLE-FRIENDLY SOIL AND COMPOST 83
- • HARVESTING YOUR VEGETABLE GARDEN 93
- • LIST OF THE MAIN VEGETABLES AND HERBS WITH DESCRIPTION AND EXPLANATION FOR GROWING THEM 104
- • SYMPTOMS AND SOLUTIONS: PROBLEM-SOLVING GUIDE 124
- • FREQUENTLY ASKED QUESTIONS 135
- CONCLUSION 142

HYDROPONICS

- **INTRODUCTION** 148
- **CHAPTER 1.** WHAT IS HYDROPONICS? 153
- **CHAPTER 2.** EQUIPMENTS 165
- **CHAPTER 3.** HYDROPONICS GROWING SYSTEM: OVERVIEW OF THE DIFFERENT HYDROPONICS SYSTEMS AND CHOOSING THE RIGHT HYDROPONIC SYSTEM FOR YOU 182
- **CHAPTER 4.** BUILD YOUR OWN HYDROPONIC SYSTEM 192
- **CHAPTER 5.** PROS AND CONS - THE DIFFERENT TYPES OF HYDROPONIC SYSTEMS 202
- **CHAPTER 6.** PLANTS TO GROW IN YOU HYDROPONIC SYSTEM 208
- **CHAPTER 7.** PLANT NUTRITION 220
- **CHAPTER 8.** SYSTEM MAINTANACE 229
- **CHAPTER 9.** GETTING RID OF COMMON PESTS ... 239
- **CHAPTER 10.** POTENTIAL PROBLEMS AND HOW TO OVERCOME THEM 249
- **CHAPTER 11.** HYDROPONIC TIPS AND TRICKS FOR BEGINNERS 255
- **CHAPTER 12.** HYDROPONICS AS BUSINESS 260
- **CONCLUSION** 269

GREENHOUSE GARDENING

- **INTRODUCTION** 273
- • **TYPES OF GREENHOUSE** 276
- • **CONSTRUCTING A GREENHOUSE** 292
- • **GREENHOUSE ENVIRONMENT** 300
- • **ESSENTIALS FOR YOUR GREENHOUSE** 304
- • **AIR FLOW, COOLING AND HUMIDITY** 310
- • **GREENHOUSE IRRIGATION SYSTEMS** 316
- • **HEATING YOUR GREENHOUSE** 321
- • **GROWING IN YOUR GREENHOUSE** 330
- • **SCHEDULING IN YOUR GREENHOUSE** 342
- • **GREENHOUSE ENVIRONMENTAL CONTROL SYSTEMS** 345
- • **GREENHOUSE CLEANING AND MAINTENANCE** . 355
- • **HYDROPONICS IN A GREENHOUSE** 359
- • **POTENTIAL PROBLEMS AND HOW TO OVERCOME THEM** 366
- • **MAKING MONEY FROM YOUR GREENHOUSE** 375
- **CONCLUSION** 383

VEGETABLE GARDENING

Introduction

Most people who practice organic gardening hope to live a more sustainable, clean, healthy, and earth-friendly way of life. However, there are many reasons that a person may choose the organic gardening method. We will go over the many reasons why you may choose organic. Whether you are a beginner or a pro at gardening it is never too late to begin the organic transition!

The Effects of Pesticides

Chemical pesticides are known to have many problems in the environment, health, and more. However, the information of these effects is often hidden by large corporations who make their money off of these pesticides. This leaves the public largely confused on the effects, despite being eager to make the best choices from themselves and their families. Thankfully, while large corporations may try to hide this information, they are unable to get rid of it altogether. In this portion, let's examine what is known about these chemical-based pesticides and their risks.

While you may think that the use of chemical-based pesticides doesn't cause long-lasting effects, the truth is that they linger for long periods of time. In truth, long after these chemical pesticides have been used they remain in the soil, atmosphere, and even waterways. As these have been used throughout the world for nearly a hundred years, there is quite a bit of chemical pollution lingering in the atmosphere due to their use. By continuing to use chemical-based pesticides, the problems they cause are only compounded upon.

Why do chemical pesticides cause such far-reaching damaging effects? The Agricultural MU Guide for Pesticides and the Environment explains the problem. In order for chemical pesticides to be effective, they must have the ability to travel within the soil. However, by having this ability the pesticides move too far within the soil, contaminating a larger area than intended. This not only contaminates more soil than intended, but it also contaminates water, the atmosphere, animals, and humans. These pesticides always travel and contaminate outside of their intended area of use.

The United States government has released reports proving that with the use of chemical-based pesticides the nutritional value of fruits and vegetables has declined. Between the years 1940 and 1991, the trace minerals within produce dropped by a shocking seventy-six percent, directly related to the use of pesticides.

Research has routinely found that many foods have a depleted nutritional value and that these foods contain residual presides from being grown with non-organic methods. Some foods contain an especially high number of residual chemical-based pesticides after being grown, including strawberries, tomatoes, spinach, potatoes, apples, grapes, celery, pears, kale, peaches, nectarines, and cherries.

These chemicals may help to fight off insects, but in the same way that they kill and harm insects, they cause harm to the environment, animals, and even humans. These chemical-based pesticides are simply not meant to be ingested by humans, as they are designed to kill and harm living organisms.

It is plain to see how chemical-based pesticides can cause a myriad of problems when ingested by humans. Because of this, there have been many studies examining the matter. One of the biggest literature reviews, a series of multi-university studies in Toronto, concluded that people should limit their ingestion and exposure to chemical pesticides as much as possible, due to them being linked to causing serious long-term illnesses.

There are many illnesses that these pesticides have been linked to. To name a few they have been found to cause nervous system diseases, infertility, asthma, depression, birth defects, Parkinson's disease, miscarriages, and even cancers such as lymphoma and leukemia. The more a person is exposed to these pesticides the larger their risk of developing one or more of these diseases. Studies have found that people with certain types of cancer are more likely to have pesticides within their bloodstreams.

You don't even have to eat these pesticides in order to be contaminated by them. As they travel within the soil, water, and atmosphere they can easily affect anyone. In fact, they can be brought indoors when pets and children play outdoors and they come inside. The pesticides stick to clothing, fur, or skin to come inside, where it can then be absorbed by the skin and get into the bloodstream or also breathed in. This is most often the result of chemical pesticides being used for lawn care.

The United States Environmental Protection Agency (EPA) conducted a study and found that indoor pollutants can be two to five times greater than that outdoors. In fact, indoor air pollution has been rated as one of the top four environmental health risks in America. As pesticides, gases, and microscopic particles build up indoors families suffer the effects.

Thankfully, you can greatly decrease this by making a change and going organic. You don't have to risk your health or that of your family. Even if you don't go organic in all areas of life, by making a change and beginning organic gardening you can greatly decrease the pesticides your family is affected by.

Benefits to the Going Organic

Now that we've explored the dangers of pesticides, let's examine the benefits of going organic. You now know the repercussions of not going organic, but the benefits of an organic lifestyle are more than you would imagine.

Organic farming greatly benefits the environment and helps it heal from the damage caused by chemical-based pesticides. This is because organic farmers know that if they take care of the environment it will, in turn, take care of them by providing them with nutrient-dense fruits and vegetables. Not only that, but it also decreases water pollution, topsoil loss, soil poisoning, toxic runoff, and the death of environmentally beneficial bugs and animals.

To this end, organic farmers greatly focus on the health of the soil that they plant their seeds in. Rather than using pesticides, fungicides, and herbicides, these organic farmers are able to use environmentally beneficial and natural methods to keep the soil healthy and also promote the health of the food grown in it.

Due to the care that organic farmers put into their soil, the vitamins and minerals found within the foods grown this way are much higher than those found in non-organic methods. This is due to the organic soil itself containing more minerals and nutrients that humans require. A systematic review by The Soil Association found that organically grown foods on average contain a higher amount of vitamin C, iron, magnesium, calcium, chromium, and other nutrients than non-organic produce. In fact, the independent review found that organic produce contains higher levels of all analyzed twenty-one nutrients. The study found that organic potatoes, cabbage, spinach, and lettuce contain an especially elevated number of minerals.

Along with elevated nutrition and decreased risk of disease by going organic, it may also benefit your mental health. Not only will the decrease in pesticide consumption likely reduce depression, but spending time in the garden is known as horticultural therapy. This is because spending time outdoors while working with plants and in the soil is peaceful and meditative. Horticultural therapy has been used in many ways, including to help people with psychological, educational, social, and physical adjustments while improving their mind and body.

This type of therapy was made official in 1973 when the American Horticultural Therapy Association (AHTA) was established. This organization works to train medical personnel and therapists on how to treat mental illness, substance abuse, and physical illnesses with gardening. Yet, even if you are perfectly healthy in mind and body, horticultural therapy may still benefit you! Studies have found that adults have much higher levels of daily stress and anxiety than in past generations. But, by utilizing gardening and horticultural therapy you can decrease your daily stress, improve your mood, and therefore improve your long-term health.

Everyone can improve their mood and mental health by feeling personal rewards from accomplishments. Imagine when you were a child, how satisfied you felt whenever you successfully hit a baseball, got praise for drawing a picture, or got a good grade. Whether a person struggles with their mental health or not, these feelings of accomplishment are an important part of staying happy and satisfied in life.

Gardening can increase a person's sense of accomplishment and reward, as they can directly see the beneficial outcomes gained from their efforts. As a person sees their sees beginning to grow, flowers bloom or bring in the harvest they can feel proud of themselves and enjoy the fruits of their labor. This process can also increase feelings of peace, patience, compassion, and gratefulness, which have been shown to increase a person's overall mood, improve their intersections with others, and decrease stress levels.

If you have children, then gardening may also help to bring your family together. The National Gardening Association claims that gardening has the ability to teach children valuable life lessons. If you bring your family into the garden, then it is a wonderful way to teach children the importance of hard work, completing chores, and helping the family. Children can also learn patience as they wait for the seeds to grow into plants, how to handle disappointment when a plant dies at the end of the growing season, and responsibility as they must properly and consistently water and care for the garden.

With a largely damaged economy and many Americans unable to afford basic healthcare, owning their own homes, or new vehicles people look for a way to save money. Thankfully, while organic living may at first appear to be expensive, you would be surprised by how much money it can save you. Even if you live in an apartment, as long as you have a balcony you can practice these methods with container gardening..

Yes, synthetic chemicals and pesticides are less expensive than purchasing organic supplies. However, there are many ways in which you can save money with organic gardening, making it less expensive in the long-run.

While chemical-based gardening supplies focus on feeding the plants, organic gardening focuses on feeding the soil. Not only does this increase the nutritional value of food grown in the soil, but it keeps the soil healthier for years to come. This means that rather than buying supplies to feed your garden time and again, the soil stays healthy with just a little work. Over time, you will find that you are spending much less money on sustaining your garden while maximizing its health and efficiency. This method is known as "feeding the soil, not the plant" as it is more sustainable and will continue to keep an entire garden healthy for years to come, rather than only feeding a plant for a single season.

One of the best approaches to both saving money and keeping your garden soil healthy is composting. By allowing organic materials, such as fruit and vegetable peels, to healthfully and naturally decompose it creates a nutrient-dense fertilizer for your garden. This saves you money so that you don't have to buy fertilizer and is also better for the planet

America is the worst country when it comes to having large landfills. While other countries have virtually eliminated landfills and replaced them with innovative recycling methods, America is behind the times in this aspect. These landfills are harming the environment. Not only that, but these landfills are filling up and finding new spaces for landfills is not easy. But, by practicing organic gardening paired with composting you can help make a dent in these landfills. Studies have shown that one-third of America's landfills are full of organic waste from peoples' kitchens and yards. You can recycle your kitchen waste, leaves, and grass in a compost bin, which will benefit the environment, your garden, and your budget.

A study by the National Gardening Association (NGA) found that a small garden with an average-sized plot can produce approximately three-hundred pounds of fresh produce, retailing at a six-hundred-dollar value. This data is based on the average gardener investing seventy dollars into their garden, giving them a return of five-hundred and thirty dollars! This is pretty impressive and can be easily achieved whether you use gardening beds or container gardening.

In order to save the most money, look at produce you already regularly eat or those which you most enjoy. For instance, if you like to cook with fresh herbs these would be a wonderful investment to grow yourself. While buying fresh herbs in the grocery store is expensive, they are easy to grow both outdoors and indoors. Similarly, if you know that you enjoy tomatoes, cucumbers, kale, and green beans then you may choose to focus on growing these items. By growing what you most purchase and enjoy you can save money and decrease your grocery budget.

If you have the time and space, rather than buying plants at the gardening center you can begin with seeds. These cost a great deal less, and if you start sprouting them in seed starters at the beginning of the season you can have a plant at a fraction of the cost. If you purchase heirloom seeds online, you can even reuse the seeds that you gain from your vegetables the following year if you save them properly.

If you find yourself with a harvest larger than you can eat, this is even more beneficial! You can learn to freeze and can excess fruits and vegetables, which you can then eat when they are out of seasoning and no longer growing. This effort will save you money in the future and provide you with delicious home-grown vegetables when they could not otherwise be grown. Because of this, you may even decide to purposefully grow more than you can eat in a season so that you can enjoy them in the offseason.

Many people who garden use chemical-based pesticides, fungicides, herbicides, and fertilizers. These people simply don't feel like there is another choice. Even if they have heard about organic farming they may have a misconception that it's difficult. Yet, these people have not stopped and asked themselves a simple question about gardening. This question is so simple that it is easy to forget, it's unnoticeable. But, the question is why do we need to use these chemical-based products in a garden if they are not needed in nature? Plants can thrive in nature without these products, without dying due to disease and insects. Why is it that these chemical-based products only seem to be needed in domestic gardens?

The answer is that they are not needed. Many people simply don't have the knowledge of how to garden without these products, largely due to marketing by the chemical-based product companies. Thankfully, learning this knowledge is easy and can be used by any beginner.

- **A New Way To Garden: Wide, Deep, Raised Bed Garden**

Raised beds combine the best features of in-ground and container gardens. Like containers, with proper mulching, you won't need to weed as often. But unlike containers, the plants' ability to send their roots into the native soil to access water and nutrients cuts down on both watering and fertilizing. Raised bed gardens, when done right, are very attractive. (Many people build raised beds on top of a solid surface such as paved ground. This design acts more like a container garden in terms of soil, water, fertilization, and drainage requirements.)

Starting a raised bed garden is a great way to accommodate that budding little gardener in your family. It is the ideal way for kids to learn about nature; they will see the wonder of a little seedling emerging from the ground, growing tiny leaves, and later develop into a mature plant with fruit. Planting in raised beds will make it convenient for both you and the young ones to reach every planet in the box without ending up with muddy feet or knees full of dirt.

Most gardeners who choose raised beds find the trade-offs to be worth it both in time saved over the season and their overall gardening experience. Almost all crops grow well in raised beds; some popular ones include tomatoes, beans, broccoli, peppers, onions, and zucchini.

Everything you are going to produce, with the assistance of this Raised Bed manual, is a way of raising fruits, vegetables, and veggies, with no usage of any dirt. The origins will rely upon a nutritionally enhanced liquid. They're nourished in warm water together with liquid nourishment. You can use different mediums, like perlite and vermiculite, or perhaps Rockwool or clay beans.

There are a variety of methods for conducting this kind of garden. Within this publication, I'll explain each procedure that will assist you in determining which works best on your situation. Following that, you'll be prepared to purchase a kit or put together your equipment, as stated by the method you pick. To do so, you want to consider the following:

What's the magnitude of this room for the Raised Beds installation?

If you're a newcomer to Raised Bed farming, then it's much better to start little.

Can it be inside or out?

If you're lucky enough to have a pretty sized lawn, then you need to consider preparing a subway system. Raised Beds may be installed outside, but you may be more likely to fleas or even the vagaries of the weather. In case you've got a spare indoor space, you'll have to consider the lighting source.

Price?

You'll need particular sorts of gear; however, you can restrict the price should you start little.

Which kind of crops do you desire to grow?

It's possible to grow more or less any plant utilizing Raised Bed growing, like fruits, vegetables, vegetables, herbs, and even blossoms.

What time do you have accessible for upkeep?

If you're a newcomer, then it's far better to develop flowering plants. You will find lots to select from, including carrot, carrot, strawberries, or berries. Not one of them demands much in the method of your own time. In this way, you know at a constant pace and may alter your system, or crops, as you're more seasoned. If you like that, then you're able to move on into the more complicated plants.

Pros/Cons Of Raised Bed Gardening

Well, to begin with, you will not get dirt on your nails, and that is a fantastic beginning!

Among the most noteworthy features of developing using this way is the crops use much less water than they ever might if grown as plants on the floor. Raised Bed farming utilizes just 10 percent of the water which conventional ground plants utilize. Now that is a guess worth considering.

Could that be the future of farming in states in which water is a scarce resource? Already it's becoming more popular. Thus, let us consider the desirable features of a Raised Bed garden or even farming method:

PROS

No Soil, Less Land

No dirt at all. Your crops will increase within a water-based system. Liquid nutrients can help them develop into adulthood. The vast acres of land used for farming may be utilized for different needs like home and woods. Additionally, it usually means that the more vegetation could be increased into smaller plots.

Less Water

You're able to grow plants anywhere, any time of the season, irrespective of climate. The system you select is only going to use a fixed quantity of water in line with the dimensions of your farming method. With the assistance of simple gear, the plant roots sit at the pool. It is similar to area plants where the water soaks off to the floor or pops up with the warmth of sunlight. The water on your system may be re-used again and more. Thus you're recycling it. No irrigation of this property is necessary, hence fewer costs to the farmer.

Comparatively Nutrients, Less Fertilizer

Nutrients are fed into the plants in a controlled environment rather than working off and tapping into the earth, polluting rivers, and land. Envision a farming globe without the necessity of spraying compost all around the property.

More Compounds, Fewer Enemies

The ventilation methods, for example, within your house or a greenhouse, possess great benefits. There's not any loss of plants as a result of poor weather. Wild animals can't consume the crops as they could with plants. Without dirt, there'll also be fewer bugs and diseases to cope with.

The external systems still get the job done effectively, but in case your Raised Bed garden isn't secure, then it might continue to be more prone to problems from insects and also the weather.

Healthier Plants

Plants increased by the Raised Bed system enjoy 100 percent of the nutrients fed into them. None will soak in the earth or be blown off by the end. The result of this is they create around 30 percent more foliage than soil-grown plants and increase 25% quicker. It's all down into the well-balanced nutrients that the roots get out of the water.

Fewer Chemicals Needed

With fewer parasitic germs, fewer weeds and insecticides are wanted. The result is healthy meals for human consumption.

Weather Resistant

Raised Bed plants grown inside aren't weathered dependent. They may be built all year round, whatever the weather or temperature. Plants are far more shielded when grown indoors or in greenhouses.

Less Labor

There'll not be any labor-intensive weeding required, either, or hand. It enhances the demand for upkeep. There'll be the first seeding, feeding, and harvesting that are accomplished with much less labor than the standard ways of growing plants.

Could be Grown Anywhere, Geographically

This process doesn't depend on accessible land. The farm may be installed close to the marketplace where the plants will be marketed. It is an excellent method of cutting down on transportation costs and contamination. It may even be portable if needed, and put up where and whenever required.

An approach to Satisfy Budgets

There are lots of procedures for developing crops with a Raised Bed system. It is sometimes a small affair in your garden or inside in a room. However, it may also be performed on a commercial scale. Massive amounts of produce thousands of plants for a country of individuals can be accomplished using Raised Bed farming.

CONS

Plants are determined by people. Nature has little to do with this kind of farming. The crops are relying upon a human focus for all, from food, into humidity and light. When the garden is ready to go, it may enter restoration for the large part. Though as with farming, a person must control it. When it isn't done correctly, entire crops can be dropped.

Requires some Experience

It isn't a conventional way of growing crops. A specific quantity of understanding of the respective systems is needed. Done incorrectly, the entire harvest of crops can perish.

Safety

Everybody knows that electricity and water are a dangerous mix. Raised Bed plants require both power and water to deal with the whole system. If errors occur, it might lead to a life-threatening circumstance.

Electric Failure

What will occur if the power supply was down to almost any quantity of time? It has to be considered from the beginning. If anything were to happen, with no emergency supply, the entire harvest could expire in hours.

First Outlay for Big Farms

There's a need to purchase gear once you first install your purchasing system. That may be expensive if farming on a considerable scale. Once created, the operating costs will be power, water, and nutrition. Additionally, a little labor force if it's a massive farm.

Quick Genital Diseases

The odds of soil disorder are nil; therefore, diseases and pests are fewer. But if your system receives a water-based ailment, this can disperse quickly to any crops on precisely the same order. A way of quantifying the water to these bacteria has to be set in place to prevent this occurring. Otherwise, you can lose your whole harvest to illness.

Figuring Out Size and Shape

Most gardeners who can give an hour per week to garden tasks during peak season can easily manage a few raised beds. Although raised beds come in a variety of shapes and sizes, I recommend sticking with a conventional size. A simple 4-by-8-foot, 4-by-12-foot, or 3-by-6-foot bed provides plenty of plant layout options.

If you choose container gardening, you will likely find your limits not in the amount of time you can give but rather in your budget. Purchasing containers and soil can become costly. You can always start with a few containers and add more as your budget allows.

Mix and Match Garden Types

What if you can't decide on the type of garden you want? Many gardeners enjoy growing with a mixture of these forms. I grow vegetables and herbs in the ground, in raised beds, and in containers. Because there are pros and cons to each method, I use each to my advantage.

Frequently harvested plants such as herbs and greens are ideal container plants. Some vegetables, such as onions and peppers, thrive in the warm, well-draining (but not too well-draining) soil of raised beds. And some crops, such as corn, are best suited to the larger space of an in-ground garden.

Regardless of the place, remember vertical gardening. Tomatoes, cucumbers, and pole beans, for example, benefit from trellising whether in containers, raised beds, or the ground.

How to Build a Raised Bed Garden

You can find a myriad of options and plans for building a raised bed, but I'll share the most basic plan.

Preparing Your Site

The most important part of preparing your site is making sure it is level. Measure out the bed size and check its slope with a leveling tool. If there is any slope to the ground, you may need to scrape one side until the land is level on all sides.

If your ground contains pernicious weeds or grass, lay down an organic barrier, such as cardboard, to smother them. An alternative is to simply scrape the top layer of vegetation and turn it over; it will compost into the soil over time. If you think you may have rodents such as voles or moles, you will need a permanent barrier (hardware cloth, for example) because organic barriers will eventually break down into the soil.

Materials and Tools Needed

If you're willing to pay for convenience, purchasing raised bed kits is an option. But to save money and go the DIY route, you'll need these tools to construct a standard 4-by-8-foot, 10-inch-high raised bed:

- 3 (2-by-10-inch-by-8-foot) pieces of lumber (or 2 by 8 inches or 2 by 12 inches, depending on how tall you want your beds)
- Measuring tape
- Pencil

- Carpenter's square
- Circular saw or handsaw
- Drill or impact driver
- 12 (2½-inch) deck screws
- Roll of ¼-inch hardware cloth (optional)
- Staple gun (optional)
- Level

The most durable and budget-friendly wood is pressure-treated pine, widely available at home supply stores.

Building Your Raised Bed

Once you gather the materials, set aside a few hours to build your raised bed. Though it can be built by one person, an extra set of hands is always useful.

1. Take one 8-foot board and mark it with the pencil 4 feet from the end. Use a carpenter's square to draw a vertical line across the board.
2. Cut the board at the vertical line with a saw.
3. Situate one 8-foot board perpendicular to one 4-foot board, where their ends meet flush. Position the other corners of the raised bed the same way.
4. Using the drill, pre-drill the holes. Then, screw each of the four corners together where the boards meet, using three deck screws per corner.
5. If you're using hardware cloth to cover the bottom of the bed (this prevents ground-dwelling rodents from getting to your plants from underneath), spread the cloth over the bed, stapling it in place. If it doesn't cover the entire

bed and you have to use two strips, make sure you have a 6-inch overlap between strips.

6. Carry the bed to its site and position it. Set the level on each of the four sides, ensuring the bed is level in all directions. If the bed isn't level, use a shovel to scrape down higher areas of dirt until the bed is level.

For a raised bed, you want a slightly "heavier" medium (soil mixture) than for a container garden.

Plants that grow vertically or taller than others should be planted on the north, east, or northeast part of your raised bed. Lower-growing plants should go on the south, west, or southwest side. This way, tall crops, such as tomatoes or pole beans, do not shade shorter crops, such as peppers or sweet potatoes, from the much-needed southwesterly sun exposure. The exception is if you plan to grow cool-weather crops, such as greens, further into the summer. These crops benefit from afternoon shade and may grow longer before bolting if provided with shade. (For gardeners in the southern hemisphere, these cardinal directions will be opposite.)

How to Cover Your Garden

Most gardens will benefit from some type of covering to protect them from the elements during at least part of the year.

Floating row covers help gardeners begin their growing season earlier and extend it later. Air- and water-permeable covers made from lightweight polyester fabric protect crops from frost, allowing a few extra weeks of growing time on the bookends of the season. For in-ground gardens and raised beds, you can make arches with PVC pipe and lay the cover on top for a dome effect. Attach the cover to the PVC with clamps to ensure it doesn't blow off. For small plantings or for those in containers, placing upside-down plastic pots or cups on top of vulnerable plants works well. (Place a rock on top of the pot or cup to prevent it from blowing away.)

In some areas, wind damage is a major concern. Siting your garden on the south or southwest side of a structure or natural brush offers some protection. Well-anchored floating row covers can also protect lower-growing or young crops from wind.

Many gardeners find their biggest challenge isn't the cold or wind, but heat. Particularly in the southern United States, the recommended full-sun location might translate to stressed plants when temperatures rise to almost 100°F

How to Make Your Own Soil Mix

The biggest advantage to growing in containers or raised beds is that you can control the soil medium.

The soil for both types of gardens contains many of the same ingredients, with slight variations. Therefore, my soil mix recipes vary. With containers, drainage is critical, because soggy soil will cause rot and plant death, which is why you should never put garden soil in containers. Raised beds, on the other hand, benefit from the moisture-holding capacity of garden soil.

Many online soil mix recipes contain a diverse range of ingredients, and although diversity is good, it's more important at this stage for soil making to be practical, inexpensive, and doable.

Here is a list of common soil components, available in most garden centers or online:

- Coconut coir: an alternative to peat moss serving the same function but with a neutral pH

- Compost: final product of decayed living matter that adds fertility; can be purchased or homemade

- Peat moss: organic material derived from peat bogs that holds moisture and nutrients and contributes to the structure and tilt of soil, but has a low pH

- Perlite: volcanic glass expanded through heat that adds aeration

- Vermiculite: a combination of heat-expanded minerals that adds aeration while increasing water retention

Container Soil Mix

3 parts peat moss or coconut coir

3 parts finished compost

2 parts perlite

1 part vermiculite

This forms the base. I recommend adding up to 1 part worm castings or up to ¼ part slow-release organic fertilizer. If you use peat moss, add 1 ounce of dolomitic lime for every 1 gallon of peat (do not do this if planting potatoes).

Raised Bed Soil Mix

1 part topsoil (bagged or native)

1 part finished compost (homemade, bulk compost, or OMRI-certified bagged)

1 part other organic materials

For the 1 part other organic materials, I've had success using peat moss, vermiculite, composted chicken manure, and worm castings. Other options include greensand, bio char, coconut coir (in place of peat moss), and perlite.

As you can see, you have some flexibility. The key is to include materials that offer both water retention and drainage, as well as rich organic material. If all this overwhelms you, however, go for bagged mixes, though I recommend choosing organic blends for the long-term health of your garden.

- **Why People Should Choose Raised Bed Gardening**

Companion planting works perfectly in raised beds. Those vegetables which need more space for their roots like carrots should be planted on top while others like leeks and onions will fill up the space on the sides of your beds. The leeks and onions repel pests and will act as a shield for the carrot plants on the top of the bed.

These are but a few of the numerous benefits of gardening in raised beds. Therefore, it is not surprising to find that our modern-day gardeners are turning their attention with more frequency to this method. They have added a twist, though; now solid frames replace these sloping sides to give the raised beds a distinct and well-defined structure. What this means is that you can make the beds as high or tall as you want them to be without the danger of soil runoff when it rains.

It might sound like a huge job, but these modern raised gardening beds are easy to assemble or build by yourself. Frames can be built with concrete blocks, timber, or bricks and then filled with many organic materials mixed with soil. You will find kits ready for assembling as well as prefabricated plastic containers at almost any gardening center. Now anyone and everyone can easily and successfully grow their vegetables in raised beds and enjoy their own fresh produce.

I will now point out some of the many benefits of this gardening method.

1.   Excellent Aeration

The older, traditional way to create raised beds is simply to dig up the soil, piling it into rows. You can follow this method and then support the two sides by using solid frames. Otherwise, place your frames in place and then fill them up with compost, farmyard manure mixed with quality soil. Whichever way you choose to do it, your plants will flourish in this enriched soil, and its loose structure will allow excellent air circulation around all the roots.

We know that the different parts of plants all need to breathe, and so do the roots. For example, during photosynthesis, the leaves take in carbon dioxide and expel oxygen. If your plant sits in compact soil, the roots will suffocate and will not succeed in developing fully. This is because they need good aeration for their roots to be able to absorb the essential nutrients in the soil. To explain further, the soil bacteria convert the nitrogen in the little air pockets into nitrate salts and nitrate, thus providing the macronutrients for the plant. Without sufficient air, there is a lack of nitrogen, and therefore less nutrients will be available to the plant.

It is clear that the population of microbes in your vegetable soil must be kept healthy, and this is made possible with good aerated soil. The balance of anaerobic and aerobic bacteria should be maintained as they all play their different roles to enhance the fertility of the soil.

2. Good Drainage

Even during a downpour of rain, your raised beds will render good drainage. No wonder this method is so popular in the tropics with its heavy rainfall. Because the soil has such a loose texture, water will seep slowly into the bed instead of a making a quick runoff with the accompanying washing away of all fertile topsoil. Furthermore, all the excess water can easily drain away.

Although most plants do not mind moisture at all, they hate to get their feet wet. Firstly, all that water around their roots will make breathing almost impossible. Secondly, too much moisture will promote fungal and bacterial diseases. Lastly, excess water drenching the soil can change its pH level and raise the acidity. Plants which prefer more neutral or slightly alkaline soil will suffer as a result.

Some plants, for example, those that live in bogs, are adapted to grow in drenched soil, but most plants prefer soil with a twenty-five percent-moisture level. Raised beds will not allow water stagnation while at the same time, they keep your soil quite evenly moist because the water soaks into the lowest levels of your beds quickly.

3. The Spreading of Roots

Although plant roots can be quite persistent in their effort to grow, they will find it difficult to do so in tightly compacted soil. In loose soil they can grow and spread out to their hearts' content. Furthermore, a framed bed will retain the moisture after watering a lot longer than the more traditionally raised beds because the frames prevent water loss on the sides of the beds more effectively. Drying out of the beds can, therefore, be prevented and good root spreading will follow.

Plants growing in non-raised garden beds generally have a very shallow system of roots since they find it impossible to penetrate through the more compact soil deeper down unless of course, you go to the trouble of tilling the soil deeply before you plant your vegetables. This means that the plant roots are unable to get to the moisture kept in the deeper layers, which in turn may lead to dehydration of the plant when the moisture on the surface evaporates. Well-developed root systems anchor your plants. It also enlarges the potential food source area from which the plant can gather its nutrients and water. Vegetable plants, in particular, need enough of both to encourage vigorous growth and maximum yield during their relatively short growing season.

4. Minimum Risk of Compact Soil

A raised bed will not completely deter your smaller pets like dogs and cats from digging and rolling around in your gardening soil, but it definitely will keep humans and larger pets or animals at bay. This will prevent the tamping down of the soil. The ideal width for your raised beds is three to four feet, making it easy for you to do your gardening chores such as weeding, harvesting, and fertilizing without having to step onto the beds.

The floods, which sometimes occur after a heavy downpour, can also compact the soil of cultivated fields. Wet soil is heavy and will sink down and fill all the little air pockets. Once the water has evaporated, you will be left with a dense, hard layer that is not very accommodating for the plants. Raised beds allow the water to drain away much quicker, preventing floods to cause soil compaction.

5. Improved Weed Control

Sick and tired of weeding? A raised bed garden is the answer. In a normal vegetable plot, you will find it hard to get rid of all the frustrating weeds no matter how dedicated you are. They just seem to take over all the time.

When you cultivate the soil for normal vegetable beds, you expose lot of the weed seeds that have been lying dormant underground shielded from the sun. The exposure to sunlight and extra moisture they receive during irrigation will provide them with the opportunity to start sprouting, just what they have been waiting for. Very quickly, they will feed on the nutrient-rich soil prepared for your vegetable plants and begin to flourish.

You can make use of the option to fill your raised beds with relatively weed-free soil and compost. If a few stray weeds appear, your raised beds with its loose soil will make weeding a breeze. A good tip is to fill up your raised beds with as many plants as will grow in it so that they will suffocate and outgrow any stubborn weeds that may try their luck.

6. Easier than Amending Existing Soil

Garden soil greatly varies from area to area; sometimes, it is more alkaline and chalky, often it is too acidic, and plants will not thrive without your intervention. Vegetables, in general, like slightly acidic to neutral soil, anything with a pH level of between 5.5 and 7.5. Having said that, there are exceptions. Blueberries and tomatoes, for instance, like more acidic soil while asparagus and broccoli prefer to have their roots in sweeter soil.

The remedy for alkaline soil is to add Sulphur, for acidic soil lime can be added. Sometimes applications have to be repeated a number of times to get the desired effect, but a downpour can undo all your hard work in a flash. It is not a simple, straightforward process to change the intrinsic nature of any type of soil.

If you plan to cultivate different kinds of vegetables, raised beds will give you the option of which soil you choose. On top of that, you can now fill up different raised beds with the type of soil each variety of vegetable prefers. The addition of lots of compost, something most gardeners usually do, makes it easier to sustain the soil's neutrality.

7. Garden on Top of Existing Turf

You have made the decision to start your own vegetable garden, but the task of having to dig up and clean the existing turf presently growing on the area you have targeted is just too daunting. Do not despair; raised vegetable beds can be built straight on top of your grass without having to dig up any sods.

Mark your area, and then place multiple layers of cardboard and newspaper on the area. Erect your frames and then simply continue to fill them with grass clippings, soil, sand, decomposed farmyard manure, and compost. Plant your seeds or seedlings in this rich mixture, and you have started your garden without too much backbreaking labor.

8. Avoid Root Run from Larger Plants and Trees

Sometimes you will find that the only available space left in your garden for your vegetables is near a number of well-established trees. These trees have massively huge roots to anchor them to the ground and will devour all the nutrients in the soil, leaving very little for your vegetable plants. You may be able to get rid of some of these invasive roots, but it is an impossible task to get completely rid of them all. Using chemicals to try to kill the roots is not an option because these very same chemicals can harm or even kill your vegetable plants. However, your raised beds will be safe from this problem since tree roots generally grow downwards and will not reach into the raised beds.

9. More Effective Pest Control

Creepy crawlies are true to their description, they usually enter vegetable patches this way, crawling away until they find food. Encountering an obstacle like a solid frame will definitely deter some of them from crawling up. They may just pick the easier option of continuing along the ground. To protect your plants from soil parasites like nematodes, line your raised beds along the sides and the bottom with plastic. If you fear annoying rodents burrowing their way into your beds, use a netting of wire, placing it at the bases of your beds.

Overall, it will be easier to rid your beds of the various offenders just because they are more accessible. Applying chemical or natural pesticides or picking out invaders by hand is a lot less cumbersome if you do not have to bend down to ground level all the time. Everything, including nasty pests, will be more visible to the eye too. Walking along your raised beds, inspecting your plants regularly, you can quickly detect infestations and deal with them immediately. Remember, the sooner you tackle any pests, the easier it will be to rid your vegetable garden of them.

10. Extra Available Space

Raised beds in the traditional fashion provide more space for plants growing along the sides of the beds. Although this advantage is not applicable to framed beds, they can provide additional space in another manner. Many of the plants growing along the side edges of the frames will extend over these side edges, leaving more room for other plants on the top surface of the bed. More light will be able to reach the plants as well.

Those varieties of tomatoes that normally will need staking can simply be allowed to grow downwards instead of upwards. Make sure the beds you plant them in are high enough. Strawberries and the vines of sweet potatoes tumbling down the sides of your raised beds will make a very pretty picture in your garden and create a luxurious aspect.

11. Extended Growing Season

We all know how long it takes the ground to thaw in spring, but raised beds speed up this thawing process. This means that you can start transplanting your seedlings much earlier in the season, giving them a wonderful head start. If the area where you live has a short window period to grow your edibles in the outside garden, this extra time will make a huge difference.

Some vegetables, for instance, onions, need a fairly long season to grow to maturity. Three to four months are needed for onions sets, and if you grow them from the seeds, it will take even longer. Seeds give you a much larger choice as only a few varieties are generally available assets. Making use of this advantage of choice means that you will need more time. Fortunately, onion seedlings like cooler weather, so plant them as soon as the soil in your raised beds has thawed.

Towards the end of the autumn, you can also extend your veggies' growing season; just place a few hoop covers onto your bed frames. This is easily done by installing pipe brackets made of metal from which you can attach or remove the hoop covers when necessary. Custom made covers in plastic or glass can be fitted for your individual raised beds as well.

12. Intensive Gardening with Higher Yield

It is a fact that a higher yield will be obtained by growing your veggies in raised beds rather on flat ground beds. Attributing factors are the good aeration of the soil and extensive root run, but the main cause is the intensive nature of this kind of gardening. Raised beds allow you to plant a greater variety of different kinds of vegetables closer together than could be done on flat ground.

Because the soil used in these raised beds contains more organic matter and compost, it is rich enough to support quite a number of extra plants, definitely more than usual. The plants will completely fill up the beds as they continue to grow with their foliage touching. The close proximity of the plants will prevent weeds from flourishing too.

13.   Solution for Mobility Challenged Gardeners

Not all gardeners are young, energetic, and healthy people. Many experienced gardeners find it difficult to continue bending down for weeding and tending their vegetable patches as they grow older and experience health challenges. Raised beds can be built or assembled to the exact width or height that will suit every individual. It can even be planned and laid out in a fashion to accommodate wheelchair users and allow them freedom of movement to plant and harvest their vegetables easily.

Even if you do not face any of these challenges, you will find it a relief to see to those vegetable plants that need constant attention if they are raised off the ground. Backbreaking work is never fun and may even cause injuries. Salad vegetables and herbs need frequent harvesting, and popping out into the garden to pick a few herbs for your meal will be a lot easier if you do not have to bend down all the time.

14.   Portability

If you find that your vegetable plants are not exposed to enough sunlight in their current spot, you can just move your raised bed without too much effort. Portability is one of the advantages of this method of gardening. Beds with wire bottoms can simply be dragged to a brighter location. Otherwise, dismantle the frames and then reassemble your beds in their new spots. With care, you can move the plants, as well as the soil, contend without any damage.

A very practical solution is to buy raised beds that are ready-made and fitted with casters. They are easily moved around, and if early frost overtakes you, they can even be rolled into your heated garage to save your plants.

There are quite a number of variations on the theme of raised bed gardening like square foot, hay bale, and keyhole gardening. They all assist in making growing your own food less of a challenge and a lot more rewarding, something the modern age gardener appreciates.

- **Planning Your Garden, Growing Your Plant**

Gardening is not as simple as simply planting a seed or transplant and observing the plant grow. After a site is chosen, there'll be other questions to take into account in the preparation stage. The size of your garden is going to be restricted by the dimensions of your lawn. You will want to construct garden beds in narrow rows so that you have room to attend the plants without even stepping on or harmful neighboring plants. It is possible to sketch out your design beforehand or put down things to picture the distance. If you do not have sufficient space for a huge vegetable garden, do not worry. A three meter by 3 meter garden is adequate, and you may also grow vegetables in containers in your own balcony if you don't own a garden.

When you think about how you are growing your plants, one of the most important things people tend to think about is the pesticides. Many people choose to grow their own vegetables and fruits simply because they know the amount of pesticides that have been put on the foods they are eating.

It does no one any good to grow their own plants if they are just going to cover them with the same pesticides that are used in commercial growing. The great thing about hydroponics is that you do not have to use any pesticides. Many hydroponics systems are indoors, which prevents all pests that come from the soil and all disease. Even for those systems that are kept outside, there is no need for pesticides because since there is no dirt for the bugs and other pests to hide in, they leave the plants alone.

Planning your vegetable garden might not sound like the funniest part of the process, and you'd be right to think so. At this stage you don't even get your hands dirty. But by planning your garden properly, you will be equipped with all the knowledge you need to have in order to understand exactly what conditions your plants are growing in. Just because it is boring, it doesn't mean it has to be hard.

Before beginning a school or community garden, it's very important to think about which kind of garden is suitable for your present and future requirements and the quantity of resources and time your situation will need. Watch the other books in this series to learn more about planning, producing and sustaining a community or school garden. While meals gardening is a superb activity to do in your lawn, it is also part of an increasing trend of people wanting to eat much better, develop some of their own meals, and have more control on the level of the food supply. What better way to make certain you eat healthful food than developing it yourself? In ancient 2009, the National Gardening Association (NGA) finished a questionnaire that characterized food preservation in the USA. Here is what it found:

✓ Around 23 percent, or 27 million Families, had a vegetable garden in 2008. That's two million over in 2007. The amount of meals drinkers rises to 31 per cent, or 36 million families, should you include those individuals growing veggies, berries, and herbs.

✓ The Average man spends roughly $70 in their food garden each year. (I wish I could keep my paying that none!) The entire nationwide is $2.5billion spent on food gardening. I clarify what you gain out of this $70 compared to what you would spend in the supermarket later in this segment.

✓ The typical vegetable garden is 600 square Ft, but 83% of those vegetable gardens are less than 500 square feet. Almost half of anglers grow some veggies in containers too.

✓ The average vegetable gardener is faculty Educated, married, female, age 45 or older, and does not have any children at home. And nearly 60% of vegetable anglers are gardening for under five decades.

✓ The typical causes of vegetable gardening In order of significance are: to generate fresh meals, to spend less, to generate better-quality meals, and also to grow food that you know is secure. There you have it. A great deal of food anglers are outside in their plants, and the numbers are increasing quicker than wheat in July. You may grow just a little food garden, but when all of the gardens have been added together, the effect is huge. Want further evidence? Allow me to show you!

✓ About 36 million families grow veggies, fruits, berries, and veggies. The typical garden size is 600 square feet. The NGA quotes you could create about 1/2 pound of vegetables per square foot of lawn annually. That is about 300 lbs. of veggies in the typical garden. The normal cost, in season, of veggies is approximately $2 per pound, therefore the typical vegetable garden generates $600 value of produce. So, Americans spend an average of 70 to afford $600 value of produce each year. Wow! That is a fantastic return in my novel!

The Economics of It

The first thing that they teach you at college is that everything leads back to economics. Unless something is economically feasible, people are not going to adopt it. Well, in the long run, growing your own food is much cheaper than buying from the supermarket or even your local farmer's market. This obviously makes sense since when you are purchasing from an outside source, you are also paying for their profit. Also, buying seeds is cheaper than buying grown products.

Initially, a few basic supplies will require some investment. If you are lucky, you might have them lying around your house or you can ask around in your circle if someone has spares. However, once you have procured the few basics, they will last your forever. After that, the only recurring cost is seeds and fertilizer. A great bargain if you ask me!

The Health Aspect of It

Freshly picked out food is much healthier. As soon as you detach the fruit from the tree, it quickly begins to lose essential vitamins and minerals. The nutritional information that you find is of fresh produce. The ones you get are at least a few days old and sometimes have also been cold stored. So you can imagine the quality deterioration that occurs. When you have the plant right in your backyard, you can pick it and cook it straight away. Getting the best health benefits.

The Activity of It

Gardening is an extremely positive and healthy activity. It is fascinating to first hand witness the miracle of creation and to be involved in it. When you start growing, you will feel a childlike fondness towards your kitchen garden. You watch the seeds transform into healthy, robust, producing plants. You tend for them, care for them and hear to what they have to say. In return, they give you great, healthy food.

Call me superstitious but I have this inherent belief that when you pour your love into something it rewards you with results. Cooking is that way and gardening is the same. When you cook and grow with love, the result if tastier, healthier and yummier food.

Gardening is also a very physically challenging activity. To tell the truth, we could all use some exercise. Being a couch potato is no way to be. Think I'm bluffing? Try taking out weeds someday. It leaves you in sweats. A great way to get some much needed exercise.

The Emotional Connection of It

Call me sentimental and stupid but I am a strong believer in developing a connection with nature. Today's world with all its grey structure and fancy gizmos has moved humans away from their origins. So many young people (children) do not even know the pleasure of morning birds chirping or the changing colors of fall. I blame this on an increased focus on indoors life. We go from house to car to mall to office and back to car and inside our homes. We have self-confined ourselves within the four walls when there is so much to the outside world.

Gardening re-establishes the connection of humans with the earth. Earth is our nourishing force. "Mother Earth" as they call it for it nurturing capabilities. Getting your hands dirty, clothes soiled and having the smell of fresh watered soil in your nose is just so important. In my opinion, it helps you appreciate the order of the world, the bounty of the nature and the system of the universe. A truly rewarding experience.

For someone who has never grown even a flower shrub in their life, kitchen gardening can seem a bit intimidating. However, if you put your right foot forward, it can be a fun and simple activity. Not as daunting as it seems. All you need is an excitable attitude, some willpower, plenty of elbow grease and you'll be good to go!

I Can Do This!

Everything in the wide world starts with the correct attitude. If you think that you can do it, then you will do it! It is that simple.

When you are thinking of getting started, a lot of thoughts will plague your mind. Like, how will I manage my time? Or what if my plants wither? Or that it will tire me too much? Do not pay heed to any such negative thoughts popping up in your mind. They are just a waste of energy. You'll be surprised that once you have set your mind to it, how easy things fall into place.

So before you even begin collecting supplies or making plans, be assured in your heart and mind that you want to do this. Do not let even a shred of doubt to creep into your consciousness. You want it! You need it! You will do it!

Commitment Phobia

A kitchen garden is not like buying real estate on the moon so don't let your commitment phobic self-creep up. All you're attempting to do is grow some plants, right? So there's nothing to worry about. If at any stage, you feel like this is too much and I can't do this anymore (though it almost never happens), you can always easily back out. You can even sell your basic supplies to get back your initial investment. So don't feel like this decision will drag you down. It is life changing but in a very small and meaningful way. Don't be scared that you won't be able to keep up.

All At Once

The common mistake that most novices make is that they think they have to do everything at once. When they think of a kitchen garden, they imagine a backyard filled with about 50 different types of plants bearing everything from parsley to strawberries. They think that once they start their kitchen garden, they will never have to buy any produce ever again.

This approach is a recipe for disaster. Piling too much on your plate (pun totally intended) can often lead to all sorts of problems. Your kitchen garden doesn't have to be this magazine worthy big setup. Even a few plants in little pots can be a good start up. In fact, when starting, it is better to grow only a few easy types so that your confidence builds up. Mint for example, is low maintenance and easy to grow. Once you discover the pleasure of home grown mint in your salads and smoothies, you'll naturally want to grow more things as well.

That's the way to go. Slow, consistent and steady.

Checking the Essentials

We learnt in our elementary science class that plants need three things to thrive. Sunlight, water and nourishing soil. Before you move on to fancy equipment and large spaces, you need to make sure that you can manage these three essentials. Consistent moisture, plenty of sunlight (be it open air or a large window) and some rich, hefty soil. If you have these three, you have everything (well almost) you need to start growing some food for your table.

A Friend on Board

I mentioned earlier that I started maintaining my kitchen garden after seeing my father turn to it after his retirement. Since my father is more experienced than me, I often ask him when I encounter a problem with one of my plants. If you can find someone like that, it can be great! That someone can be your childhood friend, neighbor, colleague, child, parent, well just about anybody. You can even forge a new friendship over your kitchen garden.

- **Step By Step Guide To Starting And Sustaining A Vegetable Garden**

Deciding Where to Plant Your Garden

If we are going to be starting a vegetable garden, then the very first thing that we need to do is pick a location for our vegetable garden. In your backyard, there are dozens of places in which you could plant your garden depending on how you space it or position it, and also the size of your backyard. Each possibility is technically in your backyard but locations aren't all made the same. Some are better than others and some are downright unsuitable for gardening.

In this stage of your planning, you should take a moment to consider each of the following environmental attributes. Some of these you can tell just by looking at your yard but others will require a little bit of data gathering. These steps are included where necessary. You can get by with growing in a location that is a little less than ideal for some of these attributes, but spots which fail on multiple fronts are best avoided.

Elevation: This one can usually be done through eyesight alone. Looking at the space you are thinking about planting your vegetables, is it elevated? Is it on an incline? Is it at the bottom of an incline? Is it rather flat? Depending on which of these questions is the most accurate, you are going to have a unique relationship to watering your plants. Generalized advice on watering your plants assumes that they are in a flat space. Plants that are on an incline will act flat. Plants on the bottom of an incline are going to need less water. Those planted on an elevated surface will require more water than normal.

Sunlight: Plants need a certain amount of sunlight a day. Some species prefer this light to be direct, others prefer it to be indirect, in the shade. Some want as much sun as possible, while others need relatively little direct sunlight. If you are going to be growing vegetables, then you are going to need to know two things. You are going to need to research the species of plant to see how much sunlight it needs, and you are going to need to know how much sun your chosen space gets. Keep an eye on the space throughout a day and see how much time it is in the sun and in the shade. Finding this out will let you know which vegetables will do best in this particular space. If you are looking to plant some veggies that want a lot of sun and some that don't want much, then remember that you don't need to grow everything in the same bed. It is better to grow multiple beds than try to force a plant out of its comfort zone.

Coverage: How much foliage or coverage from rain and wind does the space have? Are plants going to be safe from high winds where you plant them? Are they going to be able to get enough water when it rains or is the foliage going to misdirect it? Flipside, is the foliage going to help to prevent drier plants from drowning? Coverage isn't necessary when it comes to vegetable gardening but many gardeners have no choice but to work with it because of having trees in their backyards or limited space.

Security: How safe are your vegetables? Vegetable farming doesn't tend to bring out thieves the same way that cannabis or fruit farming does. Well, at least not human thieves. Vegetable farming does bring out mice, rabbits, deer and other herbivores. While seeing a deer eating your vegetables is a good sign (after all, it means they must be pretty tasty), it also means that you now have a half ruined crop. If there is easy access to your backyard or growing space then you should consider how you can add some security to prevent unwanted visitors. This can be as easy as adding a knee level plastic fence around the garden but if you can offer security in one direction (such as when growing next to a house) then you can save money by using less fencing and limiting critters from approaching.

Ease of Access: This is the one factor that causes the most problems, but new gardeners don't realize it until it is too late. When you are first planning out your garden, it is easy to forget about the fact that you are going to need to be able to maneuver through it. Maintaining your crops requires you to water each plant and inspect it for signs of problems. If you plant your crops in such a way that you can't get easy access to some of them, then you are going to end up neglecting those plants and they will reflect this in their yield. Most gardeners get a pack of vegetable seeds and then plant them too close together. When the plant you are growing is so tiny to begin with, it is easy to forget what size they are going to be growing to. This is the reason that crops are most often planted in rows. Try to keep size in mind and ensure that there is enough space for you not only to get at every plant but to be able to get down and inspect each one.

Ground or Container: The majority of this manual is written under the assumption that you are growing your plants in the ground itself. At this stage, it is important to note that, while there are some general differences between these two methods, there are also many similarities. Whether you are growing containers that are above ground or below ground, they tend to need to be watered more often than plants grown outside of a container. Beyond this main difference, they will still require as much sunlight, security and ease of access as any other garden bed you plant.

Putting It All Together: Once you have considered each of these attributes of the space, you can decide if it will be a good fit for your plants or not, as determined by their needs. Figuring out each of these attributes will take time and make it a longer wait before you are ready to plant your vegetables, but it can save you from some nasty surprises that could lead to weak veggies and poor yield. A spot that looks perfect at first glance might not get enough sunlight or shade for the plants you were looking to put there. Knowing this ahead of time allows you to match your garden to the local conditions so you can have the most productive vegetable garden possible.

Planning the Vegetables in Your Garden

Now we're onto the fun part of planning. We can start to imagine what delicious veggies we are going to be eating in the near future. Before we look at these specific examples it would serve well to take a moment to consider our location again.

As noted above, it is better to plant multiple garden beds for plants with different needs. You will know exactly how much space you have to work with and what conditions you are able to give your veggies. Use this to decide what to plant and which spot it should be in. You can grow anything you want, just research its needs ahead of time so that you know in which space to put it and how to keep it healthy

Putting Your Plan into Motion
Here's a step-by-step guide:

1. List the crops you want to grow. Divide this list into two categories: must-grow and would like to grow.
2. For each plant, decide whether you want to start seeds indoors, purchase transplants, or direct sow.
3. Based on your decisions, write down the planting date for each crop. To do this, first find your average last-frost date and use the plant timing instructions.
4. Note the harvest category of each crop. Place a star beside any plants with a quick-burst or weather-dependent harvest; they are prime candidates for succession planting.
5. For each plant, look up the recommended plant spacing. Then decide how many plants (or how many rows) you will plant for each crop.
6. List any companion planting combinations you want to incorporate.
7. Brainstorm any vertical gardening ideas you want to try (see here).
8. For raised or in-ground beds, draw a layout grid of your garden space (graph paper is a great help). Each square represents 1 foot. If you're growing in containers, sketch out a top view of each container. If the container is circular, draw a square inside, noting the distance between the sides of the square.
9. In your layout, use a pencil to sketch in your must-grow crops. Then fill any remaining space with the crops you would like to grow. For the crops with a star, decide how you will use

succession planting in those spaces. Some areas may have two crops listed, if you plan to plant a second crop after the harvest of the first one.

10. Now that your garden layout is taking shape, adjust it as necessary. You may decide to add more containers or change the quantities of crops.

11. With your rough plan in place (don't worry, you can still change it!), it's time to start building your garden.

Summary

• Seeding here refers to sowing seeds directly into the ground while planting refers to starting seeds indoors to transplant later.

• Seeds tend to take better when they are started indoors but a lot more work is involved therein.

• Some seedlings don't take well to transplanting and so they must be started outside.

• It is important to purchase high quality seeds. Make sure either the label or the seller can tell you when the seeds were harvested.

• The ground needs to be at a certain temperature before seeds can be planted in it. It is best to wait for after the last frost of early spring.

• If the temperature of the ground is too hot or too cold, your seeds aren't going to germinate properly.

• You shouldn't sow seeds into wet soil. Wait for it to dry before sowing.

• Sowing by hand takes longer but gives you better control over the rows or beds you are seeding. Using a tool to sow will speed up the process at the cost of control.

- Planting in rows is the most common approach. Dig out a small trench, sow your seeds, cover them with soil if the species in question requires it and then water them deeply.

- Many seeds won't germinate, so it is important to plant more than you are intending to grow. You will need to thin out your rows when you do this. It is the best way to ensure enough seedlings sprout.

- Sowing seeds in a wide bed is pretty much the same, except that you are working with a wider space. Wide beds should be no more than four feet in width.

- Garden beds follow the same rules as wide beds when it comes to sowing.

- You shouldn't sow most vegetables on a hill. It is better to set up a trellis and grow tomatoes or other vine vegetables on hills.

- Starting seeds indoors allows you to control the growing environment and provide the perfect conditions for germination, whereas starting outdoors requires Mother Nature's cooperation.

- Another benefit of starting seeds indoors is the fact that it allows you to begin your crop earlier in the year because seedlings can be started prior to the last frost of the winter.

- To start seeds indoors you are going to need soil, small containers, plastic wrap, and some LED grow lights.

- Start seeds indoors by first filling up the containers with soil. Then plant the seeds in and cover them with soil. Water them and then wrap plastic over the top.

- Seeds will need to be watered or misted. Taking the plastic wrap off for a few minutes every day also helps them to get enough oxygen. Remove the plastic wrap entirely once the seedlings start to sprout.

- Thin out your seeding containers by removing all but the strongest seedling.

- Seedlings should begin fertilization once the second set of leaves has begun to grow. Feed seedlings a fertilizer at half strength or less on a weekly basis.

- Before seedlings can be transplanted outdoors, they must first be hardened. When seeds are grown indoors, they don't form the natural protection against the elements that their outdoor siblings do. They need to be taught this.

- Stop watering your plants a week before moving them outside to harden off. Move them to an outdoor location with shade and protection from the wind. Let them stay outdoors for ninety minutes. The next day, increase this to two and a half hours while also moving the plants a little more into the sun. Continue adding an hour a day and giving the seedlings more sunlight for about a week before transplanting them. Wilting seedlings should be given only the smallest amount of water to hold them through this process.

- To transplant your seedlings, gently remove them from their container and check the roots for signs of rot. Dig a hole in the garden and place the seedling inside. Pack the soil around the stem to cover the roots and keep the seedling in place. Water seedlings immediately after transplanting.

- Use a soil test kit on your soil to see if it has enough macronutrients and a good pH level. Some soil test kits will even tell you how many micronutrients are present.

- Vegetables like a pH level between 5.5 and 7.5 generally. A pH level that is too high or too low will prevent your plants from being able to properly absorb nutrients.

- The texture of soil is important. You want it to be loose enough to allow quick drainage and plenty of oxygen to get the roots of your plants but also enough nutrients to keep it healthy.

- Soil is made up of clay, silt, and sand in different ratios. You want to balance these pretty evenly in your garden.

- If the soil in your yard isn't particularly fertile, then you are best off purchasing a premixed blend that has plenty of nutrients and drains quickly.

- When you grow vegetables in a pot, you start seeds in a small seedling container and then transplant them to another container instead of the ground.

- Only use containers which have drainage holes to prevent water from stagnating at the bottom.

- Growing plants in the ground leads to larger yields, but growing them in containers can allow you more control and the ability to reposition your veggies after planting them.

- Plants grown in containers are going to need to be watered much more often than those in the ground.

- **Growing A Self-Sufficient Garden**

We see that small farming can be really profitable and self-sufficient by growing special root crops, vitamin-abundant vegetables and calorie-rich carbonated crops.

Familiarize yourself with which crops are most caloric, which carbon-crops give caloric crops, and which crops are abundant in nutrients.

Calorie Farming

As we know, calories are a crucial part of our nutrition. They are present in all food to some extent.

Calorie farming refers to the production of root crops that are rich in calories, and they are space- efficient. This category includes crops like potatoes, sweet potatoes, garlic, leeks, and salsify. If a farmer reserves 30% of his area to these special crops, he can grow a sustainable diet on a small area.

Remember that everything you pluck or take from your farm contains organic matter. Those nutrients do not go back to the soil. In a case of sale of your crops, try to consider the loss of nutrients. Kitchen scraps come in very handy in this situation. Your customers can bring them to you, and you can use them for the compost.

After you have used up your land on carbon and special root crops, the remaining 10% of land you might use for growing vegetables to diversify your nutrition and diet. Remember that vegetables are real vitamin boosters like A, C but also iron (cabbage, tomato, cucumber, eggplant, lettuce, etc.).

Create Balance

Self-sustaining farming combines many elements. One cannot work without the other. We have seen that all the steps are closely intertwined and that, only if they are all supported, success can be expected.

The ultimate goal is to achieve a closed system, creating an ecosystem that generates each step of the production.

All methods and principles should be equally applied and taken care of, because if not, one might create worse conditions than at the beginning.

You may cultivate a deep soil and engage in extensive planting, but if you leave out the compost, your soil will lose structure and its fertility. The same applies to overuse of compost which can result in better crops for several years, but causes soil imbalance later and insect diseases. The key factor is to grow your own compost material in order to keep your soil rich in minerals and avoid depleting your soil. As we see, compost has to be proportionally added, not too much and not too little.

The whole process will take some time- the healthy soil, crop diversity, compost supply, but results will be visible over some time. One has to be patient, consistent and committed. The first few years might be difficult due to challenging soil, insect pests, but consistent work and following of these eight principles will eventually lead to a successful, self-sustainable farm and ecosystem that you created.

The crops will be better than the average, growing in a healthy way. One should look at a farm as just a piece of the entire ecosystem and that it is all in correlation. It would also be ideal to have a buffer zone (uncultivated area) next to the farm. That uncultivated part or land in the wild encourages plant, insect and animal diversity and in that way helps the existence of the farm.

Start with healthy soil, because it represents the backbone of all the other elements. Also, bear in mind that the interconnection and complexity of all the elements are crucial. One supports and stimulates the other. Create a healthy soil for a healthy crop, and in return, only a healthy system can preserve a healthy soil.

Mutual growth encouragement

There is the term referred to as companion planting which can be beneficial for the relationship between plant, soil, and insects.

Companion planting means to plant crops that are bearable to each other, i.e. similar, and hence, they make good neighbors and will stimulate mutual growth. Good-neighbor plants can grow next to each other, or they can be inter-planted and share the same space. For example, inter-planting of beans and corn stimulates a better soil. Tomatoes and basil go with each other as well, encouraging mutual better flavor, besides growth. Marigold is good to keep unwanted insects away.

Crop rotation is one of the methods of companion planting. Crops of the same family do not share the same space for three years in a row and in that way, they account for diversity in the garden kit. That is one way to minimize disease pressure among crops.

Gardening counsel isn't that rare. Truth be told, you can get Gardening guidance from another Gardening worker, in a planting index, planting books, gardening magazines, and even on the Internet. Despite the fact that you will have varieties with each plant, there is some Gardening guidance that is widespread and that goes for any plant.

For instance, the Gardening counsel given for planting is essentially uniform. You should put plants where they will have space to develop so they don't pack one another. Great wind stream is or more, and plants must be in a position where they will get sufficient measures of daylight. Exhortation will consistently instruct you to add some kind of supplements to the dirt to prompt better plant development, for example, mulch or fertilizer.

Gardening guidance on watering plants is somewhat more fluctuated, on the grounds that each sort of plant needs various measures of water. For instance, you wouldn't have any desire to water a desert flora close as much as you water a tomato plant. The amount you water will clearly likewise rely upon where you live, the atmosphere, and how much downpour your zone gets.

Gardening exhortation from about each source will disclose to you that your plants not just need treat when you first plant them, they will likewise should have been prepared all through their developing season. What kind of prepare utilized will rely upon the dirt substance and pH balance, however treat will be required on most all plants. Fertilizer can be utilized rather and it is anything but difficult to track down exhortation on the best way to make a manure heap just as when prepare and fertilizer should be utilized.

Planting exhortation on weeds, creepy crawlies, illness, and how to dispose of them is presumably the most looked for after guidance in the entirety of gardening. These bugs attack all nurseries and on the off chance that you don't dispose of them, they will dominate and demolish your gardening. There are a wide range of synthetic substances and pesticides that can be utilized, and planting guidance will as a rule enlighten plant specialists regarding which synthetic substances are better, which are unsafe, and which ones are simpler to regulate.

Planting isn't a simple errand; you need to battle against numerous outside powers, for example, climate, bugs, malady, and weeds. Indeed, even the most prepared of plant specialists will search out gardening exhortation now and again. Who wouldn't when there are such a significant number of powers that could take a gardening out? There is a ton of general gardening counsel available that goes for any plant, yet on the off chance that you look a little harder you will discover explicit guidance for that one plant that is the just one giving you inconvenience. Planting exhortation is moderately simple to discover, and keeping in mind that you may run over the incidental rotten one, its majority is generally solid and will help with any gardening question.

Hydroponic "life hacks"

Separate barrels or walls are planted with plants from above or from all sides. By this, however, the choice of forms is by no means exhausted. You can easily build planted columns, half columns, cubes, as well as arbitrary shapes like trellises, pyramids, garlands, hanging curtain rods and pots, etc. There is no need to dwell on the manufacture of the basis for all of these forms. Therefore, we confine ourselves to only general provisions for all forms.

When choosing a shape and determining the size of the frame, you can more closely follow personal tastes and adapt to the particularities of the place. However, it is always necessary to reckon with the following: plants must have a sufficient volume of substrate for the roots and have a stock of the solution corresponding to their size and number. The height and length of the structure can be chosen completely arbitrarily, but the width (thickness of the substrate layer) must have the following minimum dimensions: when planting with plants on all sides - at least 30 cm; when planting with plants on one side - at least 18 cm.

If this condition is met, you can be sure that the supply of nutrient solution to the plants is enough for 8 to 10 days.

We have already seen that vertical beds or walls can be stationary or mobile. They can even be put on wheels. In order to use the terrace as a flowering screen in accordance with the position of the sun, an enterprising gardener built several metal frames that could be made together like building blocks and made of the large floral walls. When decorating the stage, stands, and assembly halls, they always successfully replace the slightly treasured greenery of palm trees and evergreen shrubs.

Various vertical walls can also be used to decorate walls and parts of buildings. They can be suspended at any height, and the rear surface adjacent to the walls of the building can be impermeable to moisture (for example, from tin coated with an insulating layer, or from the roofing material, roofing felt, or plastic film) so that the walls of the building do not suffer. It is very advisable to put a couple of bars between the back surface of the base and the wall of the building, which will provide better ventilation.

Here, by the way, it should be noted that it is already possible to obtain bases made industrially from asbestos cement or metal. Since they are in good shape and made very reasonably, they certainly deserve attention.

Gardening Tricks

A wall of moss or peat can also be used for internal gardening. However, in this case, it is necessary to provide some kind of receiver to drain a possible excess of nutrient solution. The receiver can be a painted tin can or even a plastic tub installed under the base or suspended from it. With a known dexterity, you should immediately make a device for draining the liquid - it can be a faucet or just a siphon tube. If all this is provided for, we can be calm for the completely modern conditions for indoor plants that have been created.

Here, in fact, all the most important guidelines that must be observed when building the foundations for growing plants on a substrate of moss or peat. It should only be recalled that when planting young plants, you need to take into account the space required for a fully developed plant. For example, if a fully planted foundation should ultimately have a length of 2 m, then a 2.6 m long frame is sufficient because the height of the plant on the end surfaces will be at least 0.2 m. In conclusion, another indication for the site owner demanding on himself familiar with the craft of a bricklayer: a flower wall can be folded out of brick, or better yet, of uncut stone. To do this, first lay the foundation with a width of about 60 cm and the desired length. The top of the foundation is leveled and a groove is made in it to drain excess fluid with an inclination to one side.

There is no need for the whole process of work, you should only warn that cement should not be saved. The strength of the structure will increase significantly if you use a solution with a narrow ratio of sand to cement (2: 1 or 3: 1). When the masonry is finished, you need to hold the brush and cover the inner surface of the masonry and the top of the cement, i.e. all surfaces that will come in contact with the substrate, bitumen paint, to prevent the influence of lime or bricks on the nutrient solution.

A layer of coarse quartz sand with a thickness of 5-8 cm is first poured into the finished base. It will ensure the rapid removal of excess moisture. Then the substrate is stuffed, which should be very moistened to speed up the process of natural subsidence. After this, you can start planting the plants.

Another important point! You can greatly facilitate your work if at the beginning of the masonry, at the end of the wall above the lower end of the gutter, several stones or bricks are fixed so that they can be easily removed. Then, using the poker, you can easily dig out the substrate from the usually inaccessible narrow space. Another detail: curly seams made of white cement give a special decorative effect to a wall made of bright red facing brick.

- **Get To Know Organic Gardening**

Organic matter has an open-cell structure, so nutrients, when falling through the soil column, will actually become trapped within the cell structure of the organic matter and be retained. This allows for plant roots to access nutrients that would otherwise be washed from the soil. In addition, as if I have not loved on organic matter enough, it provides a superior home for beneficial bacteria and fungi. These organisms live in the soil column in what is called the rhizosphere.

Organic gardening through the season

- **Cool-season.** Plant these plants in early spring and early autumn. They're cold-hardy and flourish in spring and autumn when temperatures are below 70°F: beets, broccoli, Brussels sprouts, cabbage, lettuce, cauliflower, collards, kale, kohlrabi, lettuce, mustard, onions, peas, celery, radishes, rutabagas, spinach, Swiss chard, and turnips.

- **Warm-season.** Plant these plants following the last spring frost once lands have heated up. They're frost sensitive and flourish in summer when temperatures are over 70°F: cantaloupes, beans, cucumbers, okra, peppers, pumpkins, southern peas, squash, corn, sweet potatoes, tomatoes, eggplant, and watermelons.

- Biennial plants for example artichokes grow the initial season, and blossom, fruit and perish the next year.

- Perennial crops like asparagus and rhubarb endure for several years after established.

- When to plant?

- Strategy for yearlong production through succession planting.

- **Spring.** Plant cool-season plants early and warm-season plants in late spring. Utilize a cold frost or frame cloth to start earlier in this season.

- **Summer.** Cool-season plants will bolt since the days lengthen and temperatures rise. Use shade fabric to protect crops and expand the season. Warm-season plants planted in late spring could rise before the first fall frosts. In late summer, plant cool-season plants for fall.

- **Fall.** Cool-season plants established in late summer may keep growing through medium to freezing temperatures.

- **Winter.** Cold hardy crops (like kale, collards, and turnip greens) implanted in autumn may live through winter. In colder locations, use a cold frame or suspend fabric to prolong the season.

- Scheduling when to plant and when to crop can be carried out in many powerful ways. Composing the planting dates and proposed harvest dates on a calendar is a technique employed by a number of farmers and anglers. Another procedure is drawing a diagram of this garden and composing projected planting and harvesting dates onto the garden diagram. Understanding when an area is going to be chosen helps with preparation when to plant a different crop in that area. Employing this technique of preparing allows for a little distance to be handled to its fullest capacity.

Organic pest and disease management

Each organic garden will experience different problems and pests throughout the growing season, and until you start gardening, you won't know which ones you'll encounter. These are some of the most common issues.

Early blight or Septoria leaf spot on tomatoes. These fungal diseases cause yellowing leaves starting at the bottom of a tomato plant. Early blight may look like a target, with outer circles of yellow darkening to brown in the center. Septoria leaf spot appears as many brown dots on leaves and often shows up later in the season. Cut off and dispose of all affected stems when the leaves aren't wet. During rainy periods, you may have to do this daily to get it under control.

Powdery mildew. Most common on squash, zucchini, and cucumbers, powdery mildew is a fungal disease that looks like white powder on the tops of leaves. Left unchecked, it will spread up the plant and inhibit photosynthesis and subsequent fruit production. If you catch it early, clip off affected leaves, up to 25 percent of the plant. If that doesn't work, mix 1 teaspoon of baking soda with 1 quart of water and spray on affected and unaffected leaves once a week.

Blossom-end rot. Most common on tomatoes, this black rotted spot appears where the blossom drops off the fruit. It can also affect squash, melons, and peppers. Although this condition is caused by a plant's inability to take up calcium from the soil, simply adding calcium is usually not the best remedy. Most soils have enough calcium present (a soil test will confirm this); the problem typically lies in uneven watering or out-of-balance ph. Keep plants watered regularly, especially during the blossoming and fruiting stages. If this doesn't help, get a soil test to determine if a lack of calcium or pH issue is to blame.

Lack of pollination. When a fruit stops growing and begins to rot, usually a lack of pollination is the cause. Squash, zucchini, cucumbers, and melons are most susceptible to this condition. Without the presence of pollinators such as bees, cross-pollinating plants can't develop fruit. You may need to hand-pollinate. Find the male flower (the one without a fruit developing at the base) and with a cotton swab transfer the pollen from its stamen onto the flower of the female (the one with a fruit at the base). These flowers only open once per day, usually in the morning, so you'll need to go out early, and daily.

Aphids. Tiny, pear-shaped insects in various colors, aphids congregate on new growth of many plants such as tomatoes and peppers, especially early in the season. Avoid spraying, because most insecticidal soaps also kill ladybug, lacewing, and syrphid fly larvae, which prey upon aphids. Instead, apply worm castings to the base of the plants and water well. Worm castings contain chitinase, an enzyme that aphids cannot digest. When the aphids suck the plant juices containing chitinase, they die.

Worms. Cabbage worms, tomato hornworms, armyworms, and other worms can defoliate your vegetable plants almost overnight. If handpicking doesn't keep them under control, coat affected crops with the organic pesticide Bacillus thuringiensis, being careful to avoid any flowers. You might also consider a floating row cover to protect vulnerable crops (broccoli, cabbage, kale, and lettuce) against the moths that lay the eggs that hatch into these worms.

Beetles. Beetles such as squash bugs, stinkbugs, Japanese bean beetles, Mexican bean beetles, cucumber beetles, and others are some of the most difficult pests to control. Organic options are limited, because deterrents that might affect these beetles will also kill beneficial beetles such as ground beetles and ladybugs. The best way to control these pests is to handpick adults and remove egg clusters. Removing infested plants and practicing crop rotation also help for future seasons.

Less is more when it comes to issues in an organic garden. Early manual removal of diseased plants and pests offers the best protection. Be willing to accept some damage, and know that the healthier the soil is, the healthier the plants will be, which enables them to withstand more pest and disease damage over the course of the season.

Pest Control

Like it or not, part of gardening is dealing with the possibility of unwanted pests. These usually come in the form of insects that can damage or kill your plants, not to mention being unsightly at home.

Technical maintenance

Absolutely nothing thrives without maintenance. In our day to day activities, there are always a number of things to maintain because anything that doesn't need maintenance is either dead or not useful. A hydroponic system needs a number of measures for its maintenance to ensure the plants survive and the initial efforts are not wasted.

To grow plants hydroponically, there are certain aspects of the system that must be maintained to have great yield.

First of all, the PH of the nutrient solution has to be checked. To do this, there are various systems that can be adopted such as paper strip system which is the cheapest way. People who engage in gardening as a hobby mostly use liquid PH test kits. The tech savvy way to check PH is using the digital meter. Therefore, with any of the ways most suitable, ensure that the nutrient balance of the solution is tested at least every three days. Also, in a case where the plants have been exposed to rain, the nutrient solution must be checked to prevent the dilution of the liquid sources.

The next maintenance measure that must not be taken lightly is checking the water level in the system container at least every three days. In doing this, ensure that the water system is well enriched with the nutrient solution.

Furthermore, make sure that the plants are checked daily, this is to check for the growth patterns and to see if any pests or diseases have gotten in. In a case of such, the necessary actions to treat the deficiency or infection must be taken at once. Sticky traps, natural solutions or a good spray down can be applied.

The maintenance of light is also very important. Some plants don't need so much light while others do. Maintaining the lightning is actually not difficult because whatever lamp is being used has a life span which the user should be aware of and should therefore plan towards replacing the lamp and the reflectors after certain grows (about 4 to 8) probably every year. In maintenance of lighting, be observant to see if there's excess amount of light whether it's artificial or sunlight been used. To curb the excess light, screen clothes can be added or removed or the system can simply be transferred to a more protected area.

Again, keep the system clean at all times! Failure to do this would lead to dangerous build ups. Therefore, ensure there is a periodical flush of the piping system using clean water and hydrogen peroxide.

There must also be a total replacement of the nutrient solution at about every three weeks.

In addition, ensure the unit of the pumping system is well supervised when pumping is to be done to ensure that the pump is working well and so would deliver the nutrients to the plants.

Oh and then, just a little bonus for you! If you are growing herbs especially, to make the plants get fresh gusto, grow much better and for additives in cooking; consider topping or clipping the plants when appropriate.

Lastly, if you are making use of fans, filters and ducting, always check to make sure no issues exist in between grows. In essence, you are maintaining the ventilation system and preventing serious environmental issues.

Put all the aforementioned measures into your hydroponic system and enjoy a problem free planting!

Pest and Disease Control

You might believe growing indoors or in a greenhouse may exclude most of the pests from Becoming into your plants. That's not true; the Pests continuously find their way right into almost any harvest place even in mid-winter. If a great deal of these pests have been killed by frost, people who discovered their way in your Harvest earlier will flourish unless you restrain them. Resistant conditions inside your indoor or suburban garden are perfect for Insects Diseases, Whereas Flip Side may be controlled Using Resistant Types and Maintaining down Moisture Levels Generally, and the relative humidity of 75 Percent is great to the Plants. It is not overly humid to Market Ailments but be Cautious to Prevent any Suffering in the growing systems, which Can build up moisture Amounts and, at the same time, Turned into a House for algae. When algae grow into moist spots, they Bring Insects Such as fungus gnats, which will nourish on plant roots, particularly of the seedlings. Clean up any Escapes and Maintain the Ground dry to Stop Such Problems

CLEAN –UP BETWEEN CROP CYCLES

Whenever the harvest is terminated, and plants disposed of, the whole growing region has to be sanitized to prevent carryover of diseases and pests to another crop. Ahead of yanking the plants spray them using a pesticide to kill all those flying insects. Since you eliminate the vegetables, put them into big garbage bags to stop infested plants out of spreading insects and diseases that the plant debris may be removed into some garbage soil fill, or you may spoil them into a pit out encircling it afterward with dirt. This really can be the harder way since the hole could need to be relegated into around 3 feet in thickness. Making a pit can be a whole lot of effort, particularly if in winter if the floor is partly frozen. It's better to choose the plant that stays in a landfill. In case you're a garden gardener and also maintain mulch that the harvest debris might be composted. Vacuum up most little leaves etc. as some other plant debris left could transmit pest eggs or overwintering fungal spores.

Subsequently, spray on the whole growing region using a 10% bleach solution or alternative disinfectant. This contains the walls, flooring, and developing service trays. The rising stations, pond, and baskets, seedling trays, to hooks plant along with plant clips, ought to be saturated at a 10% Clorox solution for many hours.

Disinfectants are oxidizing agents which kill germs others apart from bleach you might utilize comprise "Virkon" (peroxide) and also "Kaleen Grow" (quaternary ammonium). Use safety gear like a respirator, disposable glasses, and also match when spraying those chemicals as their irritants for the skin. Never mix bleach with ammonia or acidic answers since these mixtures create noxious chlorine fumes. Thus, just be cautious, and there'll likely be no issues! Kleen Grow is enrolled for indoor and greenhouse harvest production centers thoroughly wet the surfaces. Utilize one teaspoon ounce each gallon of water 6--8 mL of Kleen Grow percent of water to rainwater surfaces and gear. Always read and follow label instructions precisely.

INSECT AND DISEASE CONTROL

Exclude pests as far as possible together with the use of screens onto any intakes that make fresh outdoor air. Sanitation practices such as eliminating any pruning debris and ruined or deformed fruit decreases ailments. After all, you'd be happy living in a filthy, cluttered home, so maintain your crops' living quarters tidy too to help them from getting ill! Preventing insects from penetrating can decrease infections because lots of insects suck plant cells' death on bacterial spores and spores into your plants.

Sucking pests inject viruses into the crops since they rasp or eliminate into the plant cells with their mouthparts. These pests contain aphids, mites, thrips, and whiteflies. Additionally, they carry fungal spores in their bodies also take them into plants since they suck on the juices out of the plants producing the perfect point of entrance for bacterial spore germination. Avoid diseases by maintaining the plants healthy, having an energetic origin system. Excellent hygiene of maintaining the developing region blank can decrease the existence of a substance that could harbor ailments. Be cautious in recognizing virtually any plant signs expressed from the presence of a disorder or insect. Early identification and detection of almost any ailments and pests is your secret to the effective management of the diseases. You will find numerous sites (see Appendix) which provide colored images of diseases and pests and recommend control steps.

Utilize these websites for identification and regularly take photographs for potential reference. Consider account that the plant signs might likewise be a reflection of environmental. When you've decided the origin of this illness or that pest exists, consider quickly, corrective activities to restrain them from stopping them disperse. Utilization approved compound sprays. Seek the usage of organic pesticides (bio agents). If those aren't adequately successful, then employ more powerful ones. Would not apply the same pesticides at future issues; change precisely the kind of pesticides to minimize any potential immunity build-up from the insects. A much better strategy will be to present organic predators (beneficial insects) to the harvest that will consume or parasitize the insects maintaining their amounts restricted. These beneficial insects can be found through many vendors as well as Raised Bed outlets.

FREQUENT DISEASES

Using resistant varieties will rejuvenate and boost your achievement. While Raised Bed growing considerably reduces the danger of infection in the bacterium, it doesn't stop ailments from the plant expansion over the parasite. Maintaining optimal ecological conditions, along with controlling germs, can help considerably in preventing diseases. Once you believe a disorder is existing beginning to identify specific regions within the plant that are influenced and clarify the character of these outward symptoms. Primarily, define the part changed: leaves, blossoms, fruit, developing tip, stem, crown region, or flowers. It can be a mix of them; for example, when the plant wilts through the elevated temperature and light intervals of this day, likely the most origins are contaminated, decreasing water uptake. Cut a few backgrounds to ascertain whether they are turgid and soft or white and slimy. When the latter, then you understand instantly, there's a root difficulty. Is your entire plant type stunted or dwarfed? Maybe the cap of the plant hairy with many tiny leaves and short internodes? Search for these signs: deformed, wrinkled, wrapped, curly, mottled, chlorotic, necrotic leaflets. Search for the existence of spots-concentric or curved, and white, ivory, hair-like development over the leaves (because of fungi, like powdery mildew and Botrytis). Cut the stem onto a plant to determine if the lymph tissue remains white and bright or soft and brown, which could signal that the existence of a disorder organism. Any softness or discoloration in the bark (crown) of the plant could indicate that a disorder. A fruit could have stains or lesions pointing into the existence of a disease. After taking and describing photographs for potential mention to those signs, proceed onto sites of their web to locate descriptions and photos of disorder symptoms, which may be like people your plants.

- **Nurturing Vegetable-Friendly Soil And Compost**

The first step to beginning a garden is setting one up in a satisfactory location with a solid foundation; depending on where you live, there are many ways this can be achieved. Then, focus on the soil; this is one of the keys to successful organic gardening, maximizing compost and other organic fertilizers to create a rich and bountiful bed for your vegetables. Once you have your location set up and your soil in place, then you can turn to procuring seeds, nurturing seedlings, and handling transplants.

One of the simplest ways to ensure that not a single fruit, vegetable, stem, or vine goes to waste in your garden is to feed your compost pile. Any inedible or undesirable bits of skin or core or bird-picked fruit should be tossed in the pile (or, alas, the occasional neglected scrap at the bottom of the vegetable bin). When one season rolls into another and you are clearing away the last roots from your spring plants or vines from your summer plants, be sure to grind these up as best you can and add them to the pile, as well. Each year your garden is fed by the garden of yesteryear, a true cycle of life (to paraphrase a famous film).

Soil: Food for Plants

Now that you have your garden location set up, the focus turns to the soil, the key to creating a strong and vibrant garden. When gardening organically, the importance of composting cannot be overstated. Not only is it the most successful way to improve and enrich your soil, but it is also environmentally friendly and cost-effective.

Obviously, in your first year of gardening, you must first provide some topsoil, whether from your own backyard or via a garden sourcing outlet. Over time, you may produce enough compost to replenish your soil each year, while adding some organic fertilizers when and if necessary, but at first build a strong foundation. Source your topsoil from a reputable local source or from a garden center that carries organic potting soil. Then, add your compost and get started.

Basically, composting is the method by which you break down organic matter—grass, leaves, food waste—into a kind of fertilizer. The goal is to achieve a balance of particular elements that encourage plant growth and, in some cases, discourage pests and disease. Essentially, composting takes time, some management, and a conscientious view of reusing materials.

Composting Solutions: If you truly want to garden organically, you absolutely must invest in some sort of composter. There are numerous models on the market with prices varying from the modest to the expensive, from the small indoor to the large outdoor. However, while most of these models are fuss-free and efficient, it is also possible to make your own composter with a few simple items.

Composting will maximize microbial diversity by the usage of plant materials and soil from your garden.

Compost can be defined as the broken down plant material nourishing the soil and providing it with carbon. This enables the soil to regain fertility. Compost in the soil releases enough nutrients for plant roots and microorganisms. It reduces the risk of challenging soil conditions. It is also helpful because it retains water and requires less watering.

Compost usage for your soil fertility increases your self-sustainability.

The compost pile should always have enough moisture and air.

There are some that should not be put in the compost pile like magnolia, eucalyptus leaves, poisonous plants, disease-infested plants, etc. because they do not compose very well.

Generally speaking, providing fertilizer once a year should be sufficient. Compost should be applied in proportion to your sustainable farm production.

A soil might lack particular nutrients that the compost does not provide. To solve this dilemma, test your soil for basic and trace nutrients.

Again, there are many varieties of composters on the market, and many are reasonably priced. The advantage to some of these models for purchase is that they can shorten the amount of time it takes to create usable compost. For compost to be useful to your soil, it must have a suitable time and enough internal heat to break down; thus, for first time gardeners who wish to compost in do-it-yourself mode, you must either start composting about a year before you plan to garden (or less with some composting models: check into manufacturer's claims carefully) or buy your compost from a reputable source.

Truly, composting can be virtually cost-free and simple for the do-it-yourself gardener. It simply requires an out of the way space—naturally, composting does give off some odor as it is working and can attract bugs—some basic materials, and patience. I have made my own composting set up using rebar, chicken wire, and dark plastic sheeting: plant the rebar sturdily into the ground in a wide circle (about the size of a backyard garbage can), then wrap it in chicken wire and cover the wire in dark material (recycled plastic works well). The dark covering traps in heat and encourages the aerobic breakdown of the material you put in the composter, while the chicken wire allows for adequate oxygen and moisture levels to penetrate. While not absolutely necessary, a nice covering—I used an untreated round of cedar wood, with a loop of rope for a handle—can speed up the process slightly and keep odor down.

What to put in your composter is simple, but it does require some balance. Lawn cuttings can be put in a composter but beware of overwhelming your compost with cuttings from each mowing throughout the year. Also note whether the grass you are putting in the compost has been treated with petrochemicals, such as fertilizer or herbicides. Leaves raked from the yard near the end of the growing season is an excellent source of compost, but again consider what kind of chemicals the trees in your area may have been treated with. And, of course, food scraps are imperative to creating compost rich in nitrogen: vegetable scraps, fruit peels, coffee grounds (and filters, if organically produced), and egg shells, and so on. Avoid meat and dairy products, as these take much longer to break down and can attract a host of unwanted pests.

The ideal is to create a ratio between "green" compost—food scraps, grass clippings, and the like—and "brown" compost—leaves, newspaper, untreated cardboard. Typically, a ratio of 1:3 is ideal (one part green compost to three parts brown compost), but it isn't crucial to be exacting. Basically, green compost heats things up, creating nitrogen and protein, while brown compost adds bulk and carbon to your compost while keeping down the odor. I highly recommend having a kitchen top composter to throw in your scraps while cooking that you can then transfer once or twice a week to your outdoor unit: this convenient setup ensures you keep your composter full and your trash can relatively empty. These units are moderately priced and are available at many garden stores and online.

How does one know when compost is ready? Essentially, it should be broken down by about half, should look like topsoil with few if any individual particles are recognizable, and should have lost any odor other than an earthy soil smell. When mixing in your compost at the beginning of the growing season, take from the bottom up, and leave behind whatever top layer has accumulated in the few months prior. Again, some commercial composters will not require that you take this step.

While compost is the key ingredient to your topsoil, you can also consider other organic fertilizers, such as manure and certain meals, to accelerate the health and growth potential of your garden. Manure is the most common addition to gardens, considered a complete fertilizer with lots of organic matter. Never use fresh manure in your garden during the growing season, as this can contaminate plants and lead to illness for anyone consuming them.

Organic bone meal and blood meal can also be used to assist your soil's potential: bone meal contains calcium and phosphate and promotes strong root health, while blood meal is high in nitrogen and stimulates leaf growth (though too much can burn plant roots, so apply judiciously). There are also fish and seaweed-based meals and emulsions for the garden. I can attest personally to the efficacy of fish skeletons: after a particularly successful fishing season, I will keep my fish scraps, frozen, until the end of growing season than simply till them into the soil before overwintering (even throwing in some past-their-prime whole carcasses). This technique has led to some of my lushest gardens.

Last, one option to consider when starting an organic garden is to get your soil tested. What this test will tell you is how acidic or alkaline your soil is: most plants prefer a soil that is very slightly acidic with a pH of about 6.5 (7 is considered neutral). This is the level at which the most important nutrients, including nitrogen and potassium, are most available to plants. Usually, lime is used to treat acidic soils, while sulfur is used to treat alkaline soils. This is where an extension center becomes very useful, as their testing can pinpoint exactly what nutrients your soil lacks and/or what nutrients are too prominent.

Seeds: Nurturing Success

There are many venues from which to procure seeds, such as via seed catalogs, local farms, and seed saving. Remember that, when attempting to garden organically, the seeds themselves must come from an organic source; this does not mean that hybrids cannot be used, but it does bar the use of genetically modified seeds. Thankfully, GMO seeds are not much of a problem for the home gardener, as they are typically relegated to large industrial crops, such as corn and canola, but it does not hurt to check. Some tomato varieties—the Flavr Savr, for example—are indeed GMO products, and the FDA has recently approved GMO potatoes for market.

But, for the home gardener, the biggest decision will be whether to use heirloom varieties—which are older varieties passed down through generations—or hybridized seeds. Heirloom varieties are wonderful and can expand our experience of what certain vegetables taste like, though they can be hard to grow if they are not originally local to your area. Hybridized varieties are typically hardier but can be less impressive than heirlooms. For the first time gardener, I would recommend sourcing some of both, to ensure maximum harvest while providing a valuable learning experience.

To clarify, the difference between GMO seeds and hybridized seeds is that one is a high-tech, relatively new innovation in creating almost entirely new plants while the other is a centuries-old tradition of selective cross-breeding of similar plants to produce a heartier version.

Hybridized seeds cross different strains of the same plant to maximize the best qualities of each strain. Thus, a hybridized plant may come from two strains, one that proved to be particularly abundant and one that proved particularly disease-resistant; the hybridized plant created from this mix thrives well and survives well. Hybrids have been nurtured to match human desires for centuries: the corn that we recognize today is the result of thousands of years of hybridization, selecting for the plant that produced the largest ears; corn is a grass plant, and early corn produced tiny, tough, inedible-without-processing kernels. Through crossing strains over time, we now have large ears of corn with juicy, ready-to-eat kernels. The disadvantage to using hybridized seeds is that they do not necessarily reproduce in exactly the same manner each season; that is, if you save seeds from a hybridized plant to use the following season, these may or may not produce the desired qualities initially derived from the hybrid plant. So, buying seeds each year, while not necessary, is recommended to achieve the same results in a hybridized strain.

GMO seeds have been genetically engineered in a laboratory, produced quickly by technological means and not subject to years of selective breeding. Since these kinds of seeds have only been widely used since the early 90s, there is still little known about the environmental consequence of adding these seeds and plants to the biome. GMO seeds are not limited to cross-breeding within their plant family, and thus, science has produced seeds that are genetically engineered to contain bacteria and, in some cases, viruses, along with the original plant matter.

Organically grown food is healthier: there is no other simpler way to say it. It nourishes our bodies and our environment in ways that mass-produced agriculture cannot. Gardening organically means that you are able to grow tastier food with more nutrients within a short walk from your back door. In addition, as we are well aware, organic gardening enriches our soil, our water, and our air by avoiding the use of petrochemicals and instead relying on the creation of a natural microbiome that cycles and recycles its main ingredients in order to continue thriving.

Foremost, your impact hits home—literally. The food that you grow with your own conscientious labor is both more satisfying and more delicious. Most produce that comes out of the agricultural system is bred (or modified) for heartiness and convenience, rather than taste. A bland supermarket tomato or mushy apple have been treated to ship well and to appear attractive without much thought given to the quality of taste or nutritional benefit. It really goes without saying that harvesting your evening meal—even a small part of it—

from your own backyard or terrace is immensely pleasurable, both sensually and psychologically.

This also clearly engenders a sense of accountability: if you depend on your soil and your environment for your own food, then you begin to actively support those things, even beyond your own plot of land. This breaks a cycle wherein the corporate control over our food-ways feels like our only choice. We have other paths we can choose to take.

- **Harvesting Your Vegetable Garden**

In earlier times, crops were usually grown in the spring season. So before the start of fall was the harvest period. People started harvesting from the first full moon of September. This served two purposes. One, it helped mark the occasion since it was a big yearly event. Secondly, nights were illuminated so people could harvest for longer.

How you harvest your garden, how much you harvest, and what you do with your harvest, depends (of course) on what you grow. Nothing mind-boggling about that, is there? But it is something you need to think about during the planning stages. You need to think about what you want to do with what you grow—even if all you want to do is look at it. But almost every plant has at least one purpose beyond its good looks, so why not get the most out of your garden?

Now-a-days, you don't have to wait until the autumn full moon. When harvesting, the best policy is to harvest as soon the fruit or the vegetable is ready. Just pick it from the garden and straight to the kitchen but how do you know that your vegetable/fruit has reached its harvest time.

At this point, I would like to draw the distinction between two terms that are often used interchangeably but are not quite synonymous-ready and ripe. Ripe is the stage when a fruit (or vegetable) has reached it maximum growth. When it is plump and matured to its maximum capacity. Ready, is when the part is done to your liking? For example, I like my guavas to be a little raw and firm. They are not exactly "ripe" when I pluck them but they are ready for me.

Leafy and stem based vegetables like spinach, lettuce, asparagus and celery are picked when they are "ready" and not ripe. Usually, they are picked sooner because younger leaves and stems are soften and sweeter. Later on as they mature, they get hard and loose the texture. Nobody likes to chew on something for ages. Same is the case with corn which is harvested a little early for sweetness.

On the other hand, fruit based vegetables (like tomatoes) are harvested when they are juicy and ripe. After all, nothing beats a full on juicy, red tomato. This is also the case for most traditional fruits. One thing to check for ripeness is scent. Ripe fruits give off a strong, appealing scent even when they haven't been cut. Have you ever been to a peach garden just before the harvest? It smells heavenly!

Herbs and spices should ideally be harvested as you go. They yield the best flavor when seeds begin to develop but unless you plan on drying and storing them, harvesting side by side is the best way to go. I just grab a handful of mint or rosemary and cut it off. Then use it fresh in the kitchen. The flavor and aroma is unbeatable.

Root based vegetables (potatoes, carrots and beetroots etc.) take a little more nuance. One thing to look for is the root peeking through. If the root starts to show its head through the soil then it is usually a sign that they are ready to be taken out. In the case of roots, it is better to err on the side of lateness. A few more days underground won't hurt but if you take it out too soon, you really can't do anything.

Do not feel stressed to harvest all your produce at once. That's the pleasure of a kitchen garden. You don't have to transport the produce anywhere to sell it in bulk. Just pick a tomato, cut some parsley, take out a carrot and cook them straight away. At home, all your fruits/vegetables also won't ripen at once. So do not feel pressured to "collect and hoard" them. Instead just pick, harvest and use.

The only exception to this can be root vegetables that can easily be stored long term. Some examples are onions, ginger and garlic. You can harvest them all at once and then store in a cool, dry place in your pantry.

For harvesting, usually your own hands are enough. Though in some cases, you might find that having the following tools around can be useful.

- A Sharp Knife
- A Pair of Sharp Scissors
- Long Handled Fruit Picker (if you have fruiting trees)
- Spade (for root vegetables)
- Hori Knife
- Straw Basket

Harvesting is undoubtedly the most fun and fruitful (pun totally intended) part of having your kitchen garden. Enjoy it to the fullest!

Advice for Cultivating and Harvesting

Build and Test Your Soil

Start your gardening season with a soil evaluation. This will identify exactly what your dirt lacks or has. Subsequently, you use this info to construct your dirt

Solarize

Utilize solarization to rid of the growing Moderate of soil-borne pests. By dispersing a huge sheet of plastic held in place using bricks, it is possible to grow soil temperatures high enough to destroy weeds, insects and their eggs, and various soil germs. Yes, this necessitates additional time up front in preparing your possessions, but this method can help save you trouble, time, and expense later in the growing season when you need to take care of infected plants or insects that are damaging.

Utilize Plastic Culture

Years ago, farmers used continuous cultivation to remain before weeds, but studies have demonstrated that this can break down the soil structure which you just worked so tough to construct. So use plastic culture, the way where you put black plastic over the ground and plant crops through it. Drip irrigation installed beneath the plastic offers proper moisture. This decreases the demand for dirt farming (weeding) and elevates the soil temperatures at the months when you'd like to expand the season for temperature-sensitive plants.

Plant Cover Crops

"Growing vegetables is extremely taxing on the soil and can strip off its own nutrients, "Planting cover crops in the off-season or involving harvest rotations adds back into those very important soil nutrients"

Cover crops include organic matter that is significant, and future plantings gain in the stored nutrients. These plants also enhance soil structure by reducing compaction and opening up dirt pores to keep oxygen and water. A number of the common cover crops include oats, buckwheat, rye, and clover.

Grow With Worms

Worms are excellent little dirt engineers. They split raw organic matter into smaller bits that valuable fungi will make accessible to the plant root system. They also help combine organic matter through the dirt, and their spores enhance soil oxygen and water-holding capacity.

How to tell it's Time to Harvest Your Veggies and What to Do When It Is

In order to accommodate this, we will be looking at a bunch of different veggies to see what unique signs they give us to let us know they're ready for harvest. But before we do that, there are a few tips to help us with the harvest. After we know that it is time to harvest our veggies, we'll take a look at how to harvest the more popular ones.

The first thing you need to know about harvesting is that a bigger vegetable isn't necessarily a better vegetable. Of course, we all love it when we can get nice big veggies because there is more eating to be had but vegetables like lettuce and spinach, cucumbers and beans, peas and potatoes are all tastier when they are harvested a little earlier when they still haven't fully matured. Now there are vegetables (like tomatoes) which are best when they are properly given time to mature but "bigger is better" only applies to certain veggies and not the whole garden.

You should also not harvest when the soil is wet or when it is raining. It is always better to give your plants some time to dry off before you start picking vegetables off them. This weather leaves the plants more vulnerable to disease and so they need their full strength to stay healthy. If you start picking at them, you will stress them out. This stress isn't very harmful while the environmental conditions are right but when they are wrong and there is a lot of moisture around, you are inviting danger into your crop. You might think this doesn't matter because you are harvesting and so you won't need that crop any more but this is wrong.

You don't just harvest your vegetables once and move on. In fact you should harvest them over the course of several days or even several weeks. Not every vegetable on a plant matures at the same time. The oldest veggies will mature first and need to be harvested earlier. Removing these from the plant will then help it to send energy towards the remaining veggies to speed up how fast they mature. By harvesting several times, you will end up with a bigger and better yield because of the way you are taking control of how the plant spends its energy.

- Harvesting your vegetable garden is the most time-consuming part of the whole process because you need to be checking it daily and looking out for certain signs and reacting quickly.

- By learning how to preserve your vegetables you will be able to keep your table packed high with nutritious food all year long.

- Different types of vegetables are harvested at different times throughout the year and have different signs that signal when they are ready. You will need to research your specific veggies to know what is best.

- Vegetables aren't always better when they are bigger. There are some kinds that are tastier when they are harvested a little early and there are some that go bad and lose their flavor if they grow too big.

- Never harvest in wet soil. If it rains, give the soil enough time to dry out so that you don't risk exposing your plants to disease.

- Many vegetables can be harvested throughout the season rather than just at one time and so you can get a lot of eating out of your veggies by carefully harvesting. Always remove the oldest parts of the plant first to allow younger parts to grow.

- Asparagus is ready to harvest when it is the size of your hand. Break it off by the soil and continue harvesting it as it grows back.

- Beans need to be harvested before they start to bulge out.

- You need to remove broccoli flowers throughout the season but these can be cooked and eaten. Harvest the broccoli itself when the buds are the size of an eraser. Secondary heads will continue to grow and can be eaten as well.

- Brussel sprouts mature very quickly and they are harvested all throughout the season.

- Cabbage needs to be firm and full but not too full. If left in the ground too long, then they will start to crack and split.

- Carrots can be harvested pretty much any time. Check the size of the root to get a feeling for the size of the carrot. Just because a carrot is the right thickness doesn't mean that it will be long enough. Carrots can stay in the ground for as long as you want before winter and so if they aren't big enough, then just give them a few more days.

- Cauliflower is harvested when the heads are full but smooth.

- When the silk corn husk starts to turn brown then you can begin checking the kernels. When a cut kernel starts to leak a milky substance, it is time to start harvesting.

- Cucumbers are harvested while they are still young in order to have the best flavor.

- Eggplant should be cut off the plant when it is smooth with a deep purple shine.

- The top of garlic turns brown and collapses when it is time to harvest the cloves.

- Like cabbage, head lettuce should be full and firm but it is better to harvest it a little early rather than keep it in the ground during warm weather.

- Kale can be picked throughout the harvest season. When picked only a little at a time, it lasts a remarkably long time and provides tons of nutritional value.

- Leaf lettuce can also be picked throughout the harvest season, starting from the outside in for the best results.

- Leeks can survive in the ground through winter. Similarly to carrots, simply dig them out of the ground when they are an inch thick.

- The top of the onion plant wilts when it is ready to be harvested. Carefully dig out the onions and let them dry in the sun before taking them inside.
- Parsnips can stay in the ground throughout the winter and actually taste better after a few frosts.
- Peas need to develop in the pod before they are picked but they should be taste-tested often so you can harvest when they are the sweetest.
- Potato plants start to flower when they are ready for harvest but you need to be extra careful digging them out of the soil because they are easy to damage.
- Radishes are harvested based on the size of their shoulders. It's better early than late with radishes because they lose their flavor when left in the ground too long.
- Spinach can be picked a bit at a time while growing so that it provides plenty of eating even before you harvest it fully.
- Squash needs to fill out and take on its color before it is harvested by being cut from the plant.
- Tomatoes should be entirely red before you twist them free from the vine.
- Turnips are ready to harvest based on the size of their shoulders and also take on a gross flavor if left too long.
- Drying out your vegetables requires you to clean them, Blanche them, and then leave them in the oven on low for a few hours up to a whole day. This will bake out all of the moisture in them so that they can be kept for up to a year but it will change their flavor drastically.

- To blanch your vegetables is to cook them in boiling water for a short period of time. This is important for drying and freezing and there are lots of health guides that can be found on the topic thanks to its importance to storing food.

- Canning is a complicated method used to create an airtight environment that can be used to store tomatoes, salsa, pickles, and pastes or jams. Canning isn't recommended for beginners.

- Pickling can be done to a lot of different vegetables, though it will change their taste. Boil glass jars and their lids to kill off any germs and then fill them with cut up veggies. Dissolve a tablespoon of salt into some vinegar and then add a cup of water. Fill up your jars with the liquid mixture, adding any spices you want to include beforehand. Stored in the fridge, these pickled vegetables will last several months.

Freezing your vegetables is the best way to preserve them without drastically changing their taste. Blanch your vegetables before storing them in freezer bags. Squeeze out as much of the air as you can before sealing so that these frozen vegetables can last up to a year.

- List Of The Main Vegetables And Herbs With Description And Explanation For Growing Them

ASPARAGUS

Asparagus officinalis

Asparagus plants can live 15 or more years, producing every year once they are established.

Family: Asparagaceae

Growing Seasons: early spring, plant 4 to 6 weeks before last frost

Zones: 3 through 8; because of the diversity of these zones, choose a variety best suited for yours

Spacing: 12 to 18 inches apart

Seed to Harvest: plant seedlings (crowns) the first year; harvest lightly in the second spring

Indoor Seed Starting: not recommended because your time to harvest will increase by one year; use plant crowns (dormant roots of year-old plants) purchased from a seed company

Earliest Outdoor planting: early spring once you're raised bed can be worked

Watering: water regularly

Starting

Location: full sun, part shade

Transplanting: Plant crowns in a trench 8 inches deep. Spread the roots and cover them with 1 to 2 inches of soil. You will add soil to the trench as the plants grow.

Planting: Add lime and fertilizer before planting crowns. Asparagus likes a pH near 7.

Growing

Keep asparagus watered in the first year, especially during times without rain. Do not overwater. The roots do not like to be overly wet. Mulch heavily to minimize weeds.

Harvesting

Harvest the spears before the tops develop fern-like leaves. Cut at ground level.

Problems

Asparagus beetle: Remove manually.

Fusarium wilt: Use fungicide.

BASIL

Ocimum basilicum

Try growing the large-leaf basil for making wraps and purple basil for creating a focal spot in your garden.

Family: Lamiaceae

Growing Seasons: spring, late spring

Zones: 3 through 10

Spacing: 12 to 18 inches

Seed to Harvest: 50 to 90 days

Indoor Seed Starting: 6 to 8 weeks before last frost

Earliest outdoor planting: after danger of frost; ground should be 60 degrees Fahrenheit

Watering: needs 1 inch of water per week during the growth cycle

Starting

Location: full sun

Planting: Cover seeds with ¼ inch of soil when planting directly in the garden.

Growing

Basil should not be allowed to dry out. Regular watering is best. To create bushy plants, pinch off the plant tops when they start to flower.

Harvesting

Pull off the leaves as desired.

Problems

If you are growing your basil in a warm area, pick varieties that are slow to bolt.

BEET

Beta vulgaris

Beet greens and roots are edible. They can be roasted, pickled, grilled, or boiled, and they freeze well.

Family: Chenopodiaceae

Growing Seasons: early spring or late fall in warmer climates; late spring or early fall in colder climates

Zones: 3 through 10

Spacing: 12 inches apart

Seed to Harvest: 50 to 60 days

Indoor Seed Starting: not recommended

Earliest Outdoor Planting: in cooler climates, early spring once your raised bed can be worked; in frost-free areas, sow in the fall

Watering: 1 inch of water per week

Starting

Location: full sun, part shade

Planting: Beets do not like acidic soil; they prefer a pH between 6 and 7.

Growing

Too much nitrogen will make the tops grow better than the roots.

Harvesting

Harvest beet greens when they are 4 to 5 inches long. Harvest the roots at 1 to 3 inches in diameter.

Problems

Leaf miner: Handpick and destroy affected leaves.

Leaf spot: Keep water off the green tops.

BELL PEPPER

Capsicum annuum

Family: Solanaceae

Growing Seasons: in warm climates, early spring; in colder climates, late spring to early summer

Zones: 3 through 10

Spacing: 14 to 16 inches apart

Seed to Harvest: 65 to 70 days

Indoor Seed Starting: 8 to 10 weeks before last frost; in the Deep South, seeds can be planted directly in the garden

Earliest Outdoor Planting: early spring after danger of last frost

Watering: 1 to 2 inches of water per week

Starting

Location: full sun

Growing

Too much nitrogen will cause the plant to produce more leaves than peppers.

Harvesting

Cut peppers off the stem rather than pulling them off. Peppers develop more flavor as they mature.

Problems

Aphids: Use natural soap and water.

Blossom end rot: This condition normally clears up on its own. Cut out the affected portion and eat the rest of the pepper.

Cucumber mosaic virus: Pull and dispose of infected plants; choose a different planting location next year.

BROCCOLI

Brassica oleracea var. italica

If you live in a warm climate, a fall planting is best, because broccoli thrives in cool weather.

Family: Brassicaceae

Growing Seasons: spring, fall, cool weather

Zones: 3 through 10; if in a warmer climate, plant heat-tolerant seeds

Spacing: 18 to 24 inches in rows 3 feet apart

Seed to Harvest: 45 to 60 days

Indoor Seed Starting: 7 to 9 weeks before the last spring frost; give seedlings 14 to 16 hours of light using fluorescent lighting

Earliest Outdoor Planting: 2 weeks before the last spring frost; in fall, in warm climates, 85 to 100 days before the first frost

Watering: moderate and even; water only the roots, not the heads

Starting

Location: full sun, can tolerate some shade, but plants will grow more slowly

Planting: Broccoli prefers a temperature between 64 degrees and 73 degrees Fahrenheit. It can be sowed outdoors with soil temperatures as low as 40 degrees Fahrenheit.

Growing

Broccoli can tolerate frost. Because it has a shallow root system, the use of mulch, rather than a cultivator, is recommended.

Harvesting

If you see yellow flowers, harvest the heads and use them immediately, because they are slightly beyond their prime. Harvest the central head of each broccoli plant with a pair of garden shears to encourage growth on the side shoots, which will continue to grow heads for several weeks.

Problems

Aphids: Use an insecticidal soap or a heavy spray of water to remove them.

Cabbage worms: Remove them manually, or use row covers to keep them off.

CABBAGE

Brassica oleracea var. capitata

Some varieties of cabbage grow flowers. The leaves of those plants are edible, but they are usually used as a garnish. Check your seed packets to verify you have edible cabbage leaves.

Family: Brassicaceae

Growing Seasons: plant in early spring, late fall

Zones: 3 through 10

Spacing: 12 to 18 inches apart

Seed to Harvest: 50 to 60 days

Indoor Seed Starting: 6 to 8 weeks before the last frost

Earliest outdoor planting: Early spring once your raised bed can be worked

Watering: keep well-watered during dry periods

Starting

Location: full sun

Planting: Plants will withstand a light frost.

Growing

Cabbage has a shallow root system. Avoid damaging it when weeding or cultivating.

Harvesting

Harvest when the heads are firm.

Problems

Cabbage aphids: Use an insecticidal soap or a heavy spray of water to remove them.

Cabbage worms: Remove them manually or use row covers to keep them off.

Club root: Remove the affected plants.

Cutworms: Remove them manually.

CANTALOUPE

Cucumis melo var. cantalupensis

Most people will grow their cantaloupes on the ground rather than on a trellis, because they "slip" off the vine when they are ripe.

Family: Cucurbitaceae

Growing Seasons: in warmer climates, early spring; in colder climates, late spring to early summer

Zones: 3 through 10

Spacing: 36 to 48 inches apart

Seed to Harvest: 70 to 85 days

Indoor Seed Starting: 3 to 4 weeks before planting, but direct sowing is recommended

Earliest outdoor planting: after danger of frost has passed

Watering: 1 to 2 inches of water per week

Starting

Location: full sun

Growing

Melons have a shallow root system; avoid damaging it when weeding or cultivating.

If you are growing melons on the ground, use plenty of mulch so they do not sit in the soil.

Harvesting

Ripe melons will "slip" from the vine. You will not need to exert much pressure to get them to release.

Once they start to smell like a melon, they are ripe.

Problems

Aphids: Use an insecticidal soap or a heavy spray of water to remove them.

Powdery mildew: Spray plants with a solution of 2 to 3 tablespoons of white vinegar per gallon of water.

Squash bugs: Remove eggs from the underside of leaves in the morning and later in the day.

Wilt disease: Use a fungicide.

CARROT

Daucus carot

Plant carrots every couple of weeks for nonstop harvesting.

Family: Apiaceae

Growing Seasons: spring, fall, depending on location; check your zone for specific times

Zones: 3 through 10

Spacing: 3 to 4 inches apart in rows 1 to 2 feet apart

Seed to Harvest: 50 to 80 days

Indoor Seed Starting: plant directly in the garden because they do not like to be transplanted

Earliest Outdoor Planting: after danger of heavy frost; in frost-free areas plant in fall

Watering: keep moist but not saturated; best done by drip irrigation; do not water foliage

Starting

Location: full sun

Seeding: Do not start indoors. Plant direct.

Planting: Cover seeds with ½ inch of soil. Plant them in deep, loose soil so the roots can grow.

Growing

Only weeding and watering are needed. Carrots need 1 inch of water per week during the growth cycle. Do not try to grow them in clay soil.

Harvesting

Simply twist and pull the roots, being careful not to pull the tops off. Clean the carrots and cut the green tops to just above the root for storage.

Problems

Aster yellows disease: Spread by the aster leafhopper, this disease causes shortened tops and hairy roots. Control the pest and keep this disease away using a sticky trap found at hardware stores.

Fusarium: This fungus causes dry rot of the root when carrots stay in the ground past their prime. To prevent fusarium, pick carrots at maturity.

CHIVES

Allium schoenoprasum

Chives are a great focal point in a garden bed and a welcome addition to many cuisines. For best production and healthiest plants, divide clumps every 3 to 4 years.

Family: Amaryllidaceae

Growing Seasons: spring, late spring

Zones: 3 through 10

Spacing: 3 to 4 inches apart

Seed to Harvest: 80 to 90 days

Indoor Seed Starting: 8 to 10 weeks before last spring frost

Earliest Outdoor Planting: after danger of heavy frost

Watering: water seedlings thoroughly after planting; plants need about 1 inch of water per week

Starting

Location: full sun

Seeding: Seeds can be started indoors or directly sown in the soil.

Transplanting: Plant seedlings with plenty of room for the root ball.

Planting: In the garden, cover seeds with ¼ inch of soil.

Growing

Weeding and watering are the only maintenance needed.

Harvesting

Clip plants to 1 inch above the ground. The tops will regrow.

Problems

Chives usually remain pest-free.

CILANTRO

Coriandrum sativum

Cilantro can be harvested as cilantro (the fresh herb) or coriander (the seed). For cilantro, harvest plants once green leaves are present, before the plants flower. For coriander, harvest the seeds once they turn grayish-brown.

Family: Apiaceae

Growing Seasons: spring, early summer

Zones: 3 through 10

Spacing: 10 to 14 inches

Seed to Harvest: 60 to 90 days

Indoor Seed Starting: 6 to 8 weeks before danger of last frost

Earliest Outdoor Planting: after danger of frost

Watering: needs 1 inch of water per week

Starting

Location: full sun

Seeding: Plant indoors 6 to 8 weeks before the last frost.

Planting: Cover seeds with ¼ inch of soil. Plant every 3 weeks if you want a continuous harvest.

Growing

Cilantro needs 1 inch of water per week. Do not fertilize.

Harvesting

Cut with scissors to 2 inches above the ground.

Problems

Keep soil moist so plants don't wilt.

CORN

Zea mays

Keep different varieties away from one another so they do not cross-pollinate, which could affect the flavor and quality of your harvested corn.

Family: Poaceae

Growing Seasons: spring, late spring

Zones: 3 through 10

Spacing: 5 to 6 inches in rows 2 to 3 feet apart

Seed to Harvest: 70 to 85 days

Indoor Seed Starting: directly sow in the garden

Earliest Outdoor Planting: after danger of frost

Watering: needs 1 to 2 inches of water per week during the growth cycle; soaker hose or drip irrigation is best

Starting

Location: full sun

Planting: Cover seeds with 1 inch of soil. Mix slow-release fertilizer into the soil when planting, according to the instructions on the label.

Growing

Weeding and watering are the only maintenance needed.

Harvesting

Each stalk usually produces two ears of corn, but hybrid varieties may have a higher yield. Harvest when the silk at the end of the ears is dry and brown and the ear feels plump. You may need to pull back the husk a little to see what you have. Give the ear a twist and a good tug to release it.

Problems

Corn earworms: These pests are found at the ends of the ears. Either trim and discard the ends, or do what I've done successfully for 20 worm-free years and squirt food-grade mineral oil into the ends of the ears when the silk turns brown.

CUCUMBER

Cucumis sativus

Cucumber plants are prolific, so do not plant too many. Buy pickling cucumber seeds to make pickles and slicing cucumber seeds to eat fresh. Do not use slicing cucumbers to make pickles; they soften when pickled.

Family: Cucurbitaceae, sometimes called curbits

Growing Seasons: soil temperature at least 60 degrees Fahrenheit

Zones: 3 through 10

Spacing: 18 to 36 inches apart; bush varieties can be planted closer together

Seed to Harvest: 50 to 70 days

Indoor Seed Starting: 3 to 4 weeks before the last frost, but direct sowing outdoors is recommended

Earliest Outdoor Planting: after the last frost

Watering: steady supply of water; drip irrigation on a timer is best

Starting

Location: full sun

Planting: Do not plant cucumbers until the soil reaches 60 degrees Fahrenheit.

Growing

Bush cucumbers do not need to be staked, but regular cucumber varieties do.

Harvesting

Cut rather than pull cucumbers off the vine. Do not leave overripe cucumbers on the vine, because the plant will take that as a signal to stop production.

Problems

Slugs and snails: Handpick and discard them.

GREEN BEANS

Phaseolus vulgaris

Beans are available as bush beans or pole beans. Bush beans do not need the support of a trellis, but pole beans do.

Family: Fabaceae

Growing Seasons: early to late spring, depending on zone; check your zone for specific times

Zones: 3 through 10

Spacing: 2 to 4 inches apart

Seed to Harvest: 50 to 55 days

Indoor Seed Starting: not recommended

Earliest outdoor planting: early spring once the danger of frost has passed

Watering: 1 inch per week

Starting

Location: full sun

Growing

When watering, do not wet the leaves. If they do get wet, do not handle them when wet because disease may result.

Harvesting

Beans are easy to pick right off the vine.

Problems

Aphids: Use an insecticidal soap or a heavy spray of water to remove them.

Bacterial blights: Use copper fungicide.

Spider mites: Use neem oil.

KALE

Brassica oleracea var. acephala

Kale has many health benefits. It is good for digestion, high in iron and vitamin K, and filled with antioxidants. You can plant it from early spring to early summer, but if you plant it in late summer, you can harvest it from fall until the first ground freeze.

Family: Brassicaceae

Growing Seasons: spring, fall

Zones: 3 through 10

Spacing: 12 to 18 inches apart

Seed to Harvest: 50 to 55 days

Indoor Seed Starting: direct sow outdoors up to 3 months before the last expected frost

Earliest Outdoor Planting: early spring once your raised bed can be worked; will germinate as low as 45 degrees Fahrenheit

Watering: do not let the plants dry out during drought periods

Starting

Location: full sun, part shade

Planting: Kale is easy to grow and prefers well-drained soil.

Growing

To reduce disease and pests, do not plant kale in the same location as other Cole crops (cruciferous vegetables like broccoli or cabbage) for 3 to 4 years.

Harvesting

Kale harvested after a frost will have a sweeter flavor.

Pick the outer leaves and leave the center.

Problems

Kale is relatively pest- and disease-free.

LEEK

Allium porrum L.

Leeks grow through the winter in the Deep South. Some varieties are bred to overwinter in colder eastern climates.

Family: Alliaceae

Growing Seasons: spring, fall

Zones: 3 through 10

Spacing: 18 to 20 inches apart

Seed to Harvest: 98 to 105 days

Indoor Seed Starting: 6 to 8 weeks before danger of last frost, or direct sow in the garden

Earliest Outdoor Planting: 4 weeks before last frost

Watering: 1 inch of water per week; keep evenly watered

Starting

Location: full sun, part shade

Growing

Leeks have a shallow root system and do best in a loose, well-drained soil. They should be kept well-watered and weeded. Mulching is a good way to hold the water and suppress the weeds. Avoid damaging when weeding or cultivating.

Harvesting

Leeks should be harvested when they are about 2 inches in diameter. Rock them back and forth to loosen them. Once harvested, the roots and all but 2 inches of the leaves should be cut off.

Problems

Damping off (pathogen-caused seedling collapse): Spray with a mixture of 1 tablespoon hydrogen peroxide per quart of water.

Downy mildew: Remove and discard affected parts of plants. Do not get water on leaves. Do increase airflow by thinning plants.

- **Symptoms And Solutions: Problem-Solving Guide**

Greenhouse Insect Management, Pest Control, Fertilization

Insect management

Solutions to insect problems include insect predators or other predators like you. When you put beer out for slugs, squish aphids with your fingers, or discard an infested plant, you are functioning as a predator. If no other solution works, you can spray. Sometimes simply a strong spray of clear water will wash insects off plants; many bugs are too fragile to survive this.

Showers

Some very successful indoor gardeners give most of their potted plants (not cacti and similar kinds) a weekly shower. They put the pot in the bathtub and turn on tepid water from overhead. This gets rid of many insects before the gardener has even begun to notice them, and the "rain" is good for most plants.

Other Sprays

The next step is a soap spray. You can buy an insecticidal soap solution, or you can put a drop of dishwashing liquid in a gallon of water. Other popular organic sprays involve garlic, onion, hot pepper, or a combination thereof, ground up and mixed with a great deal of water. A certified organic farmer I know makes "nettle tea" by leaving nettles in water in a barrel outdoors "until it stinks to high heaven," then diluting the tea ten to one or more. He recommends it highly; it may smell up your greenhouse, but it will kill many bugs.

Other Organic Poisons

A few years back, rotenone and pyrethrum, or pyrethrins, were all the rage with organic gardeners, including me. Now I never use them. They are organic in the sense that they are made from plants; rotenone is made from the root of a South American plant, and pyrethrum from a variety of chrysanthemum. Unfortunately, both can kill creatures you don't want killed, like spiders and ladybugs, or, in the garden, bees. Rotenone is particularly deadly to fish. You may not keep fish in the greenhouse, although a few greenhouses do, but pesticides have a way of getting into the water table.

Traps

Insect traps are not usually used in the greenhouse, except for one kind. Aphids, whiteflies, and many other undesirables are attracted to bright yellow. You can buy sticky 3-by-5-inch "cards" of this color, or circles of the same material, and set them up as traps. Hundreds of bugs will get stuck on them; when one gets too gross, throw it away and set up another one in the wire holder that comes with it. If you are really thrifty, you can buy a bottle of the sticky stuff, clean dirty traps with cooking oil, and recoat them.

Pest control

Gardeners like you often choose the path of gardening because plants can enjoy optimum growth under greenhouse conditions. However, the moderate warmth and moist also made a greenhouse the perfect nest for most pests. Greenhouses can act as a barrier of protection but pests can always sneak through small gaps. Below are the tips that will help in eradicating pests from your greenhouse

Greenhouse cleaning routine

Just like any other space in your house, you need to have a cleaning routine for your greenhouse. During the summer, you can move all the plants and gardening tools out from your greenhouse so cleaning activities can be carried out. Scrub the walls and floor with hot water and detergent solution. Pay particular attention to the corners and cracks as these are the likely places where pests will lay their eggs.

Freeze your greenhouse

If the environment inside your greenhouse is always warm and nice, pests will love it. It is good if you can freeze your greenhouse during winter season as cold temperature is the best way to kill or get rid of most pests. Before you do this, make sure that you have an alternative storage for your plants. It can be your warehouse, min indoor garden or you can simply freeze them inside the greenhouse. This is because pests might hide themselves and their eggs within the plants. If you have chosen the greenhouse plants that are able to grow without optimum growing conditions provided by the greenhouse, they should be able to be frozen inside the greenhouse. Even so, you should pay particular attention to their growth.

Sterilize gardening tools and soil

Before moving any new gardening tools or gardening materials into your greenhouse, make sure that you have properly sterilized them. Instead of using a normal garden soil, you should opt for a sterilized potting mix that are often pest free. As for your gardening tools, bleach them in a detergent solution. You must be very strict when it comes to this. Most of the time, you only have yourself to blame if your greenhouse suffers a pest infestation because you are the one showing them where the paradise is.

Constantly look out for pests

To prevent a total outbreak of pests, you need to monitor your plants closely. Destroy any eggs, larvae or bugs that you suspect to be harmful to your greenhouse garden. You may want to consider treating a particular plant separately. This is to avoid pests from moving effortlessly to another plant while treatment is being conducted. Do not be lazy because one a pest infestation takes place; it will take a long time for you to get rid of the whole colony because the environment inside the greenhouse provides a great breeding ground for these notorious creatures.

Introduce biological pest control

Consider deploying beneficial insects within your greenhouse. These predatory insects will feed on pests that are present inside your greenhouse in no time. Some of the beneficial insect that you can consider are ladybugs and praying mantis. You can get these from your local nurseries or even order them online. This method is not only organic but it will also save you a lot of time and effort trying to pick up harmful pests while performing your greenhouse gardening chores.

Use potting soil

Often ordinary garden soil will be packed with a lot of insect eggs, creepy crawlies and other pests. Therefore, for the plants inside containers in the greenhouse, its best to use a good potting soil or compost for potting them. The soil should be rich in nutrients, sterilized free from any diseases and pests to help the plants grow.

Practice crop rotation

If you plant directly into the ground in your greenhouses, obviously you will not have much better control over the spread of pests and diseases inside the soil. Crop rotation is a better way to combat this by growing different type of plant in the structure each year. It will discourage the building up of pests in the soil since the same plant usually promotes similar kinds of pests.

Use netting

Greenhouses require proper aeration, and it is not ideal to seal them up absolutely to prevent pests from entering. But you could reduce the number of big flying insects that come in by hanging netting, open windows, or other vent points.

Move pots outside in the heat

In the summer periods, a greenhouse will usually become hot and dry through the day. Taking plants in pots outside will not only help in cooling down the plants but also cut down the buildup of spider mites on them. Spider mites multiply in numbers in warm climates, so the ideal thing is to keep the greenhouse aerated and also use a mister to keep the humidity up. If you are leaving the house for the day, it's ideal to douse the floor of your greenhouse with water, which would evaporate into the air through the rest of the day.

Fertilization

Your greenhouse is the best investment you have ever done in terms of productivity and hobby. You can get a good source of income even from a small greenhouse by growing some vegetables, fruits, or flowers. But remember that greenhouse gardening is not like traditional gardening and you have to do utmost care of your plants for best production. Greenhouse plants need more amount of nutrients than outdoor gardening and you must provide them through proper means.

Keeping your soil fertile should be your major concern because many plants die in the absence of proper nutrients. Plants use a process called photosynthesis to produce some major nutrients on their own. So, unlike animals, plants only need some inorganic compounds to produce essential nutrients for their growth. Some of these nutrients like carbon, hydrogen, oxygen, nitrogen, phosphorus, potassium, Sulphur, calcium and magnesium are required in large quantities by plants and hence are called macronutrients.

The term pest control often conjures up images of people using sprays filled with chemicals. You might think that using such methods is rather extreme. But if you spot your wonderful tomatoes surrounded by ants or your beautiful flowers suddenly attacked by flies, then you might think of drowning those creatures in pesticides.

The thing about pesticides is that they have an instant (and noticeable) effect. You can see the number of pests on your plants reduced. Nevertheless, there are certain effects in the long term – such as depleting the health of your soil and slightly poisoning your water – that might prove disastrous for you in the future. You might have to change the soil entirely. If you are using a raised bed, then this might not be a problem. However, if you have decided to plant directly into the earth, then getting rid of all that pesticide residue is a strenuous process.

Here is another thing that you should keep in mind; sometimes, getting rid of the pests may not be necessary. If you have aphids roaming around on your plants, then see if you have helpful insects that dine on these aphids. In fact, certain farmers are known to let the pests live. This is because they usually have some form of predator that can take care of the pest problem. This has two beneficial results:

- You do not have to spend time (and money, in some situations) on pest control activities.

- You let someone (or something) else take care of the problem for you. A friend in need is a friend indeed. Even if that friend just happens to have four legs, wings, or antennae.

Mixed Plants

Most insects have receptors that allow them to target their favorite plants. It is how bees can seek out nectar so easily. If you have the plants that insects are waiting to attack and you have done nothing to protect those plants, then you might as well schedule buffet hours for the insects! What you can do to avoid this situation is to plant your crops in small batches throughout your garden. Then you can add other plants into the mix (preferably those that have resistance against the pests in your area). This confuses the insects, tricking them into believing that perhaps your garden does not have the food they are looking for. Additionally, you might be able to avoid diseases from spreading when you mix plant breeds.

Timing

Certain pests often arrive during certain climates. This fact might give you an idea of the kind of threat you are dealing with. When plants are young, they do not have the strength to ward off pests effectively, which is why you can plant your crops early so that by the time pest climate arrives, your crops have strong tissues. In some cases, insects often leave eggs behind in gardens. When the larvae hatch, they find a ready source of food in the plants around them. For this reason, you could also plant your crops a few weeks after the larvae have hatched, allowing you to starve the pests before working on your garden.

Here is a pro tip: speak to farmers in your area about the emergence of pests. They have extensive knowledge about when these pests might come out during a particular season, allowing you to know how long to wait before planting your crops.

Crop Rotation

You can move around the crops to new locations in your greenhouse each year. This does not give pests a particular spot to target. Shifting locations confuses the pests, who might be used to finding plants in a specific spot of the garden. Certain insects often lay their eggs in one location when they realize that they know where they can find a ready supply of food. However, by moving your crops around, larvae that hatch might not find their food source. Before they can discover food, they might starve and you might be able to get rid of them without much effort

Go Easy on the Fertilizer

This might be a common mistake committed by beginners. Gardeners who are starting out might worry about the amount of fertilizer that they use. Many use too much to avoid using too little. Unfortunately, too much fertilizer can cause harm to plants, just the way too little can. In fact, you could say that increasing the amount of fertilizer to a plant is like giving steroids to them! For example, soil nutrients provide nitrogen to the plant. This is good in moderate quantities. By adding more fertilizer, you increase the supply of nitrogen. Providing excess amounts of nitrogen might cause rapid growth in plants. This causes them to end up being juicy

Clean Up Other Materials

If you notice fallen leaves, fruits, or other objects in your garden that should not typically be there, then make sure you clear them out. These objects and debris might carry organisms and pests on them that could be transferred to your plants. This increases the chances of infecting your plants with diseases or sending pests into their midst. Once you have cleaned up, see if you can also cultivate the soil when you get the opportunity. This reveals any hidden pest eggs. Additionally, if there are any larvae, you might just let predators (or even the weather) get rid of them.

Make Friends with Creatures

I am not asking you to invite creatures into your house for tea and supper. What I mean is to allow the growth of certain organisms that could help you get rid of pests. For example, certain types of spiders leave your plants alone, but find abundant food in the pests that might live there. You can always encourage the growth of these pest-hunters, as you can call them.

Insecticides

These are a form of pesticide that are specifically made to harm, eliminate, or repel one or more species of insect. You can discover insecticides in various forms such as sprays, gels, and even traps. Pick one based on the pest that is attacking your garden.

Once you have selected your insecticide, it is better to know the below tips:

- I would recommend using just one type of insecticide in your garden. Adding two or more insecticides diminishes their effect and may inadvertently cause harm to your garden.

• Remember that not all insecticides take the same time to remove pests from your garden. You might have to wait longer for certain types.

• Try to see if you really need the spray. For example, if you want to get rid of ants, you could use a bait instead (after all, ants are attracted to nearby sources of food).

Fungicides

These are pesticides that are made to kill fungal infections on the plants and any fungi spores that might have latched onto your crops. In some cases, fungicides are used to mitigate the effects of mildew and mold. The way they function is by damaging either the fungal cell structure or stopping the energy production in cells.

When you are ready to use your fungicide, do make note of the below tips:

• In many cases, people might accidentally diagnose fungal diseases for their plants when in reality, it might not be a disease at all. Make sure you use the help of local experts to give you a second opinion. They might just prevent you from buying a fungicide needlessly and might recommend another solution.

• Make sure that leaves are not kept wet for too long. Simply keeping the leaves dry after watering them helps reduce the spread of fungi.

• Keep your tools sanitized. Sometimes, the fungi could spread from one plant to another because they stuck to the tools you were using.

Herbicides

The main purpose of herbicides in a garden is to get rid of all the weeds.

When you have gotten your herbicide, do make note of the following tips:

• Always make sure that the instructions on the herbicide suit your purposes.

• Go easy on its application. Adding more herbicide might sound like a safe bet, but it might end up damaging your plants. If you feel unsure, read the instructions provided on the herbicide to understand its usage quantity.

• Certain herbicides show immediate results. Others take a while to get rid of the weeds. Always check with the seller or supplier for details before using the herbicide. This way, you are not left wondering if you had bought a defective product when you see weeds present even after the third day of using the herbicide.

• Herbicides also have an effect on the soil, so make sure you speak to experts about your garden's soil types before you make a purchase.

- **Frequently Asked Questions**

I cultivate my garden, and my garden cultivates me.
~Robert Brault

I have tried to give you a basic, but thorough beginner's guide to the most common and popular gardening methods. The emphasis has been on the mechanics of gardening. Now I want to bring it all together by answering the questions people tend to ask once they decide to try their hand at gardening. Some of the answers may be repetitions of things you have already read, but that is okay. If it is important enough to put in here twice, it's important enough to read it twice. So, without further ado…

Q: Is it better to start from seed or seedling plants?

A: Most of the time you will do better if you start your flowers with seedling plants. The main reason for this is that flowers take much longer to mature than vegetables. The exception to this is zinnias and sunflowers. You will also find that planting iris and lilies using just the chromes will work just fine, too.

When it comes to vegetables, however, it is almost always better to start from seed, with the exception of tomatoes, which need to be started indoors if you want to enjoy the fruits of your labor before the growing season is over.

Q: Is there anything to the old sayings about planting according to the signs of the moon and other such things?

A: Yes, most definitely! For example, a new moon pulls water up from the ground, which in turn, swells a seed and causes it to burst open (germinate). That is why planting within a day or two of the new moon causes quick productivity.

Q: What's the difference between garden soil and potting soil?

A: Potting soil is less dense. It contains little or no actual dirt/soil, but is a combination of peat moss, vermiculite or perlite, sand, and even finely ground tree bark. Potting soil has also undergone a sterilization process to kill any weeds and seeds that would interfere with plant growth. Garden soil contains actual soil, so it is much denser and doesn't drain as well as potting soil, and it tends to get packed down in pots.

Q: What about succulents? Are they easy to grow?

A: Yes. Succulents, which include cactus, are very easy to grow. They require next to no care and prefer not to be watered very often. In fact, I know people who have beautiful cacti that grow well with only a tiny bit of water every month or so. There are so many varieties of succulents to choose from, you can have a diverse and attractive display with very little work on your part. NOTE: Succulents do best in containers in most parts of the country.

Q: Are berries easy to grow, and can they be grown in small areas?

A: Strawberries are very easy to grow and can be grown in an area as small as 5x5 feet. Strawberry plants are a lot like bunnies—they multiply rapidly. You will need to thin your plants out each spring before they begin to bloom. You do this by simply pulling some of the plants out of the ground. You will also have to break their runners to separate them from their 'parent' plant. Sell or give your excess plants to someone. Blackberries, blueberries, raspberries, and all other berries require a lot more room and attention.

Q: Is one kind of mulch better than another?

A: Mulch is a matter of opinion. When you think of mulch, you tend to think in terms of cypress, cedar, or pine wood chunks. But there are actually several other materials you can use for mulch. They include rubber, pea gravel, creek gravel, nut hulls, cocoa bean hulls, and lava rock. Deciding what you use to mulch your gardens (if you use anything at all) depends on a number of things. For example, if your garden consists primarily of perennials, or if you have an area of your yard designated for pots, rock is often your best option. It doesn't have to be replaced, it doesn't attract insects (like wood does), and it requires next to no maintenance. Vegetable gardens or flower beds you will be tilling or spading every season don't need mulch. And finally, be sure your pets won't ingest the nut hulls, cocoa bean hulls, or rubber, as all are toxic to them.

Q: What are community gardens?

A: Community gardens are gardens used and tended to by several individuals. Most community gardens rent space to people to use for growing vegetables and herbs. Each person is responsible for keeping their own area of the garden weeded, watered, and tended to. I'll be honest—I don't know how community gardens keep people from taking things that aren't theirs. I assume it's based on an honor system, which should work. If you participate in a community garden venture, you still need to have your own tools, fertilizer, pest prevention, and so forth. Community gardens can be a great way to enjoy raising your own herbs and vegetables as long as you don't get tired of traveling back and forth to take care of your space.

Q: How do I know what planting zone I'm in?

A: This map shows the different planting zones in the United States.

Q: What flowers attract hummingbirds and butterflies?

A: Impatiens, petunias, hollyhocks, honeysuckle, bee balm, columbine, lilies, and phlox are a few of the most popular hummingbird attractants. Hibiscus, coneflowers, butterfly bush, sunflowers, lilac, zinnias, sweet William, petunias, and dianthus are just a few of the many flowers that will bring butterflies to your garden.

Q: Is it better to overwater or underwater your plants?

A: Neither. You need to make sure your plants get the amount of water they need AND that their home (ground, raised bed, or container) has proper drainage. When your plant is getting too much water, leaves will become pale and yellow and the plant will look limp. If they aren't getting enough water, leaves will drop in an effort to conserve food and energy for the main part of the plant.

Q: I see all sorts of unconventional things being used as flower or vegetable containers. What special preparation, if any, needs to be done to use these things?

A: Using 'unconventional' items to pot plants and flowers in is a great way to add a bit of whimsy and personal flair to your landscape. Flowers and plants look fine in traditional pots, but they look spectacular in an old suitcase, a cowboy boot, a vintage child's dump truck or lunch box, a dresser no longer in good enough condition to hold clothes, or whatever else appeals to you. The only preparation you need to make is to ensure the container has adequate drainage, so plants don't become waterlogged.

FYI: Other unusual items you can use for your container garden include:

- Old tins
- Purses
- Wheelbarrow
- Baskets
- Old tires
- Wooden boxes

Q: What things are compostable?

A: The most compostable materials are:

- Vegetable peelings
- Leaves
- Straw
- Sawdust
- Pine needles
- Small sticks
- Bark
- Paper towel and toilet paper tubes
- Newsprint (not glossy)
- Dryer lint
- Egg shells
- Coffee grounds
- Dead plants
- Stale bread, crackers, cereal
- Burlap
- Livestock manure

Q: What things can't I compost?

A: You cannot compost:

- Diseased plants
- Meat, pasta, bones
- Synthetics
- Walnut hull, leaves, and twigs
- Pet manure
- Human waste
- Plastic
- Glossy paper
- Dairy products

Q: How do I know if my soil is too acidic?

A: You can have a professional soil test done without spending a lot of money. You can also do it yourself using nothing more than a sealable clear glass jar, soil from your garden, and water. To test your soil, fill the jar about half full of soil from the garden you want to test. Fill the jar the rest of the way with water, leaving about an inch of space at the top. Seal the jar and shake it vigorously. Let it set untouched for 24 hours. During this time the soil will separate into layers of silt, clay, and sand.

You also need to notice the color or tint of your soil. The lighter the soil's color, the less organic matter it contains. If this is the case with your soil, you need to add compost matter to it to help your plants grow.

Conclusion

Planning a garden, preparing the soil, nurturing plants, outsmarting pests, harvesting, preserving, and preparing meals are many of the numerous benefits to both body and soul that come out of such an endeavor. Not only are you contributing to the health and well-being of yourself, your friends, and your family, but you are also actively participating in creating a healthier environment and a better world.

I hope you have appreciated this journey through the seasons and now have the confidence and knowledge to begin your own backyard garden. Advice on how to set up a garden; how to prepare the soil; how—and when and what—to plant; how to combat pests and diseases; how to harvest and preserve; how to succession plant to ensure continuous garden growth: these tips, techniques, recipes, and more are all here. In addition, the many positive reasons—from avoiding petrochemicals and their detrimental effects to the fostering of tastier and more nutritious food—for undertaking an organic garden are outlined throughout.

Now that you have all the information needed, it is time to get going. Walk around your available space during the day to find a sunny location. Once you have decided where you want to place your raised bed, decide on the size and dimensions. The next step is to make a list of everything you will need, from the soil, compost, and other materials, to the frames. Once your bed is up and filled up with the soil mixture, it is time to turn your attention to the plants. Select the type of veggies you want to grow according to the guidelines I have provided. If you want to grow plants from seeds, you will have to do some prior planning since it will take time for them to develop into seedlings ready to be planted outside in your box. Otherwise, you can purchase seedlings to plant directly into your raised beds.

Now, most of the work is done, and the fun part starts. While you wait for your veggies to grow, a little attention is needed; water them regularly and keep your eyes peeled for any pests or weeds. Then wait for the fruit to mature and start harvesting!

Growing vegetables in raised beds makes gardening a pleasure. With limited time and space, you can grow an abundance of food in a small area. The benefits are numerous; fewer weeds and pests, better drainage, better soil, no compacting of the soil, less pain potential for you, the gardener, to name but a few. Your friends will envy your neat, attractive garden and harvest of healthy, tasty vegetables.

In order to properly grow houseplants, you'll have to invest more money in ensuring you have a suitable environment for them. However, much of this money is used in the early parts of the installation, such as purchase grow lights, fans, and humidifiers. Once you have made the investment in this gear, you will be able to reuse again and again for harvest after harvest. Seen this way, the investment becomes easier to justify. Not only that but if you decide to indoor gardening is not for you, then you can resell this equipment to recover some of their money. Just remember to start small when you start; otherwise, the cost of investment and the time you need to make will be much higher.

Creating an indoor garden is no more difficult than growing one to the outdoors. In fact, the level of control we have over an indoor environment makes it easier in many ways. Rain, drought, cold, or snow and half death for your plants, and by using electric lights, which are capable of providing enough "sunlight" to ensure that your plants stay healthy and happy.

As we deal with issues such as global warming and changes in the environment, indoor gardening will continue to grow in popularity. In the future, it seems likely that a substantial proportion of our food will be developed and raised inside, rather than outside. From your indoor garden, today will give you the practical experience you need to teach others how to start yours. Not only is indoor gardening a great choice to enjoy fruits and vegetables grown organically from the comfort of your home, but it is also an investment in you and your family's future.

We have only been able to cover a small selection of plants that can be grown indoors. Instead, you should take the lessons we've been here, and apply to fruits, vegetables, herbs and most.

Interest you. Just remember to do your research to make sure you can provide the right environment for your plants, whether blueberries, basil, squash, or anything else. Each plant is unique and should be respected as such. With this attitude and a little care, you will be able to grow anything your heart desires.

When we develop our own food, we understand exactly what's gone into developing it. Lots of men and women worry about pesticide residues in food. Even if science demonstrates these pesticide residues from foods are totally harmless since they're under a particular threshold, a lot of individuals simply prefer to consume food which has raised naturally with no artificial inputs and hopefully raised by themselves. Personally, I'm a dedicated organic gardener and I never utilized synthetic fertilizers or synthetic pesticides and that I believe there's not any demand for this. Nature itself takes care of this.

We hope that you find this information helpful. While there are many ways to garden and many things to garden, choose one simple thing to do this year.

Maybe choose 1-2 plants to plant this year and focus on setting up your garden. When you feel comfortable and successful in your gardening endeavors, you can add more plants and do more elaborate things with your gardening space. I started with a single plant and now I am growing hundreds of them and making it my main source of income. People come to me all the time to get gardening advice and buy from my own garden. I can say this is the most fulfilling hobby anyone could ever have. It will help not only your family but also the environment!

Have Fun!

HYDROPONICS

Introduction

The concept of indoor gardening has been well practiced since ancient times. Plants make decorative statements indoors, but people soon realized that they don't have to go out into the sun just to till the garden and see some fresh blooms! A number of indoor gardening methods have since then developed, giving gardeners instant access to herbs and fruits, as well as place a patch of foliage and blooms inside the home.

Indoor gardening, of course, first began with soil as a medium. However, several studies found that garden soil may not be the most ideal medium for indoor gardening. According to the University of Illinois, garden soil may contain diseases and pests that can damage your indoor plants. To mitigate the risk of disease and pest attacks, the potting soil for your indoor garden must be amended and should include a variety of mediums. Peat and moss, for example, provide good indoor gardening media, are free from diseases and pathogens, and provide good aeration and drainage.

The potting soil mix also depends on the type of plants you wish to grow indoors. Herbs planted in container gardens, for example, do not very well with peat-based soil mixture because they tend to lose moisture quickly. However, you have the option to choose from several types of potting soil mixes such as vermiculite, perlite, and pumice, or you can simply create your own potting mix composed of organic materials.

Another method for indoor gardening is hydroponics. Hydroponics comes from the Greek words "hydro" meaning "water" and "ponos" meaning "labor." The practice of hydroponics can be traced back as early as the 1950s when some scientists experimented with water-soluble nutrients fed to plants, instead of deriving nutrients from the soil. Although the growth and development of hydroponics wera not so rapid, it is now enjoying its share in the limelight as demand for food and fresh produce increases and the number of fertile soil for planting decreases.

Basically, plants grown hydroponically have roots submerged into a water solution where nutrients are mixed. The roots get constant contact with these nutrients, instead of having to seek these nutrients out in the soil. Because the nutrients are readily available for the roots to absorb, indoor hydroponic gardening has provided higher success rates than most traditional gardening techniques.

Indoor gardening with soil and hydroponics can be quite challenging for beginner gardeners, however, the rewards are worth it. Plants grown in both mediums require maintenance in various aspects and levels. For instance, different plants have different reactions to different light and temperature levels. Some plants, like broccoli and cauliflower, like cool hydroponic gardens. While some varieties don't produce heads that are big enough to your liking, hydroponically grown broccoli and cauliflower tend to be more tasty and tender than their soil varieties.

Some plants also like different lighting systems. A soil-mixed container garden full of tomatoes may grow well with full sun, just like your hydroponically-grown varieties, however, hydroponic tomatoes tend to seep so much water and nutrients from your reservoir as they grow.

If you are thinking of starting an indoor garden, whether with soil and hydroponics as a medium, it is best to first understand the nature of the plants and meet their requirements. This can help extend their growing season and you'll have a bounty supply of fresh produce all throughout the year.

Science has always advanced the course of bettering the lives of humans. Every day, scientists spend hours trying to improve on present living conditions or create new ones that are better than what is currently obtainable. They discover fun ways of making our processes efficient.

This easy-to-implement guide will ultimately make hydroponics your best choice when you want to plant. Being an important part of the future of farming, understanding the intricacies of hydroponics requires informed guidance. We will guide you through the practice, the types, the best forms of hydroponics, and so much more.

Hydroponic gardening is a great way to keep your fruit and vegetable garden year-round. It also means that the crops you grow will not be exposed to pesticides, chemicals, and shipping rigors over long distances-all these factors will hinder nutritional content and vegetable and fruit taste.

Hydroponic gardening's productivity may only be exceeded by its relative ease of use, in terms of understanding the ease with which it works, once properly prepared and informed, you can start your own garden.

Hydroponics is soil-needed gardening. Water, light, nutrients are all needed. For a beginner, it's very important to know exactly what you'll need based on your intended end result and what kind of space you've got. Visit a local hydroponic supply shop, search forums and blogs, and ask as many questions as possible.

Hydroponic gardening has many key advantages as compared to traditional soil-based gardening methods- hydroponic gardening ensures you're never at the mercy of the environment, no matter where you stay- hydroponic gardening is absolutely seasonless.

Where you live it could be extremely cold and your hydroponic garden will definitely flourish as long as you provide the right light, nutrients temperature, and humidity.

If you can sustain these factors, whether in a small, wardrobe-sized system or a large greenhouse set-up, you can enjoy tropical fruits and off-season vegetables all year round! Hydroponically grown fruit and vegetables tend to be larger than their natural counterparts, offering more edible food.

Hydroponically grown food always has a constant and maximized amount of nutrients and oxygen supplied to it - the plant will never lack essential nutrients and this, coupled with a regulated temperature, helps the garden and its contents to grow much faster than a conventional soil-based garden that relies on ideal weather conditions and many other factors without a greenhouse.

Hydroponically grown vegetables and fruit will never need to be treated with multitudes of pesticides and other chemicals that are regularly applied to commercially grown fruit and vegetables-this alone will ensure a much higher nutritional value.

This "pure" technique is combined with the fact that the yield from your hydroponic system does not need to move past your greenhouse to your kitchen - the vegetables you consume will not have been transported hundreds of miles and will be spared the loss of shipping and transport rigors.

Obviously, all these wonderful benefits come at a cost. The cost of setting up a hydroponic garden is initially expensive in many aspects, but once you set up your system, it can be managed at a reasonable cost. If your goal is to live solely on your hydroponic production, you will probably spend considerable money to get started.

Of course, available space would also be a factor in how much you can grow anytime. Once the hydroponic system is properly set up, the plants will grow bigger and wider very quickly... they will easily outgrow the room you initially allocated to them, so you should overestimate the space requirements if it's your first time.

Hydroponic gardening is safe, economical, and relatively easy! Nonetheless, like any initiative deserving of your time and resources, it is simply a matter of good planning and foresight to look at all the facts beforehand and get to know the variables before purchasing any materials.

Whether you just want to grow a few plants or a whole food-worthy greenhouse, hydroponics will make you eat well all year round-you can never go to the grocery store again!

This is the perfect guide for you to learn all the basics of hydroponic gardening as a beginner. I hope you'll make the best use of it.

Let's get started!

Chapter 1. What is Hydroponics?

Plants mainly grow with the help of a process called photosynthesis. They use sunlight and chlorophyll to convert water and carbon dioxide into oxygen and glucose. There's no implicit or explicit mention of soil anywhere in the process and therefore, it could be concluded that plants only need nutrients and water to survive. Water and nutrients can easily be obtained from soil or any other source or medium.

Hydroponics is a process by which plants are grown without using any soil. The procedure involves the use of a water solvent along with a mineral nutrient solution, which aids in the efficient intake of various nutrients by the plant. This whole process is a subset of hydroculture.

The Objective of Hydroponics

The main objective of hydroponics is to provide the ideal environment for the plants through which they can obtain the required nutrition essential for their sustenance. Climate and lighting can also be controlled to improve the yield of plants, including a greenhouse set up with natural and supplemental lighting.

A Timeline of Hydroponics System

Even though the procedure of the Hydroponics System might seem like a new-age technology, the process has been in use since 600 BC. The following is the respective timeline of the Hydroponics System:

600 BC

Currently located in Iraq and one of the Seven Wonders of the World, the Hanging Gardens of Babylon is the 1st incidence to show the use of hydroponic principles. The gardens used an hydroponic system procedure for the plants to grow.

1100 AD

In Central America, Chinapas or commonly known as Floating Gardens were created by Aztec Indians. These gardens were developed with the use of layers of vegetation and mud to hang plants above freshwater lakes in the area.

1275 - 1292

In China, 'Floating Gardens' was also discovered and therefore written by Marco Polo. He was an Italian explorer, merchant, and writer, who used to travel throughout Asia.

1492

It was discovered by Leonardo da Vinci, who was also known as 'Renaissance Man' that, trees get necessary benifits. This finding of his had remained in his books for they didn't go out to the public.

1640

Jean Baptista van Helmont, who was a Belgian chemist, had carried out his famous 'Willow Tree' experiment and had proved that plants obtain nutrients and substances from water.

1920

The 'Hoagland's Solution' was created by Dennis R Hoagland. The solution was a nutrient formula and still to this day is being used as a basis for the Hydroponic System.

The Late 1920s - Early 1930s

The term 'Hydroponics' was coined by Dr. William F Geriche. The main reason for coining this term was that he started his research process in practical outdoor conditions which included large scale crop cultivation.

1940

American troops during World War II started to grow vegetables using the Hydroponics System. The reason was to ease the pressure of deporting foods that are perishable to different locations, such as the arid regions of the Middle East, barren islands of the Pacific, etcetera.

The soldiers who were protecting the Arabian Peninsula's vital oil fields used to eat vegetables that were locally grown in one of the harshest desert conditions.

1952

The special hydroponics branch of the US Army had freshly produced over 8 million pounds of plants growing vegetables, due to the high military demand.

1960

Two new methods were introduced for the Hydroponics System, known as the Drip Irrigation System and the Nutrient Film Technique (NFT).

1969

The Canadian and American industry of growing marijuana at home was demonstrated due to the wide usage of the hydroponic principles.

The Early 1980s

Starting in the 1980s, the High Times magazine started detailing simple ways to carry out Hydroponics Systems, so that millions of people could be introduced to this new way of growing plants without soil. During that same time, Disneyworld's Epcot Center introduced a futuristic ride through its hydroponically grown gardens, known as the 'Living with the Land'.

1989

Operation Green Merchant was launched by the US Government to crack down the illegal growing of homegrown marijuana, using Hydroponics Systems. While the arrests did try to drive the industry further down, it instead showed people new ways for growing plants with more efficiency and security.

1995

The High Times magazine stated the merits and demerits of growing plants organically, either in water or soil, with the help of chemical nutrients. This aided the hydroponics principles to go more mainstream among the common people.

1999

Four years later, the High Times magazine published its first annual hydro report, with the help of Kyle Kushman. The report highlighted the best products related to the hydroponics process and also the best hydro systems as well.

The Use of Hydroponics through History

During The 600 BC

The Hanging Gardens of Babylon, built-in Mesopotamia or Babylonia, was established along the Euphrates River. The place had a dry climate that showed very little signs of rain. Therefore, the plants in the garden were generally watered using the chain pull system.

The system consisted of water that was carried up from the river and then the water was allowed to trickle down through each section of the garden structure. The process helped the lush gardens of Babylon to survive even in the scarcity of rainfall.

During The 1100 AD

The Aztecs had developed a floating garden system, which was based on the principles of hydroponics, around the 10th and 11th centuries. The Aztecs had settled at Lake Tenochtitlan and were unable to grow any crops due to the mashy shore. Therefore, reeds and roots were used to build rafts, which were then topped with soil from the bottom of Lake Tenochtitlan.

These rafts were then made to float on the water. When crops were grown on the rafts, their roots seeped through the soil, into the surface of the water. A similar process was also used by the Chinese, at the end of the 13th century, which was reported by Marco Polo.

During The 17th Century

A British scientist, politician, and philosopher, known as Sir Francis Bacon, started to do his research on gardening without using soil, in the 1620s. After the publication of his work in the year 1627, the topic of hydroponics was instantaneously picked up by other researchers too.

Then in the year 1699, an English scientist named John Woodward started doing tests on the spearmint plant, in different solutions of water. Three types of water were used, namely - drained water mixed with soil, rainwater and also river water.

The experiment had concluded that the plants grow healthier and faster in the water that was mixed with soil. Therefore, the scientist believed that plants grow slower in distilled water than in less pure water. The reason behind this observation was that the less pure water (mixed with soil) had all the essential nutrients and minerals, needed to make the plant flourish.

During The 19th Century

In the year 1851, a chemist based in France had carried out an experiment using no soil but other insoluble mediums. He was known as Boussignault. The mediums that were used - quartz, sand, charcoal, along with water and chemical nutrients. The experiment had concluded that plants only need air, water, nitrogen, hydrogen, and nutrients.

The theory was solidified in the year 1860 and 1861 when Wilhelm Knop and Julius von Sachs found the first formula for the hydroponics solution. It's known as 'nutriculture' or 'Water Culture', which contains all the essential nutrients for plants to be grown in a water solution. Macroelements and micronutrients such as potassium, sulphur, magnesium, phosphorus, nitrogen, and calcium were the main elements.

During The 20th Century

William Gericke, who was a scientist at Berkeley, USA, had started the promotion of commercial agriculture with the use of hydroponics. The process that was used was 'aquaculture', which demonstrated the growth of massive tomatoes at his home.

It was one of the benefits that he obtained while used the no-soil gardening procedure by using various nutrient and water solutions. Since the term 'aquaculture' was used to study water organisms, William Gericke changed the term to 'Hydroponics'.

At the same time, two scientists from Berkeley started to expand upon the investigation and experiments of William Gericke. They were known as Daniel Arnon and Dennis Hoagland. These two scientists helped to develop different nutrient solutions that still used in the hydroponics procedure, to date.

In the year 1938, an article was published by them, known as 'The Water Culture Method for Growing Plants without Soil', which helped in shaping the entire world for this new way of growing plants.

Due to the publication of the above article, various commercial uses of hydroponics was on the rise. Vegetables, beans, and tomatoes were grown inside tanks containing mineralized water, in Wake Island, located in the Pacific Ocean. The island was generally used as a refueling station for the Pan-Am Airways. Thus, the food that was successfully grown, was used to satisfy the feeding requirements of the staff and the crew, working in the airline company. Similar methods were used in World War II, by American soldiers, on the barren Pacific Islands.

The 21st Century

Due to the numerous benefits of the Hydroponics System, the process is being used all over the world. It is undoubtedly agriculture's fastest-growing sector. The process has become an indispensable tool for all greenhouse plant growers. Every greenhouse farm nowadays uses the hydroponics procedure for crop yields.

It was reported by the 2017 statistics of the International Greenhouse Vegetable Production that the overall production of commercial greenhouse vegetables is measured at more than 1.2 million acres. Some of the countries that have adopted the hydroponics process and greenhouse farms are the Netherlands, the USA, Canada, and Australia. Countries like Israel, which has a hot and dry climate, has been able to grow massive quantities of fruits (more than

1,000 times the normal yield) with the help of hydroponics.

The USA also has the largest hydroponic farm in the world, located in New Jersey, Florida. The farm produces about two million leafy and fresh lettuce annually.

The Future

The hydroponics mode of agriculture can easily dominate the production of food over the next few years. Combined with technologies such as vertical farming, additional ways of crop production can be experienced. It's believed that by the year 2050, the total population of the world will reach almost 9.2 billion. Since only 3 percent of the Earth's surface can be used for agriculture, traditional agriculture should be compensated by Hydroponics Systems.

It has also been reported by NASA that hydroponics can be an extensive way to grow crops in various space exploration programs and thus aid in the colonization of the Moon and Mars.

The Science behind Hydroponics

It is very essential to understand the internal tactics of how hydroponics work, because the future of agriculture depends on them. In a process like hydroponics, plants are mostly grown in inert mediums, for example - peat moss and clay pellets. This allows the roots of the plants to stay directly in contact with water. Further, the nutrient-rich solution promotes the plants' growth.

The typical requirements needed for the growth of plants have always been on the simpler side. They obtain water, carbon dioxide, sunlight and essential nutrients from the soil. With the help of photosynthesis, plants convert light energy into chemical energy.

During the process of photosynthesis, plants also release oxygen and require minerals like potassium, nitrogen, and phosphorus. These minerals can be easily obtained from commercial agricultural fertilizers and from the organic soil itself. The thing that needs to be understood here is that - plants only need the minerals from the soil and not the soil itself. This is what hydroponics is all about - removing the requirement of soil altogether.

The process of hydroponics is generally carried out indoors with the help of greenhouse farms. Special LED lighting equipment is used to substitute the need or direct sunlight and hydroponic farms are constructed inside large warehouses. Hydroponically grown plants are placed vertically on top of each other, using a number of shelves. This setup is much easier when compared to growing plants horizontally, as in typical agricultural fields.

Is The Process Organic?

There has been a long laid out controversy if the entire hydroponic process is organic. It is said that agriculture carried out via hydroponics should not be considered as organic production because the soil is not used in the mixture. Since the foundation of organic agriculture is based on soil, thus not using the soil will make the process inorganic.

It was recommended by the National Organic Standards Board that agriculture which is done soil-free should not be labelled as 'organic'. Still, nowadays, hydroponically supported agriculture is termed as organic, only if the process doesn't involve any use of chemically-supported fertilizers (synthetic fertilizers) and it follows all the conditions of cultivating organic food.

The Types

Aeroponics

It is a system that is based on water and therefore no medium is required. All the plants are suspended. The free roots of the plants dangle below a tray. The tray is then put into a box having a mixture of nutrient solution and water. There is an in-built pump system where the water is taken out of the box and then sprayed in a mist-form over the whole anatomy of the plant, continuously. Since the process is difficult to set up, it is only used for large, commercial uses.

Ebb and Flow

In this process, the plants require a form of a medium, which will provide stability for their roots, like perlite. The medium is not responsible to provide any nutrients to the plant. The process is similar to aeroponics where the medium is placed onto a tray and a reservoir full of water and nutrient solution is placed under a tray.

Instead of spraying the reservoir solution, the solution is pumped into the tray. This fills the tray with the solution and it gets absorbed by the plants. Slowly, due to gravity, the nutrient solution and water will drain back to the reservoir. The process is recommended to be used with small hydroponic home setups.

Drip Irrigation

An identical method like Ebb and Flow is deployed, except for the fact that water and the nutrient solution are pumped through many small tubes instead of a single large one. The procedure works best for smaller plants that haven't generated a pronounced root system yet.

NFT or Nutrient Film Technique

NFT doesn't require any medium and is water-based, similar to aeroponics. Wooden channels are set up which help in supporting the film liners made up of polyethylene. The process is carried out for plants like cucumbers and tomatoes - plants that have developed root systems. The plants are kept on a sloped channel and the water combined with the nutrient solution is then pumped on the high slope.

The mixture solution runs through the entirety of the slope, plant and its roots, and then finally reaches the bottom slope to be collected again and reused.

Wick Systems

Here, rockwool or perlite medium is used as a medium. At each plant's root base, a nylon thread is attached which is then extended beyond the bottom of the plant tray. The tray is then placed in a reservoir. The nylon thread absorbs all the nutrients and water from the reservoir solution and the same gets transported to the root of the plants. Since no water pumping action is required, the process is simple and easy to set up as well.

Water Culture and Barrelponics

Barrelponics is defined as the process in which fishes are kept in a barrel to produce wastewater, which is then pumped up onto the plants. The wastewater gets absorbed by the plants and the rest gets filtered through the settlement layers again into the fish barrel.

This system of water culture works on the physics of pumping air through an air pump into an airstone. The air stone is placed at the bottom of the reservoir, on top of which the plants are floating on a platform made from styrofoam. On pumping air, the airstone releases all the nutrients upwards towards the roots of the plants. The nutrients then get absorbed by the plants. The process should be carried out manually.

Chapter 2.   Equipments

Irrigation

One of the key factors to a hydroponics system is its water supply. Getting the correct nutrient-to-water solution balance is imperative to the growth of the plants and crop production.

Most hydroponic systems work on a recycling principle where the water stored in the reservoir is pumped from the tank to the plant's root system. Once the roots have taken their share of the moisture, what is left over is usually drained back into the tank or cycled off. Most hydroponic systems that do not use the recovery cycle only feed the plants the amount they need which tends to leave little to no waste runoff.

A lot of hydroponics irrigation systems also tap into natural water sources like natural drain runoffs or rainwater tanks. Hydroponic innovative irrigation systems make it possible for arid countries to farm fresh produce.

The irrigation management in hydroponics is a bit more complex than soil-based systems as the water needs to be constantly monitored for its pH and nutrient balance. The irrigation is usually on demand and because of it being a root based system, any sudden changes in the irrigation schedule could do harm to a plant or an entire crop.

Irrigation is generally held in a specific tank that has a balanced amount of nutrients-to-water volume that is required for the nourishment and watering of the plants. The water-nutrient solution is then pumped to the plant's roots by means of a submersible pump held in the reservoir. The water is dispersed by means of some form of hose, sprinkler, or misting system. Or the plant roots are suspended in the water-nutrient solution and oxygenated by an oxygen-stone in the water tank.

There are many different irrigation schemes that work well with hydroponics, aeroponics, and aquaponics. But it is all classified as on-demand irrigation with the plant's water needs determined by its type and environment, such as temperature, vapor pressure, and humidity.

Pots and Trays

Each hydroponic system has its own pots and tray requirements. They can differ quite drastically depending on the hydroponic system type. There are six different types of hydroponic systems.

Pots

The pots are either solid pots with large drainage holes at the bottom, they can be soft and flexible or hard and solid.

Which one you choose depends on what it is going to be used for and is also based on your personal preference.

Pots that are used for systems such as deep water culture, Nutrient Flow Technique, and vertical gardens use netted pots. These are best for systems that require the roots to be free of medium and accessible to the spray or water solution.

Pots are chosen to accommodate both the size of the plant and the hydroponic growing system. They must be able to fit in it comfortably without touching another pot on the grow tray or grow tube.

Deep Water Culture (DWC)

They are usually double the depth of the grow tray and no more than the recommended number of pots for your system should be placed on a grow tray at any one time. This is to ensure that the plants are being fed the correct nutrients and to promote optimum growth and yield.

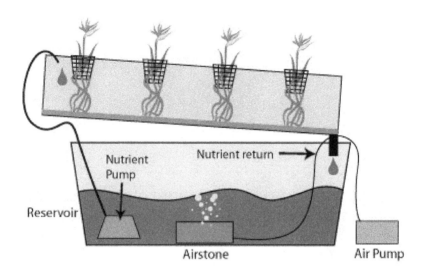

Trays

All hydroponic systems need some form of grow tray, lid, or tube upon which the plant either stands in a pot or netted pot, and is suspended over the water or encased in a grow tray.

The trays come in many different shapes and sizes which cater to a wide variety of different plants as well as the different hydroponic systems. These trays usually have sections where the pots stand, and an inlet and outlet opening for the feeder and drainage pipes.

The tray should be the same size, if not slightly bigger than the reservoir tank and the plant capacity should never be exceeded.

Trays are usually made out of some form of plastic, polystyrene or PVC.

Growing Lights

Hydroponic lighting can be quite costly but is needed in a growing house-type environment. These lights are specifically designed to give the plants the exact lighting they need for the daily maximum required time.

Normal vegetable plants require up to 10 hours of light a day, which can be both indirect and direct sunlight. For indoor hydroponic gardens, a grow light that can mimic something close to this is needed. The lighting system will need to be on for at least twelve hours a day.

To do this a lighting system, an automatic timer is needed; one that is energy efficient is always the best idea here too. The grow lights that have automatic timers can be a bit pricier than the manual grow lights, but they are well worth the investment. Without automatic lights, you could lose an entire crop over one forgetful moment.

Before going out and investing in a grow light, it is important to do some homework first.

The type of light you need will depend on the plants that are being grown, as some plants may need a bit more sunlight than others and so on. For a mixed garden, this will get a little more complicated.

Before investing in a grow light, make a list of the plants that are going to be grown in the hydroponic system. Then check how much recommended daylight they require. From this, a person can start to work out what schedule their plant's lighting system will need. Once a person has a clear cut vision of how and when the light is going to be used, you will have a better chance of choosing one that is right for your growing environment.

All of the components of the grow light must be chosen carefully for your environment. These all have to be taken into account when buying a grow light.

The three main parts of a grow light are the bulb, the timer, and the remote ballast.

The bulb

Actually, this is one of the most important parts as it is what determines the quality and brightness of the light for your grow room environment. Another important factor to take into account with the bulb is how energy efficient it is.

Hydroponics usually need a bulb that is around 400 - 600 Watts.

The preference is a HID (High-Intensity Discharge) light which produces a nice pure white light that is the closest to actual sunlight.

Conversion lamps can easily switch between the two types of bulbs available which are the Metal Halide and High-Precision Sodium bulbs.

The High-Pressure Sodium bulbs are better suited for plants that are starting to flower in the fruit-bearing stage. These bulbs tend to last the longest out of the two types but are also more expensive.

Metal Halide bulbs are the most commonly used and can be used in nearly all hydroponic growing applications. They provide an adequate lighting situation for most crops and will need to be replaced every two years or so as they tend to start to lose their power at around fifteen months or so.

If you can afford it, these two work very well in conjunction with each other.

Timer

Although the lights with timers do seem a bit more expensive, the timer on the lights is not that expensive and can actually cost a lot less than the actual bulb itself.

There are two types of timers, manual and automatic. The manual types use pins to set them. The manual timer tends to be a bit harder and less prone to going wrong or breaking than the automatic ones. They can also be attached to two different lights at the same time. This makes them the more popular choice of the two.

Automatic timers are prone to breaking, going wrong, and if there is a power outage, they won't work. They may seem a bit more convenient than the good old fashioned manual ones, but they can also be a bit more troublesome as well as expensive.

Remote ballast

This is the box that powers the fancy grow light. They are heavy and very susceptible to moisture so they should be kept above ground level at all times and far away from water or damp conditions.

They are usually sold as a set with the bulb because the ballast has to match the bulb in order to effectively power it. They are usually only used in home system environments.

Substrates and Growing Media

Hydroponics is the growing of plants without soil and using a water-nutrient solution to feed the roots. But some of the system types still need materials to help anchor plant roots, absorb moisture, or provide drainage. This is called a growing medium or substrate. There are different kinds of growing media and the ones you choose depends on the hydroponic growing system being used.

Growing media is divided into different types:

- Organic Growing Medium
  - Coco Coir
  - Peat Moss
  - Pine Bark
- Foam Matrix
  - Rockwool
  - Oasis cubes
- Grains and Pebbles
  - River Sand
  - Pebbles
  - Lightweight expanded clay aggregate
  - Perlite
  - Vermiculite

Equipment for Growing Indoors

The indoor equipment for hydroponics is pretty much the same as it would be for larger hobbyist. Only not on such a large scale.

Many of the hydroponic systems come with ready to assemble kits complete with:

- Growing medium

- Nutrient solution

- Pumps

- Tubing/pipes

- Water Nozzles/sprayers/hose pieces and piping nipples

- Grow Tray(s)

- Reservoir Tank
- Grow Pots
- Set up instructions

The above kit is generally the basis for most of the six hydroponic systems and can be used both indoors and in grow tunnels and greenhouses.

You may need to add a grow light, decent pump, and an oxygen stone but that is about it.

The kit size will depend on the plants that are going to be grown.

All the hydroponic systems can also be done DIY style and most of them are not that hard to make as a DIY project.

The trick is managing the water to nutrient balance, the pH balance, and getting the temperature, humidity, and lighting just right. But these things take practice to master and everyone has to begin somewhere.

Meters

The hydroponic system relies on the quality of the water-to-nutrient solution ration and the pH balance of the solution. Sometimes these values will fluctuate and become a little out of bounds. This is normal especially when the system is a recovery system that recycles the nutrient solution. Each time the solution is used, the plants extract nutrients from it. It also affects the pH balance of the water. The two main levels that need to be constantly tested are the pH and EC levels.

These can both be done quite easily with meters or one meter that can test both.

pH

This is what determines the acidity level of the water solution. It also demonstrates how various plants are reacting to the nutrient mix and how various other organisms are affecting the system.

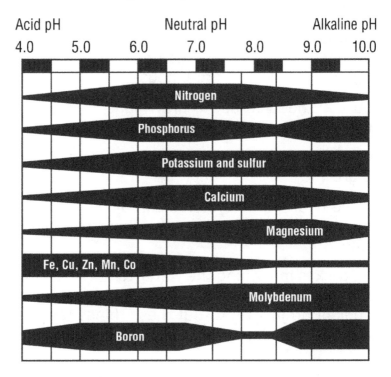

Effect of soil pH on the availability of plant nutrients

Each growing environment has its ideal pH range in which it can function normally. Kind of like testing the levels of acidity in a swimming pool to keep it clean and clear. For instance, a good example of an optimum pH range for the growing of leafy greens and herbs would be around 5.5. In order for it to maintain a good balance, the pH level should not move beyond or below .5 each day.

The pH rarely rises in a hydroponic system. It is more common that it will drop. To adjust the pH solution, you may need to simply apply a base solution to the mix.

EC

This is the level of nutrients in the water (also known as the salts in the system) and should be kept within a range of no higher than 2.0 or lower than 1.2.

EC Values differ from region to region, depending on your local water supply. So remember to always take a reading of the base water supply before adding any nutrient solutions and add this to the target ranges outlined.

If the EC solution is too high, you simply need to add more fresh-water to the reservoir until the level evens out to a more acceptable level. If it drops, you will need to add more nutrients to the mix as per the manufacturer's recommendations.

EC and pH Meters

You can get individual meters to test each one, but it is more economical and easier to get a dual meter. The dual one can quickly help a person determine what needs to be adjusted in order to bring the pH and EC levels back within an acceptable range.

Delivery System

Plants in a hydroponic system rely on three things to help them grow:

- Water

- Nutrients

- Oxygen

There are six different hydroponic systems each offering a different delivery method of these three elements to the plants.

These six systems are:

- Drip Hydroponic Solution: This delivers a steady drip of solution directly to the root of each plant by means of a dedicated nozzle.

- Wick Hydroponic Solution: This system uses an absorbent wick type rope, string, or felt to suck up water to the root system.

- Nutrient Film Technique: In this system, the roots of the plants are constantly in touch with a thin nutrient film that is set to constantly flow over them.

- Ebb & Flow System: As the name describes, in this system the plants are flooded to a watermark with nutrient solution pushed through on a timer then drained until the roots dry out.

- Water Culture System: Here, the plants are floating on top of the reservoir with their roots in constant contact with the nutrient solution.

- Aeroponic System: With this system, the plants are suspended, and their root system is subjected to a light spray of nutrient solution.

Nutrient Film Technique (NFT)
Water flows like a stream in a continuous loop past plant roots.

Wick System
Wicks are used to draw water up to the root zone from a reservoir of nutrient solution.

Drip Recovery System
An irrigation line and drip emitters are used to deliver the nutrient solution exactly where plants need it.

Deep Water Culture (DWC)
Plants float directly on top of the nutrient solution. An air pump and air-stones provide oxygen for the roots.

Ebb & Flow
Nutrient solution is pumped into a planting tray filled with gravel or clay pelets. The plant tray fills up with nutrient solution that is then flushed back into the reservoir on a timed cycle.

Aeroponics
Plant roots are misted with nutrient solution on a timed schedule.

Timer

There are different types of timers that are available for hydroponic systems, from the easy manual pin timers used to control the smaller grow systems to large sophisticated ones that are used by commercial farmers.

Timers give growers more environmental control over their grown rooms. This is a piece of equipment every hydroponic grower will eventually invest in, especially indoor growers.

There are timers that are used to control the lighting and then there are the timers that are used to control room ventilation. Then there are those that are used to control the nutrient solution dispersal intervals. This is perhaps the most important of all the timers as it is the one that determines when and how long the garden gets watered for.

Before you even look at buying a timer you should invest in a power strip that has a really good surge protector on. This is also a necessary piece of equipment that usually gets overlooked until it is too late.

The type of timer will depend on the hydroponic system being used. It will also be dependent on the type of plants being grown and how often they will require nourishment.

The timer will be something that is chosen once the size and type of hydroponic garden have been determined, along with the plants that are to be grown. This does not have to be anything fancy. It can be a standard mechanical timer as long as it can operate in the needed time frame.

Pump

You get air pumps and water pumps with a hydroponic system.

Air Pumps

Usually, a standard air stone attached to a pump is enough to aerate the reservoir tank and feed the plants. When buying an air pump, it should be able to generate at least 500 ccs of air per minute.

The general rule of thumb is that for every 1 gallon of water in the reservoir tank there should be at least 1 watt of power.

Water Pumps

There is no precise way to choose a water pump for a hydroponic system. The only thing to be aware of is that getting one that is a bit too big is better than getting one that may be too small. You can adjust the flow down on one that may be a bit too big, but you cannot increase the flow on one that may be too small.

The pump will be determined by the type of hydroponic system that is being used. The thing to keep in mind when choosing a pump is how high the pump needs to push the water to its designation. Once that is determined a person will have a better idea of how powerful a pump is needed.

Most pumps will need to be water submersible as they will sit in the reservoir and for smaller systems, usually, a standard fish tank pump is adequate.

Chapter 3. Hydroponics Growing System: Overview of the Different Hydroponics Systems and Choosing the Right Hydroponic System For You

The Basic Hydroponic setup

Hydroponic gardening makes for a fun hobby and can be exceptionally fulfilling, especially if you see your crops growing healthily and beautifully. Although it can be incredibly fun and rewarding, you need to understand the science behind this type of gardening to ensure bountiful harvests. It is not as simple, after all, as soil gardening.

Understand that hydroponic systems are not inherent in nature. It is a system devised by man to beat the natural design - grand scientific research propelled by the need to grow food faster and yield more produce in smaller spaces. To achieve this level of success, people had to understand the very basics of plant growth; and for someone planning to set up your hydroponics garden, you would have to undergo the same process of learning. Of course, this essential understanding will be condensed to a few pages, so there's no need to worry.

Below are the aspects of hydroponics that will determine the success of crop proliferation. In other words, these are the ones that will need meticulous attention.

Water

Water is the life of a hydroponic system, just like soil is to regular gardening. Not all water is created equal however, so you can't just carelessly gather from the tap and assume it will work correctly.

Apart from its chemical contents, hydroponic gardeners should also know the density of salts, metals, and minerals of the water. Fortunately, no hard laboratory knowledge is needed to calculate this. There is a device (available in both online and brick and mortar stores) that can measure this, making use of the unit called PPM (parts per million).

If it measures at around 200 to 300 PPM, the water is categorized as soft. Once free of any harmful chemicals, it can be used for a hydroponics system, and without the extra steps needed for its opposite.

Any higher than 300 PPM and that's already categorized as hard water. Hard water is usually rich in magnesium and calcium. Although these two are essential for plant growth, too much will cause deficiencies on the crops instead, and will disrupt the balance of the nutrient solution. Therefore, to make it hydroponics-friendly, its mineral content should either be filtered out or diluted with distilled water.

pH

The only reason this is a primary topic in hydroponics gardening is that water is more prone to fluctuations and shifts compared to soil. Incorrect pH levels will lead to growth deficiencies; and, should it remain uncorrected, will lead to death.

The entire process may sound easy, but the reality for beginners may be a little crueler. Since it's difficult to know at first how much or how little to add, everything will have to undergo the tiring process of trial and error. Newbie gardeners would have to measure, then adjust, and then repeat from step one until they reach the ideal pH level. This is necessary unless the gardener uses buffers instead of adjusters.

pH shifts do not stop there, however. Once the plant roots start sipping on its nutrients, the pH will once again fluctuate. And this time, not even the buffers would be able to control it. Therefore, after leaving the system for a day, be sure to measure the water's pH again, and adjust if necessary.

Oxygen

It is common knowledge that plants use carbon dioxide, then release oxygen. This is true, but only for the above-ground parts of the crop.

Water and carbon dioxide are the main food sources of plants. Just like the digestion process in humans, they undergo photosynthesis to convert these two to energy. The resulting materials are sugar and oxygen. As everyone perfectly knows, they release the oxygen back to the atmosphere, then store the sugar and use it to grow. But as already mentioned, this entire process applies only to the leafy parts of the crops.

The roots cannot undergo photosynthesis because they are below the ground. But just like the leafy parts, they need to grow and need the sugars to do so. Since they cannot produce their own, they would have to transport those stored in the leaves.

This is not a problem in traditional gardening because soil (if loosened well enough) contains millions of tiny air pockets. Water, on the other hand, is a different story. If you know the basics of

Nutrient Solution

Plants collect the nutrients they need to grow from the soil, and it may have been apparent to you already that in hydroponics the nutrients are supplied by the water. But water alone doesn't have the 14 nutrients plants require, thus there is the need for nutrient solutions.

The first thing to know about nutrient solutions is that it comes in different ratios. Plants constantly change their requirements as they grow; thus, gardeners can't stick to a single solution throughout. Furthermore, different crops require different nutrient ratios. What will make a tomato crop bloom may not do the same for an orchid.

Nutrient solutions can be bought in hydroponics stores, and their ratios are clearly printed on the bottle's label - the three seemingly random numbers at the bottom (e.g. 2-1-6, 0-5-4, or 5-0-1). Each number stands for the three primary macronutrients, commonly known as NPK or nitrogen (N), phosphorus (P), and potassium (K). Although they are called 'ratios', these numbers are the percentages of each macronutrient against the entire bottle. Therefore, if the label says, 2-1-6, it means it contains 2% nitrogen, 1% phosphorus, and 6% potassium.

Main Hydroponic systems and techniques

The following are the various types of active system:

- Ebb and Flow system
- Drip System or Top Feed
- Aeroponics
- Raft Method
- Dutch Bucket Method

Ebb And Flow System

Maintenance and set-up are not expensive and hence is a popular system. Both long-term and short-term produce grow well in this type of system. Here, the nutrient solution can flood the material for 15 minutes every hour or two.

Popular growth material is expanded clay pebbles, Perlite or Rockwool. Ebb and Flow system can be automated using a computer

Drip System or Top Feed System

One of the main advantages of this system is that it can withstand short-term power/equipment failure. Rockwool is the medium used here. The nutrient solution is dripped onto the plants, and the remainder of the water is pumped back to the tank. It is timed to supply the nutrient solution. Setting up a drip system is costly and difficult. However, it is popular with growers of tomatoes and peppers.

Dutch Bucket Method

This method is properly named as it was first developed in the Netherlands and is now commonly used for strawberries, tomatoes, and cucumbers by commercial growers there. The Dutch Bucket method enables the grower to use almost any growing medium, including coconut fiber, perlite, LECA stone, gravel, and even sand.

The Dutch Bucket is a 2.5-gallon bucket with a unique drain fitting which, as a preventive measure, maintains a small nutrient reserve at the bottom. For vast, long-term crops like vine tomatoes, cucumbers, and roses, this approach is best suited. Each bucket is fed by a single or double dripper independently of the nutrient solution and drains a common drain tube made from a 1.5-inch PVC pipe through the bucket.

The reservoir of the system is positioned just below the drainpipe level, and gravity carries the solution back to it the solution. Then a pump recirculates the nutrient solution back to the drippers to restart the feeding cycle. The inset photo outlines how a small recess on the bottom of each bucket allows it to sit flush on top of a drainpipe.

Dutch buckets can be placed at just about every suitable distance, but farmers (and plants) prefer not less than 10 inches spacing in the middle. Rafting System The rafting method is an effective procedure for growing lettuce and other crops of short height. Styrofoam sheets are used in this system to float plants set in baskets on top of nutrient solution.

What should I choose?

If you are looking to grow plants without soil, then this is the answer for you, hydroponics. "Hydro" means water and "Ponic" means labor, which determines working water. In hydroponic gardening, plants are cultivated by feeding them by water, and no soil or dirt is used.

The hydroponic system has numerous benefits when we compare it to the traditional type of gardening. In this system, no dirt is involved; it averts topsoil erosion. You need water and light to grow them. You can do it indoors as well, all year round you can grow your fruits and vegetables and there and endless benefits of it.

First, let us understand the types of hydroponics:

1) Wick - This is the most basic system of hydroponics. The good part about this system is that it uses 40-50% less water as compared to the traditional garden beds. You just need five components to build it.

These are:

- A container with the plant in it
- A reservoir

- Hydroponic growing media such as perlite or coconut coir
- Long strips of string or rope
- Nutrient solution

The drawback of it is that they are a little complicated to make. The system works well but is not like other systems as in this the wicking ability reduces as salt and organic locks in it. So ensure that you remove the salt regularly through the medium.

2) Ebb and flow systems - This is one of the most popular hydroponic systems, in this system pump is also attached. In this pump floods growing media with a nutrient-rich solution and after that drains the water back into the reservoir. In this the plants have no contact with water, they are planted in a growing medium in the tray above the tank. A pump is connected with the timer in the reservoir. And when the timer turns the pump on, the water fills the bin and pots. Also, it helps in providing the soil with fresh oxygen which is suitable for the ground. In this, the tray gets water many times in a day with the help of timer and pump, which keeps the plant roots wet and also gives nutrients to it.

3) Deep Water Culture - This one is said to be the purest form of hydroponics. Additionally, people who have experience also say that it is the most natural and most effective types of hydroponic and is very similar to the wick system. The difference between them is that instead of water being pulled in the root system, the roots of the plants are dipped in a well-oxygenated solution which is full of nutrients and water as well all the time. The deep in this means that the roots would be immersed deep in the water. The reservoir that you would take for this should be such that can contain a

tremendous amount of water. It is because the more water it would hold, the less would be its maintenance. The main thing that you have to care about is that the roots should be sunk 24/7 in oxygenated water.

4) Top Feed Drip - This system is somewhat the same as the irrigation that you do in the yard. If you are looking for a system which is simple and works well, then you should opt for this one. In this, the plants are hung on the top of the tray which drains back in the reservoir of nutrients and plants in the growing medium. In this, the plant gets water by the drip. It is placed at the base of every plant, in which the water goes by the pump. The plants get water regularly but not too much as the oxygen gets restricted.

5) Aeroponic - They are the most high-tech setups that you can make. Usually, people think that they are involved, but that is not the truth. Once you start working on it step by step, you quickly understand how it works. Experts tell that with the help of this system, you can get the fastest and most significant growth of the plant. The best part of this system is that in this, the roots are exposed to oxygen than getting submerged in the water. Here the plants are put in the basket which is full of growing medium. In this, the roots hang in the air, and they are misted with nutrient solution. There is a little extra work in it that the misting is needed after every few minutes as the roots are exposed to the air and the roots might start drying if misting is not done in time. If the plants are given everything, they require at the time; you would get the best and fast yield and that too in less time. There is a timer that controls the nutrient pump, but aeroponics requires a short cycle timer which starts the pump for just a few seconds every couple of minutes.

But there are a few drawbacks as well in it. The first reason is that it is complex to set up. Second is that you need to ensure that the pump works all the time appropriately; as if the pump stops, the plants can dry out very quickly. The third thing is that it is expensive than all the other hydroponic systems.

6) Nutrient Film Technique (NFT) - This system is said to be an active recovery hydroponic system. NFT is one system that usually people think of when planning hydroponic. In this system, the plant is inserted in a round net pot, which is fitted on the top of a square or round PVC. In this system, you need a constant flow of water, so there is no time is required in it. The solution of the nutrient is pumped into the tray, and that flows over the roots of the plants after that it drains back in the reservoir.

The pump in this system is always running, which provides the nutrient film that would give enough nutrients to the plants but not so much that it submerges in the roots. A support collar helps the plants in NFT. In this, there is no growing medium used except air. In this, air stones are must to use so that there is proper flow of oxygen in the grow tube. Same as aeroponics, there is one disadvantage that you should continuously check that the pump is working. As if it stops working, then the plants would dry very quickly.

These were the six types of hydroponics so that you can choose according to your choice. But whichever system you select hydroponics has so many advantages as compared to the conventional soil gardening. Hydroponic is a system that is giving you the benefit of growing fruits and vegetables indoor and outdoor both and without soil. It is becoming a necessity in recent times as this way you can cultivate fresh fruits and vegetables under your eyes and that too without using chemicals which means it would be organic.

The reason why people like hydroponics is that they have a satisfaction in their mind that they are growing their own food, and getting better flavor. You also save money when you grow vegetables and fruits on our own. The significant part of this gardening is that it consumes 20 times less water than soil gardening.

If you do hydroponic gardening with proper techniques and knowledge, you can yield excellent results in a short period. It is not only beneficial for home gardeners, but commercial farmers can also use it. There are many benefits of it, such as scarcity of water can be easily conquered, reduction in arable land, and there are many environmental benefits too. People say that it is one more method from which you can maximize the usage of your greenhouse space and try hands at a different type of growth strategy. This system maximizes space and increases the yield of the greenhouse.

As you have read about so many types of hydroponic gardening, you can choose one according to your preference and usage. If you do not want to go for a complicated setup, then you can select the wick system. But if you can manage and set up a slightly complicated system which has more benefits, then you can opt for aeroponics. Every order has its advantages and disadvantages. It is you who have to decide which method you can manage and get good results. The harvesting in it is easy, and you do not require to go for any soil set up.

Chapter 4. Build Your Own Hydroponic System

We have every reason to prepare in good faith for our experiments and, from the very beginning, to eliminate all sources of possible failures. It is extremely annoying to stop a well-started experiment without achieving results, just because not enough attention was paid to some "trifle". About vessels for experiments should not say much. Their size and shape can be completely arbitrary. Of course, they should not leak water at all and should not in any way affect the properties of the nutrient solution. Therefore, it is not permissible for the walls of the vessels to secrete any substance or absorb anything from the solution.

How to Build Your Own Hydroponic System

A wide variety of materials from which experimental vessels can be made (metals, plastic, ceramics, porcelain, concrete, etc.). It compels us to give one completely justified advice: each vessel should be covered with an insulating layer in places where its surface comes into contact with the nutrient solution. Double coating with good bitumen paint fully meets the purpose and eliminates unpleasant surprises. However, in this case, you should not confuse bitumen paint with often very similar preparations from coal tar containing substances poisonous to plants.

Earth excavations, wooden troughs, and other tanks can be made waterproof with plastic films. Many amateur and vegetable growers- producers use earthen ditches for growing plants, and these dredges fully justify themselves provided that they were coated with phenol-free films. The fact is that some of the plastic films, in contact with the nutrient solution, release substances poisonous to plants. For this reason, you have to constantly recommend when you buy a film and indicate its intended purpose. In this case, you will be offered the most suitable type of film.

Substrates or Fillers

What requirements should material use as a substrate meet? It must be a substance with the following properties:

• with rather large particles that would not spill out between the battens of the crate or between the mesh cells;

• able to absorb and retain a large amount of water so that it is not required to moisturize it daily with a nutrient solution;

• resistant against decomposition and not able to rot;

• chemically neutral, that is, one that does not emit any products that can damage plants, and in no way affects the nutrient solution.

What materials meet these requirements and which of them can we use?

The cultural substrate in which the plants will take root must be selected very carefully and, if necessary, subjected to preliminary processing. In recent years, suitability for this series of materials has been studied, many of which have been deemed suitable. We will consider only the most important of them, which have already become widespread.

• In principle, it can be stated that all used cultural substrates differ in the following qualities:

• they are chemically neutral and, thus, have no effect on the properties and chemical composition of the nutrient solution; high resistance to weathering and decomposition allows them to maintain their structure for a long time;

• they are loose, and you can dig into them with your bare hands without fear of injury;

• they are all more or less hygroscopic and, thus, provide capillary lifting of liquids.

We now turn to the description of individual materials that have passed the test in practice. Let's start with the substrate, which is often indicated in the literature as ideal. Since recently it can be purchased in many and most countries, it may be of interest to us as well. Let's see what experts say about "vermiculite".

"Vermiculites" are secondary minerals that have arisen as a result of hydrothermal changes in two types of mica: biotite and phlogopite. These are water-containing magnesium-aluminum silicates, mostly found as inclusions in such highly basic rocks as dunite, serpentine, and pyroxenite, and often, and vice versa, including these rocks. So far, deposits of vermiculite have been discovered in South Africa (Transvaal), Tanganyika, USA (Colorado, Montana), Western Australia, the USSR (Urals), and Japan.

Now, 17 varieties of vermiculite are already known. The following composition can be indicated as an approximate composition: 5% AL_2O_3, Fe_2O_3, 22% SiO_2, 40% H_2O_2. Vermiculite ore is stratified like mica and is colored from dark yellow-brown to light brownish yellow, green or bronze. The specific gravity of the rock is 2.3 - 2.9, and after stratification - 0.9. Hardness 1.5, melting point about 1360 degrees, water content 4 to 20%. Mining is carried out in open pits and to a lesser extent by explosive means. The rock is coarsely ground and dried to facilitate further processing. After this, the rock is milled and sorted by particle size using pneumatic devices. Heating the ore to dry it is permissible only for a short time and not more than 140 degrees.

The value of vermiculite lies in its property to increase in volume when heated by almost 15 times. Heating causes the conversion of chemically bound water into steam, separating microscopic plates that are layered on top of each other. At a temperature of 900-1100 degrees, the ore is brought to a red glow, but this temperature should not be maintained for more than 4-8 seconds. After that, the ore is cooled as quickly. As a result of these two processes, it turns into a granular, extremely light, stable, free-flowing product. This treatment of vermiculite is called delamination. After processing, the final product turns from silver to gold.

The following properties make layered vermiculite valuable and explain the rapid growth of its use, limited only by its insufficient production: low weight (1 cubic meter weighs 100-125 kg), incombustibility, impermeability (only 6.2% moisture after content at 100% relative humidity for 300 hours), indestructibility, indecomposability, resistance to insects and rodents, and above all an insulating effect in relation to heat, cold, sound, and electricity.

Here is the complete chemical composition of South African vermiculite: SiO_2 - 39.37; TiO_2 - 1.25; Al_2O_2 - 12.08; Fe_2O_3 - 5.48; FeO - 1.17; MnO

- 0.30; MgO - 23.37; CaO - 1.46; Na_2O - 0.80; K_2O - 2.46; H_2O - 11.09,

CO_2 - 0.60; P_2O_5 - 0.15; Li_2O - 0.03; BaO - 0.03; Cl - 0.02; SO_3 - 0.02; S

- 0.18; * at 105C. From this technical description, we can conclude that layered-in vermiculite is an ideal material as a substrate for growing plants without soil: it is chemically inert, free-flowing, absorbs water well, and retains its structure perfectly. According to US practice, it can be used to grow plants without any pre-treatment.

In Europe, coarse-grained pumice and foamy lava are currently preferred. We are talking about igneous rocks, somewhat similar to a sponge, and therefore, have extremely high absorption capacity. Both breeds have a stable structure and loose, but their chemical properties are not ideal. They contain quite a lot of free lime and other compounds, which subsequently very readily enter into undesirable exchange reactions with a nutrient solution. In this case, various important components of the nutrient solution pass into a form in which they can no longer be absorbed by plants.

However, these shortcomings can be eliminated through very simple operations. So, for example, we can wash gravel from the pumice of highly diluted sulfuric acid until the evolution of gas bubbles ceases. After this, the gravel from which the lime has been removed is left for many hours in clean water, after which it is thoroughly washed in running water. At the end of the flushing, such gravel can be used without any concern.

Another method of neutralizing gravel is keeping it for a day in a solution of superphosphate in boiled water (750 g of superphosphate per 10 liters of water). After a day, the excess solution is drained, and the gravel is washed with clean water, which ends its processing.

In many areas, you can easily purchase blast furnace slag, which after special treatment can also be used as a substrate. What is this? It is made from the slag from blast furnaces, a liquid by-product of iron smelting, converted by the action of water vapor into a gravel-like, highly porous material.

Unfortunately, blast furnace slag has even higher alkalinity than pumice or foamy lava (up to 43% CaO). Despite this, it can be prepared in the same way as pumice, but only in this case, you need to be even more careful to completely remove lime from the substrate. The advantage of thermite is its low cost, which compares very favorably with the previously mentioned materials. For the same reasons, special attention should be paid to coal slag, which can be purchased at a very low price.

For the profitability of industrial soilless plants in most cases, the cost of the culture substrate is a significant burden. Therefore, it is quite natural that the search for cheap substitutes for pumice and similar materials began long ago. Suitable slags are substitutes that are found to be complete in all respects. Amateur gardeners are fortunate in that they can benefit from the experience already gained in the production environment.

Suitable for use are well-calcined coal or coke slag; all other types of slag (for example, brown coal slag) are generally unsuitable for this purpose.

The required amount of slag is thoroughly cleaned of foreign debris and then mechanically crushed.

With a large demand for production plants in the substrate, stone crushing machines are mostly used for grinding slag, but we will do with a simple tamper and sledgehammer. From the crushed substrate, we need to select fractions with a particle diameter of 0-15 mm, and here, our assistants will be sieves with the corresponding hole diameter. After that, it is checked whether the substrate needs preliminary chemical treatment.

There can be quite a big difference between the two types of slag, especially regarding their suitability for growing plants without soil. Source material, combustion temperature, and other factors play an important role. It is often necessary to pre-treat the slag to remove toxic substances from it, especially sulfur compounds and, of course, lime.

The test is very simple. About 1 liter of the test material is taken from the slag mass and poured into a glass jar for canning. About 0.5 l of water is poured into the second jar of the same and very carefully add an equal amount of concentrated sulfuric acid to this jar (Sulfuric acid is diluted by pouring it into the water, but you can never pour water into acid. This is very dangerous!). This diluted acid is poured into the slag until it is completely coated with the solution. If foam begins to form on the surface of the solution, gas bubbles with the smell of rotten eggs appear, then all the slag must be chemically treated. However, if nothing like this happens, then we are extremely lucky and managed to get a completely usable slag.

The small amounts of slag required for our purposes are best immediately poured into vessels coated with bitumen paint and filled with sulfuric acid diluted in a ratio of 1:10 (10 l of water per 1 l of acid). After waiting when the formation of foam and gas bubbles ceases, a small sample is again taken from the water-washed slag and subjected to the above test with an acid in a glass jar. This is necessary because it is very likely that the first pretreatment of all substrate weights could be insufficient to convert all hazardous compounds into gaseous hydrogen sulfide (with the smell of rotten eggs) or into water-soluble sulfates. Thus, if foam appears again in the glass jar and gas bubbles rise, then the whole procedure should be repeated with a freshly prepared acid solution.

Before the final use of the slag, it is very thoroughly washed with ordinary water to remove all compounds that have been converted into a soluble state as a result of processing, as well as sulfuric acid residues. To verify the completeness of acid removal in drain water (after repeated washing), a litmus paper is lowered (such paper will be needed in the future to check the pH of the nutrient solution); in this case, only a slightly acidic reaction is permissible. After that, the slag is ready for consumption.

We will not hide that slags, in one respect, do not quite meet our requirements: the sharp edges of the particles make the slag somewhat less loose and you have to work with it more carefully. However, this disadvantage can be largely eliminated by adding to the slag (before the treatment just described) about 10% silica sand.

Quartz sand, basalt chips, and crushed granite are chemically neutral due to the high content of silicates in them. Unfortunately, they do not absorb moisture and their particles have very sharp edges (in particular, granite and basalt). They can at best be used as impurities to other materials, such as slag or pumice.

When growing certain crops that prefer moderately moist habitats (such as cacti, etc.), it is very useful to add basalt chips to other water-absorbing substrates.

We refrain from using crumb brick, although it was often recommended in some publications. Here, in most cases, you have to reckon with a very high content of lime, which must be removed. In addition, the crumb brick does not have a particularly stable structure. After a very short time, sludge deposits form at the bottom of our earthen excavation or vessel, which is agitated when the nutrient solution is drained and leads to blockage of pipes and other interferences. The nutrient solution itself is colored with silt in a reddish color, which complicates the analysis of the solution, and in some cases simply makes it impossible. Finally, in the brick crumb, very often, there are many extraneous impurities of an indeterminate nature (resins, metals, etc.), which, as substances, that are potentially toxic to plants.

In recent studies, it was possible to prove that the presence of humic substances in the cultural substrate of a plant for growing plants without soil has a direct and beneficial effect on plants. This in no way contradicts our reasoning, since humic substances, in this case, do not act as a source of plant nutrition. The action of humic substances is manifested due to the following features.

- They contribute to the absorption of nutrients because they increase the solubility of mineral salts and prevent them from precipitating from solution (the formation of complexes with organic compounds). In addition, it turned out that plant roots coated with a layer of humic substances better absorb inorganic nutrients.

- Due to the presence of humic substances, the nutrient solution acquires "buffering", that is, greater resistance to reaction bias.

- Humus contains various soluble humic substances or related products such as antibiotics, growth substances, estrogen substances, etc., which can be absorbed by the plant and contribute to its better development.

Given these circumstances, it is not difficult to understand why, at present, some organic matter, mostly peat, is willingly mixed into the substrate. A mixture of half volumes of inorganic gravel and peat has proven itself, and in some places, they work successfully with pure peat. In the following, we will return to this issue and trace the development of individual plants in pure gravel, as well as for comparison in a mixture of gravel with peat or in pure peat. In this case, it is necessary to carefully note which particular plant species respond particularly well to the presence of humic substances.

The substrate from a mixture of peat chips and bed peat is well aerated. No matter how wet the substrate is, the roots of the plants still get enough oxygen for respiration, in addition, this mixture does not melt. Peat is difficult to decompose, and even with strong moisture and high temperature, it is unlikely to rot.

Chapter 5. Pros and Cons - The Different Types of Hydroponic Systems

In order for everything to be calm at the home hydro farm, you need to know what advantages and disadvantages of different types of hydroponic systems have. The secret to the success of any undertaking is in choosing the right tools. It is unlikely that you can hammer a nail with the help of a banana. In progressive gardening, such a rule is present everywhere, including when choosing the type of hydroponic system. Each system has its pros and cons, which are worth paying attention to, so as not to fall into frustration.

Wick System

The wick is lowered into a nutrient solution, which rises up under the action of physical laws. The so-called passive system works wonders in the context of the relevance of the motto "cheap, but it works."

Pros:

- Availability. I took a container, poured a substrate - you can plant plants. Hydroponics for dummies;
- Minimum cash costs for maintenance. There is no technology - there are no problems with sensors, programs, and complex systems for providing plants with necessary substances. We need only the initiative of a cheerful water-carrier feedman;
- Without a feed pump. Since physics is the main driving force of the process, then additional assistance for the supply of nutrients to the roots of plants is not necessary.

Disadvantages:

- Limited access to oxygen to water or solution. It can cause a whole bunch of problems - stale water, problems with the root system, and so on.
- Slow growth. An independent plant cannot fully grow in breadth and height as a beginner would like if he had seen enough of the giant strawberry bushes on other hydroponic farms;
- No nutrient recycling. And why? That's right; because there is no pump. There is nothing to add.

Deepwater Crop System (DWC)

Higher than passive systems, but not having all the charms of hi-tech and engineering peaks, choice. A simple device, but with a "whistle" - a compressor that delivers oxygen to the nutrient solution, nourishing the root system. Which, in turn, is located in a mesh pot and installed in the lid of the tank with a nutrient solution.

Pros:

- The cheapest option from active systems. Savings - a necessity in a precarious American economy;
- Ease of setup and reliability. Based on the foregoing, an undeniable plus for advanced beginners;
- Without a feed pump. The same plus as in the wick system;
- Reliable, due to the small number of brittle elements;

- A decent supply of solution guarantees the safety of your plants;
- Everything is growing and fast.

Disadvantages:

- Risk of root rot with insufficiently regular cleaning.
- With a high level of solution and excessive over moistening, the likelihood of decay of the root neck is high;
- The need to constantly replenish the tank. A regular run for water and nutritious mixtures is a good help for losing weight, but not for progressive crop production.

Periodic Flooding System

A method that is also striking in its simplicity. Plants can be placed on top of each other, and the liquid flowing from one pot gets into another. Simple and tasteful. Of course, you can make an advanced option, with valves and sensors, which will allow you to control the liquid level in the substrate, which is good for the hydroponics and his wards.

Pros:

- Availability. In order to make an average hydroponic installation, you do not need to order tons of equipment and spend a lot of time choosing a manufacturer and understand a billion nuances;
- Low costs. The simplicity of the technology entails a small amount of money for maintenance;

- Good saturation with a nutrient solution. Nutrients pass through the entire substrate. Vigorous growth and high productivity available.

Disadvantages:

- Like any reversible system, there is a risk of contamination of the solution with pathogens'
- The risk of mold and other "water" weeds. If there is a lot of water, then parasites will certainly appear, which will live there freely;
- Technical malfunctions can lead to a decrease in yield. If any valves get stuck, or the water separation system itself is de-energized, then goodbye to normal watering, and as a result, caput to the mountains of vegetables.

Drip Irrigation System

This is hydroponics "as it is." A description is not required, however, this system has its advantages and disadvantages. First of all, it is worth noting that drip irrigation does not require special intervention in the process by humans. But it is worth decently investing in so that everything works like a clock.

Pros:

- The nutrient solution goes to "5+ stars". The system is so good that it is used by most hydroponic firms in the West;
- A sufficient supply of oxygen to the root system. This means that there should not be any problems with the circulation of nutrients. Consequently, the seedlings will grow and turn into the pride of a gardener, just as per the instructions.

Disadvantages:

- The biggest minus is the need for regular cleaning to eliminate blockages in the irrigation system. And a similar method is fraught with the development of mold on the roots and containers.

Aeroponics

"Ferrari" hydroponics. The most effective method for growing vegetables, fruits, and other flora on an industrial scale. But for a home farm, it suits well enough, although you have to sweat in order to understand all the intricacies of technology. Although the profit from this is rather big.

Pros:

- Maximum absorption of nutrients. Due to aeroponic technology, as many substances as the plant needs come to the roots;
- Efficient use of space. You can arrange the trays at least in three layers, the "kids" will only be a joy. There will be no empty space for sure. So, the harvest will be such that before spring is enough.

Disadvantages:

- Blockages, blockages, and again blockages. Nowhere to go from them. Therefore, you need to regularly check all nodes, contacts, and sensors. You can say goodbye to personal life and cheating;
- Aeroponics is poorly suited for thick nutrient mixtures. This cannot be called a drawback, but for the ignorant, it can serve as a motivation to throw crop production into the

far corner along with cross-stitch and modeling.

Chapter 6. Plants to Grow in You Hydroponic System

Valerian

Valerian is an herbaceous plant that originates in central Europe and Asia but is now widespread also in western Europe and North America. The valerian develops very broadly and can reach a height of one and a half meters. The rhizome of the valerian plant is composed of many roots that are characterized by an unpleasant smell.

The typical environment of the valerian is the areas rich in humidity, the margins of the courses of the rivers, woods, etc.. However, we can cultivate it very well even in our gardens when it has no particular needs. The optimal climate for the cultivation of valerian is the temperate one, however, this plant can withstand even temperatures of fifteen degrees below zero; likes sun exposure but also semi-shaded.

Valerian is multiplied by seed, by the division of the rhizome or tuft. Before proceeding with sowing, the soil will be worked deeply. If seed multiplication is chosen, it will be done during the spring period starting from the seedbed; this operation takes a long time because the valerian has a very slow development.

Basil

Basil is one of the most cultivated aromatic plants in Italy; in fact, it is a small herbaceous plant, native to Asia, which came to Europe centuries ago, and has been cultivated both in Europe and in Asia for a very long time. In fact, the basil we are used to eating and seeing in the garden is a hybrid plant, whose botanical name is ocimum basilicum "Genoese", testimony to the city where the use of basil is more widespread. It is a perennial plant, generally cultivated as an annual, as it fears the cold, and temperatures below 10°C cause its rapid deterioration. Basil, as we know it, is just one of several varieties spread in cultivation; in fact, in the Italian kitchen we particularly appreciate the so-called sweet basil, with a large leaf and a delicate aroma

Borage

Borage alias cucumber. Borage has a taste of fresh green cucumber, which makes it excellent in salads or on spreads. In medicine, the seeds of the plant or the borage oil derived from it are used mainly for skin complaints.

Watercress

Watercress, also called bach or watercress, botanically belongs to the family brassica (Brassicaceae). In addition to the genuine watercress (nasturtium officinale), the small-leaved watercress (nasturtium microphyllum) is very common in Germany. The original range of the two species probably extended over Europe, north Africa, and southwest Asia. Meanwhile, watercress as a neophyte, however, can be found almost worldwide. It likes to settle on shady, clear, shallow waters with a slight current, for example, at sources or in the shallow riparian zones of clean streams. Watercress is a beautiful water plant for gardens: it does not only look pretty, but it is also delicious. Watercress: location, and cultivation.

Watercress is a marsh and aquatic plant and thrives best in water depths of 5 to 20 centimeters. It is, therefore, quite expensive to grow them in gardens.

A natural source of water is best for planting watercress. Which makes it suitable for hydroponics. It often grows in nature at the edge of small streams and moats.

You can grow watercress in the pot by pressing the seeds lightly on the ground and keeping them moist. At a temperature of 20 degrees, the seeds begin to germinate after about a week. If the young plants have reached a height of 8 to 10 centimeters, you can put them at the appropriate watering place.

The true watercress was already in ancient times as a medicinal plant cultured. Due to its high vitamin c content, the plant was especially valued as an anti-scurvy. It is also considered a blood purifier. Its name derives from the Latin name "nasus tortus", a twisted nose in English - an expression that results from the reaction to the consumption of the slightly pungent cress type.

The cultivation of watercress is worthwhile not only because of the beautiful sight, but it is also extremely healthy: watercress is rich in vitamins c, a, k, and b2 and was, therefore, one of the few foods in the winter months against scurvy. In addition, it contains iodine, iron, and calcium, as well as mustard oils. They provide a slightly pungent taste and have an antibacterial and digestive effect.

In natural medicine, the fresh leaves of watercress are recommended as a home remedy for cystitis and congested respiratory tract and to stimulate digestion and kidney activity.

Fennel

Fennel is native to the Mediterranean but is now grown worldwide. There are various sub-forms, of which the seeds and the fennel green are used for seasoning or the fennel tuber as vegetables.

Fennel has a sweet, aniseed taste. The leaves and tubers are used, especially in the Mediterranean cuisine for fish and salads. The seeds spice soups, sauces, grilled meat, and fish, but also taste in bread and cake in alcoholic drinks such as pastis or absinthe, fennel rounds off the taste of anise.

Fennel needs warm and sunny locations with light, not too moist soil; it is relatively sensitive. As medicinal plant fennel has many effects: it helps against flatulence and abdominal pain, in diseases of the upper respiratory tract and as an infusion against eye pain and inflamed eyelids.

Strawberries

Hydroponics technical system that allows the greenhouse cultivation of fruit and vegetables on a sluggish substrate or not, by optimally managing the elements that determine the quality of the plants and the product: temperature, irrigation, light, etc.

The hydroponics in general and the strawberry, in particular, allows to improve all the elements responsible for the quality of the plant and the final product, through higher production and higher quality, u the solution to the problems arising from the culture soil (dirt, slowness, fungi, mold...) And standardization of production. Hydroponics strawberries can also be adopted for smaller plants, such as home, thanks to the cost rather than content and ease of installation.

In the fruit and vegetable sector, the introduction of strawberry technology was favoured by specific structural and ecological conditions of this crop: in recent years, the cultivation of strawberries also encountered rapid development, moving from classical cultivation in open land cultivation land substrate and especially bags of peat.

With hydroponics, strawberries are constantly kept in optimal nutritional conditions, because the techniques used guarantee phytosanitary conditions best and cleanest product. The result is higher quality strawberries, with a better look, a consistent size, inherent properties better to endure (less crude fibre content, higher percentage of sugar fats, vitamins, a higher density), lower availability and increased capacity of long-distance transport.

Cultivated strawberries are hydroponically protected by the adoption of different types of tunnels, depending on the investment cost and depreciation, openings of have been tested and afford by the side or side and is usually made of plastic films each takes an average of 3-4 years, with average brightness and good thermal insulation properties. Grow bags can be placed in a set of files of pedestals or hung in the height of the structure, which can be useful to receive the product in the palms of individual farmers. Strawberry plants are planted in plastic bags (from 4 to 6 per bag) of 10-12 litres per lot, with sizes of 20-25 cm width 35-40 cm long. The contents of the bags are usually made of white peat and pear in a variable portion.

However, there are many types of hydroponics for the production of strawberries that reach each other for how the water reaches the roots of the plant.

Cucumbers

Hydroculture for cucumbers with your own hands will be very welcome in the economy if you want to get a good harvest of this vegetable quickly. Cucumbers are climbers, so it is better in small hydroponics to sow them along the wall of the pallet, and after the shoots appear, bind them to the installed at an angle stops. This method helps breeders looking for a way to grow cucumbers quickly. Such placement of cucumbers does not disturb other plants that may also be in this range, and the bound cucumbers eventually produce fruits of much higher quality. Optimal growth of cucumbers contributes to the bright day up to 14 hours.

Varieties of cucumbers for growing in hydroponics

The most popular cucumbers for hydroponic cultivation are "European" or "long English" cucumbers. Beit alpha (ba), Japanese or Persian varieties are becoming increasingly popular (photo 2). They are similar to the European cucumbers but are smaller (usually 10-15 cm) and in contrast to the European cucumbers with an average size of 30 to 35 cm. These cucumbers are gutted and have thin skin and do not need to be cleaned when preparing salads. Due to its thin skin, the necessary moisture in the room must be maintained to avoid weight loss. European species - occupy the second place for hydroponic crops with high yields in confined spaces. Unlike tomato plantations, which are more robust, cucumber is more tender. They must be constantly kept under special growth conditions in order to achieve maximum yields. When cucumbers are left unattended, they quickly get entangled, and yields drop dramatically. They are then almost impossible to untangle, unlike tomatoes. Therefore, proper care is required throughout the growth cycle.

What you need to grow cucumbers in hydroponics

If you want to grow tomatoes and cucumbers in your own cottage, you will need to purchase a hydroponic installation. If the purchase is not possible, you can create it yourself. This requires:

- Expanded clay
- Plastic pipes for further planting

- Pump
- Mineral wool
- Mineral fertilizers
- Compost layer
- Selected medium gravel
- Capacity for plants, mostly glasses
- Water

The technology of growing cucumbers with hydroponics

Hydroponics will help to cultivate cucumbers in the home, comparable to those grown in the garden. It is necessary to follow the technology of cultivation strictly.

Sowing seeds in cassettes

First, the cork stoppers are soaked in a nutrient solution; then, a cucumber core is placed in the centre of each cork. Hydroponics contains many nutrients in the solution that help to saturate the seed from within. Powder vermiculite will help to create an optimal humid environment. After planting, the seeds of the cassette are covered with a plastic wrap, which is removed after 3 days. The temperature to be followed is 23-25 ° c.

Replanting sprouts into cubes

Cubes, such as cassettes, are subjected to a solution treatment (as described in the article) to prepare a hydroponic solution, after which seven days of shoots can be transferred there. You should take a seedling with a cork and transfer it to a cube to reduce the temperature by 1 degree. The increased distance between the cubes contributes to the normal development of the plants. Sprouting seedlings in such conditions are 1.5 months.

Transplanting cucumber seedlings in mats

Before you plant cucumbers at home, the mats must be soaked in a solution. Make small holes in the packaging that serve as a drainage function. It should take place at a temperature of +22-25°C. After the beginning of flowering, the seedling forms a stem, after which the fifth leaf must remove all flowers. The germination of the roots in the mat should be done at a temperature of +21-22 °C.

Features care for cucumbers

If we have decided to grow cucumbers at home, we have to take good care of them. Before the formation of the first fruit, the stalk must be constantly removed. As the number of cucumbers increases, it is worthwhile to control the transition from vegetative to generative growth. Cucumbers should be carefully watered, with sprinkling begun 2 hours after sunrise and 2 hours before sunset to avoid deformation of the fruit. The temperature should not exceed + 19-22°C and + 24°C on sunny days. It is necessary to ventilate the greenhouse regularly, maintaining a humidity of 70-80% to avoid mildew and botrytis.

Advantages and disadvantages of growing cucumbers with hydroponics

The advantages of hydroponics are:

- Fast growth of cucumbers
- Fruit does not accumulate harmful chemicals, which has a positive effect on human health.
- Space saving in a similar type of cultivation,

- If necessary, plants can be transplanted to another location,

- One of the main advantages of the method is that no land is needed, which is particularly important in areas with a lack of fertile land.

- Cucumbers do not need to be poured frequently.

There are virtually no disadvantages to this type of cultivation, but there are negative features:

- Spending on equipment

- Performing frequent monitoring of the temperature regime of plants.

Melons

Melons probably come from the subtropical regions of Asia and have been cultivated for millennia. As their botanical name suggests cucumis melo, they are related to the cucumbers. The cucumis melo is distributed as sugar or honeydew melon, cantaloupe melon, and nettle melon. The watermelon (citrullus lanatus) belongs to a different genus.

Cantaloupe melons are usually recognized by their firm orange flesh. The shell is hard, scaly, and traversed by longitudinal grooves. The variety of 'Charentais' is considered precocious. Depending on the variety, honeydew melons have a smooth or ribbed yellow to greenish skin. Inside they are yellowish to white or orange. Net melons can be recognized by the net pattern of the shell. The flesh is green to white or salmon-coloured. The fruits of the variety 'hale's best jumbo' can weigh up to two kilograms. Melons germinate at temperatures between 20 and 30 degrees Celsius. Therefore, we recommend that you prefer plants in warm conditions. In April, you can sow the seeds one to two centimetres deep and place them on a warm, sunny windowsill. Our tip: if you sow in small pots, you do not need to pimp them. The plants are sensitive to cold. Therefore, it is best to plant them in the second half of May or early June - ideally in the greenhouse. The distance between the melon plants should be 80 by 80 centimetres.

Location and care

Melons need a lot of heat. The more sun and heat they get, the better the fruits will grow, and the sweeter and more aromatic they become. Some varieties thrive well in partial shade, as long as it is warm enough.

They also make some demands on the ground. He should be relaxed and nutritious. The best way is to prepare the bed of compost and give them some slow-release fertilizer in the planting hole. Additional fertilizers during the summer need the strong-consuming plants. In addition, you should always pour it sufficiently.

In order for melons to plant many fruits, it is recommended to cut them: cap the main shoot after the fourth or fifth leaf so that its branches. Repeat the procedure for the side shoots after four to eight leaves. The following shoots then form the flowers and later the fruits.

You can pull melons on trellises or spread on the ground. Then put a board under the fruit, so they do not rot.

Melons are considered to be sensitive to fungal diseases such as fusarium wilt. They can also be attacked by powdery mildew and downy mildew.

Harvest and use of melons

Depending on the sowing season and season melons mature from august. Whether you can harvest them, you will recognize by their colour and their sweet scent. For some varieties, the stalk dries. It is best to harvest the melons quickly by separating them from the plant with a sharp knife. Overripe fruits do not taste that good anymore.

You can eat melons in the summer just like that. You can also use them for salads, desserts and cold drinks. Since they are not very durable, you eat them right away.

Tomatoes

Hydroponic seedlings, including tomatoes, are grown in small pots floating or suspended over water so that the tomato roots absorb the necessary amount of nutrient-rich water necessary for the tomatoes or other hydroponic plants to grow. An unsinkable support system must first be built or purchased in order to plant and grow using the hydroponic method.

Instructions

Purchase hydroponic plant trays for growing tomatoes. Trays with larger holes are used to better support adult tomato plants (remember, if you want to grow the tomatoes completely in the hydroponic beds or pimp them in a garden or pot during the warm growing season).

Use a cutter to cut larger holes in hydroponic plant trays with holes for adult tomato plants too small. Be careful not to let the lower ends taper conically to allow the root system to fall through to provide better watering results.

Purchase or build a waterbed to place the trays. Build the beds of wooden frames on the inside covered with a single solid sheet or plastic.

Fill the plant tray holes halfway down the ground and drop a tomato seed into each hole. Cover the seeds, fill the tray with holes, and then place in the waterbeds, where the trays remain over water at the surface of the water, with only enough of the tray so that the tomato plant roots can absorb the necessary amount of water.

Tips and warnings

Monitor the growth of the plants. Of course, as the plants grow, they will become heavier; if the plants are too heavy to be supported by the trays, you will need to use other materials to support the trays. You do not want to soil the trays by more than an inch deep and risk drowning the root system of the tomatoes. Bricks work to support the shells and prevent them from sinking too deep into the water.

Chapter 7. Plant Nutrition

Nutrients for Hydroponic systems

Hydroponic nutrients can be a perplexing issue or as straightforward as blending and pouring. Anybody inexperienced with hydroponic nutrients should stay with a demonstrated recipe from a trustworthy production, and essentially old the bearings on the holder. This will give you a chance to get familiar with the nuts and bolts of growing hydroponically before testing.

Anyway, a ton of off the rack hydroponic nutrients can be costly, costing upwards of $0.30 +cents per gallon of supplement arrangement, or more. In any case, there are supplement makes that sell financially savvy nutrients. Indeed, even down to as low as under 2 pennies for every gallon of supplement arrangement. We have a rundown of a portion of this financially savvy supplement produces for you. Don't hesitate to get in touch with us on the off chance that you are aware of more we can add to the rundown so we can share them too.

Nutrients are one of the nuts and bolts of any hydroponic system. All together for manure to be joined into a hydroponic system, it must be dissolvable in water. If not, the plant can't get to it. With Hydroponics, the producer has full oversight over the usage of compost in regards to type and fixation. They additionally can quickly screen and keep up a relative consistency, gave a supplement meter is accessible. The creation of the nutrients is significant, and there are more than twenty components that are required for a plant to develop. Carbon, hydrogen, and oxygen are assimilated from the air and water.

Make sure to utilize nutrients intended for Hydroponics in a Hydroponic system. The synthesis of components in nutrients designed for soil is altogether different from that for Hydroponics since soil developed plants get the greater part of these components from the soil. With Hydroponics, there is no soil to get the ingredients from, so the two are altogether different in the organization since they are not intended to be finished plant nourishment, and they may not water-solvent. For instance, Nitrogen as urea isn't promptly accessible to a plant in hydroponics since urea isn't dissolvable in water. Thus Nitrogen must be conveyed in its Nitrate structure to be used in hydroponics.

One thing that is frequently overlooked with regards to nutrients is the supplement arrangement temperature. The foundations of plants develop underground in nature, and to copy what they would get in life; it is essential to keep the root zone to 68-72 degrees. This shouldn't imply that if the supplement temp arrives at 73 or 74, the plants will bite the dust. However, it ought to be kept as near 68-72 degrees as you can. Plants with supplement seducers too high can have issues including (however not restricted to) blooms turning yellow and tumbling off, harmed leafy foods absence of new development.

Hydroponic Nutrient Solutions

The hydroponic supplement arrangement is the sole wellspring of nutrients to the plant. Subsequently, it is essential to apply a fair settlement that contains all plant nutrients at the correct parity.

A few significant elements must be viewed as while picking composts and setting up hydroponic supplement arrangements:

- Water quality - saltiness, the convergence of potential hurtful components (like sodium, chlorides, and boron)

- Required nutrients and their focuses in the hydroponic supplement arrangement

- Nutrient parity

- The pH of the hydroponic supplement arrangement and its impact on the take-up of nutrients by plants

Standard Nutrient Solutions

There are different standard supplement arrangements, for example, the Hoagland arrangement, Steiner, Bollard, and others. These standard arrangements are excellent as a general rule, yet are not adjusted to specific growing conditions. Regardless of whether you choose to utilize one of the standard supplement arrangement, make a point to use the supplement fixation as a rule, and not the manure formula that relates to them. The underlying method of the rough water that you use will influence the natural nutrients that must be included with composts.

The Electrical Conductivity Of The Hydroponic Nutrient Solution

The electrical conductivity is a proportion of the complete salts that broke down in the hydroponic supplement arrangement. It is utilized for checking the utilization of manures. Note that the EC perusing doesn't give you data concerning the specific mineral substance of the supplement arrangement.

In shut hydroponics systems, the hydroponic supplement arrangement is recycled, and components that are not caught up in high amounts by plants (for example, sodium, chloride, fluoride and so forth.) or particles discharged by the plant, develop in the hydroponic supplement arrangement. For this situation, there is a need for more data about the supplement arrangement content, that EC can't give. Testing the hydroponic supplement arrangement much of the time will assist you with settling on the planning for supplanting the supplement arrangement or weaken it with new water.

pH Of The Hydroponic Nutrient Solution

The ideal pH scope of the hydroponic supplement arrangement is 5.8-6.3. Micronutrients are increasingly accessible in lower pH, yet when pH levels dip under 5.5, you risk micronutrient lethality, just as hindered accessibility of calcium and magnesium. In hydroponics, particularly in shut systems, the roots promptly influence the hydroponic arrangement pH, so pH will, in general, change. Proper items for acidifying the hydroponic supplement arrangement are sulfuric corrosive, phosphoric corrosive, and nitric corrosive. Ammonium/nitrate is one of the central points influencing the pH of the supplement arrangement.

Plant Nutrition In Hydroponics

Hydroponics development is viewed as better than a traditional event because of the various favorable circumstances it offers. Both business scale generation and little scale crop development utilizing hydroponics procedures have demonstrated to be worthwhile in many regards. One of the upsides of hydroponics is its effortlessness. Be that as it may, what is a genuinely straightforward, straight forward method may now and again appear to be confused, particularly to the recently started. This is especially so viewing issues, for example, plant nutrition in hydroponics. Given the plenty of tonics, added substances, development enhancers, and different mixtures that guarantee quickened development, higher yields, etc., one of the essential parts of hydroponics viz. plant nutrition may appear to be frustratingly muddled. It isn't, however.

Supplement Formulations

All plants, regardless of whether they are developed in soil or with hydroponics, require an equalization of nitrogen, phosphorus, and potassium (N-P-K) and follow components to prepare appropriately. These nutrients are accessible to plants in soil in modest quantities; however, after some time, they get drained and should be provided independently to make up the deficiency. In hydroponics, it is even more essential to guarantee that plants get the correct nutrients in the perfect sums.

Hydroponics definitions are structured for explicit phases of the plant life cycle. A plant's nutritional necessities shift as per an amazing phase's period. At the point when plants are in the vegetative stage, they require more noteworthy measures of nitrogen, which is the critical component being developed of leaves and stems. Lack of nitrogen during the development time frame prompts hindered development with yellowing of leaves. This is the most regularly observed insufficiency in plants. During the blooming cycle, the proportion of nitrogen, the plant requires less nitrogen, more phosphorus, and potassium.

Utilizing high-quality definitions that contain the indispensable components for plant development ought to be the principal thought in accommodating plant nutrition in hydroponics.

Keep it Simple

Following a decent supplement system and keeping it straightforward will go far to guarantee sufficient take-up of all the fundamental nutrients. It fits not to utilize such a large number of details as it might be tough to follow the precise reason for the issue if there are numerous added substances and enhancements in the supplement blend.

Development Enhancers, Boosters, and Fortifiers

Certain business items have been built up that can animate quicker supplement take-up and accelerate stem and leaf development. Vast numbers of these items are best left to the progressed and experienced producers. Amateur hydroponics lovers should move toward such things as development supporters with alert. Likewise, there are a few items accessible in the market that guarantee to function as blossom fortifiers. These definitions demonstration to animate blooming and increment essential oils in plants. While choosing a sprout fortifier, the best activity is to select one with an NPK proportion of 0-50-30. Such fortifiers have no nitrogen and are wealthy in Phosphorus and Potassium. These essential minerals animate the arrangement of super blossoms.

Natural Formulations

Natural gardening has gotten on lately, and the hydroponics business has tried to incorporate natural growing practices in hydroponics development. A few logical definitions have been expertly created, worked, and advertised. Natural recipes for use in hydroponics ought to be solvent, independent items that leave no residue in the holder. Ensure the logical equation doesn't require shaking other purposes as any dregs are probably going to obstruct lines and siphons. Additionally, observe that natural definitions implied for soil developed plants are not reasonable for use in hydroponics as these will stop up the siphons and lines bringing about consuming of plants.

Different Considerations

Plants need to have crisp nutrients accessible for stable development. Guaranteeing ordinary repository changes each week is fundamental. pH and electroconductivity ought to be checked while blending the supplement arrangement. While the electroconductivity perusing will help decide the measure of broke up nutrients, the pH perusing will help in keeping up pH esteems at levels that will empower plants to ingest the nutrients. Filtering or flushing ought to be done the multi-week before reap. This should be possible utilizing standard faucet water through the system to clean out abundance salts that stay in the growing medium.

Keeping a gardening diary will help in maintaining a strategic distance from botches and build up pointers to the correct game-plan. Making diary sections over time will assist work with increasing a veritable fortune trove of essential data on different parts of nutrition, pH, EC, and so forth. Plants require two kinds of nutrients for stable development, full-scale nutrients, and miniaturized scale nutrients. Plants utilize full-scale nutrients in enormous sums, while smaller-scale nutrients are necessary for follow amounts. Following is a rundown of Macro and Micro-Nutrients and their functional significance in plant development:

To get started are the four main nutrients that all plants are going to need in order to grow well. These include:

Carbon—this takes up over 50 percent of the composition of your plant. Chlorophyll is the best way for your plant to get hold of this and the sugar that come from chlorophyll is important as well.

Hydrogen—this one is good for helping the roots absorb the nutrients that it needs. In most cases, you will see that the plant will get its hydrogen from the water you provide.

Oxygen—this helps the plant go through respiration so it can grow through the process of creating starches and sugars.

Nitrogen—the nitrogen is able to create chlorophyll and amino acids that help to manufacture the sugars it needs to grow.

Without these nutrients, the plant is going to have some issues with growing and producing the way that you would like. Make sure that when you create your own nutrient solution or purchase one, you are careful about getting the right amounts of these into the mixture for a happy and healthy plant.

While the macronutrients are the most important for your plant because the plant will not be able to grow at all and develop without them, it is also really important to get those micronutrients in place as well. The plant will need less of these compared to the other nutrients, but adding them into the mix will help your plant to flourish and look as amazing as you had hoped.

There are many micronutrients that you can choose for your plant, and each of the premade soils will come with different varieties. Some of the nutrients that you should consider include:

Calcium—this one is great for helping the plant create more cell walls. If there isn't enough of this in your plant, it could have a slowing down of growth.

Sulfur—this nutrient helps the plant to synthesize proteins.

Iron—this one is good for sugar creation as well as chlorophyll development.

Magnesium—this one helps with creating enzymes and chlorophyll that help keep the plant strong. If your plant doesn't get enough of this, the leaves could start to yellow.

Boron—this one works hand in hand with calcium to make more cell walls. Too little of boron in the plant diet could result in some weak stems.

Manganese—creates oxygen during the process of photosynthesis. This one can also cause yellow leaves if not properly taken into the plant.

Zinc—zinc is really important to the plant because it helps with nitrogen, chlorophyll and respiration metabolism. If your plant has smaller leaves, it is probably short on zinc.

Copper—this nutrient helps with photosynthesis, respiration, and enzyme activation. Yellow and pale leaves are common in plants that are short on this nutrient.

Making your own nutrient solution, or purchasing one that is already made, that has the right amount of these micronutrients can make all the difference in the kind of growth you get out of your plants each year. Take the time to check out your nutrient solution to ensure you are giving your plants the very best.

Chapter 8. System Maintanace

Hydroponic gardens need to have the proper care and maintenance, or they will not produce healthy plants. Not only do they need to be constantly cleaned, but there are various maintenance checks that need to be carried out in order to make sure the system remains functioning correctly.

A faulty drain, or a leaky pipe or switch could do serious damage to a hydroponic garden as most of the systems rely on their equipment and parts to work smoothly.

Cleanliness

In order to stop the build-up of algae, mold, and fungus or to stop attracting pests, keep the growing room as clean as possible.

Equipment should be flushed and cleaned at least twice a month to maintain water levels, stop algae growth, and ensure that there are no pests lurking about the system.

In order to stop pests and various fungal growth, growers should always make sure their hands are clean. Hands should be kept washed especially after handling anything that was dirty or in contact with a harmful substance.

Do not let old fallen leaves, stems, fruit, produce or growing media or even pots or discarded trays lie around the growing areas. Rather throw out any debris or broken items, and wash and pack away any unused equipment.

Wash all equipment after use and only reuse a growing medium if it can be reused and it has been thoroughly washed and sterilized. In fact, all growing mediums, whether old or new, should be thoroughly washed before being used as not to contaminate the grow pots, grow trays, and the reservoir.

Keeping the growing area and equipment clean cuts down on the chances of infestation and development of frustrating diseases that are a nuisance to get rid of.

Nutrient Solution

The proper nutrient solution for the plant type and system type should be used at the correct ratio of solution to water.

Only use good quality nutrient solutions with an organic base. Advance nutrients are only required should there be a problem that needs to be fixed, such as a nutrient deficiency in a plant.

The nutrient solution balance should be checked on a regular basis especially is it is a recovery system where the solution is being continuously recycled.

Make sure that the solution is flushed and completely refreshed on a regular basis and that there is no salt buildup, since this is very acidic and toxic to the plants.

Watering

Watering is done in many different ways and is delivered to each of the hydroponic systems differently.

Make sure the water is always fresh and checked on a regular basis. Algae is a common problem, as is nutrient build up in the system. An oxygen pump should be installed in order to ensure the water is being well hydrated and to keep the water fresher for longer.

Water solutions can come from the tap, drain systems, or rain collection tanks.

Watering can be on a continuous flow basis or set by a timer that switches on and off at different intervals during the day.

If possible, a person should always have a backup water solution available in case of an emergency and their primary watering source is unavailable. Some plants are very sensitive to their watering schedule and even a few minute's downtime and a missed watering schedule can cause some damage.

Reservoir Temperature

The water in the reservoir should be around 65 to 75 degrees Fahrenheit, which is basic room temperature. Water that is either too hot or too cold can damage the plant's root systems and their leaves.

The reservoir should be topped off with water in order to keep pH and nutrient levels constant. Change out the water on a regular basis.

Humidity

Different plants and hydroponic systems need the humidity to be on different levels. There are thermometers that can measure the humidity and temperature to ensure that the plants are comfortable. Keeping an optimum level does not encourage the growth of unwanted diseases and fungi.

Make sure plants that love the hotter temperatures get enough humidity by giving them a regular misting spray. This will help to keep the humidity constant for the plants that do not like too much humidity.

Inspect the Equipment

The equipment should be thoroughly inspected on a regular basis.

There are a lot of things that can go wrong in a hydroponic system, especially with the equipment. And the best way to troubleshoot is to try to avoid as many equipment malfunctions as possible.

The best way to inspect equipment it to keep the entire system in mind. When doing the inspection start at one point and work your way through your system.

Start with the reservoir and all the systems that are dependent on it.

- Water feeding pipe

    - This should be thoroughly checked for crimps that may not be feeding the solution correctly.
    - Nutrients build up in the pipes so they may need a thorough flushing out or replacing.
    - Check for any blockages in the pipe.
    - Check for any holes or leaks that could deter the flow of water pressure in the pipe.
    - Check for any algae or mold that may be growing in or around the pipe.
    - Determine if it may be time to replace the hoses.
    - Give them a good cleaning if they are still viable.

- Nozzles and hoses

    - Check the nozzles that feed the root systems, sprinklers, or misting systems.
    - When last were they changed?
    - Check for blockages or leakage.
    - Check any joins and washers for leaks.
    - Check for sediment build up, algae, or mold growing in or around these attachments.
    - Give them a good cleaning if they are still usable.

- Drain siphons and hoses

    - Check the drain pipes for blockages

- When last were they replaced?
- Check for leaks.
- Check for algae or mold growing in or around these pipes.
- They may need to have a good cleaning as part of the system maintenance.

- Check the reservoir water pump
  - Test the pump
  - Make sure it is still working correctly and pumping the water at the optimum flow.
  - Check that all pump attachments are not leaking air.

- Check the reservoir
  - Check that there is no build-up, algae, or mold growing on the reservoir.
  - Check for any leaks.
  - Make sure the water is at the optimum temperature for the hydroponic system and plants.
  - Check that any air pumps are functioning correctly and adequately oxygenating the tank.
  - Make sure any oxygen stones do not have unwanted algae or mold growth on them

- Growing trays
  - Make sure the growing tray(s) do not have any leaks in them.

- - Make sure the growing tray(s) are clean and have not unwanted algae or mold growing on them.
  - Clean off any nutrient build up and make sure the trays are clean.
  - For a closed system, the trays must be given thorough flushing out.
- Growing pots
  - Check that each of the pots is still intact and not broken.
  - Replace any that are not functioning correctly.
  - Make sure any growing medium is clean and does not have any unwanted algae or mold growing on them that could upset the plant's natural balance.
- Lighting equipment
  - Check that the bulbs are still functioning correctly.
  - Check that the lighting is still adequate for the environment.
  - Check the timers are working correctly.
  - Clean any residue off the lighting system.

Temperature

- Make sure that any thermostat is working correctly, and that room temperature is normal.

- Check that the humidity is correct for the growing environment.
- Check both the temperature and humidity thermometers to ensure that they are still working correctly.

Ventilation

- Make sure that there is adequate ventilation in the growing room.
- Not enough ventilation can cause mold.
- Check that all fans and cooling systems are working correctly.

- Support Systems
  - Check that any hanging supports for the plants are working without causing the plant or system any undue stress.
  - Make sure that the environment in which the hydroponic system is housed offers the correct infrastructure for the system to function correctly.
  - Make sure the plants are all supported and planted correctly to ensure a successful infrastructure.

Tools

- Are all the gardening tools in working order?
- Are they cleaned?
- Are there any that may need to be replaced?

Look at Your Plants

Make sure you keep a vigilant check on your growing plants. Measure their growth rate, root growth and when they are ready to harvest.

This gives a person a good measure of how the next batch should perform and something by which to determine if the growing medium, solution, or systems structure may need to be changed or optimized.

The plants must also be checked to make sure they are getting enough nutrients, they are growing as they should, and there are no pests or other infestations. A lot of growing problems and deficiencies can be caused by various infestations. Some are easy to spot, others may take more of an experienced eye, but as a gardener gets to know their plants they will come to instinctively know when something is wrong.

Look for the signs in seedlings such as slow growth , looking sad and droopy, white fluffy stuff growing on the leaves, etc.

Take the time to look over the plants; do not just rush through it. If there are a lot of plants to look over, break them into sections and do a revolving sweep of one section on this day, and the next section on another.

If there is an outbreak, you will need to go through the entire growing area right away.

Spending time with the plants in a hydroponic environment can also be quite good for the mind and spirit. Plants and running water are rather therapeutic and can reduce stress, anxiety and ease tension.

Change One Thing at a Time

If you are wanting to change or expand your system, do not try and do it all at once.

Choose a section to change, switch it around, or upgrade and start with that.

Before rushing out and buying expensive parts, why not try a bit of DIY and try to make it yourself. Or at least look around to see what you have available before rushing off to spend more money on an item you do not really need.

Hydroponic systems are not only flexible and versatile in what they can grow or how they deliver their solutions, but they can also be easily adapted to suit the grower's needs and lifestyle.

There are so many great DIY ideas on how to create the perfect hydroponic garden online these days that it is well worth a try. The money you save building the system yourself can be better spent on plants, growing media, or nutrient solutions.

In order to keep a system simple and working for you, think carefully about an upgrade or addition. Plot it out and then work through one section at a time getting that part right before moving on to the next.

Chapter 9. Getting Rid of Common Pests

We've made it through setting up our own hydroponic garden, picking plants, learning about nutrients and figuring out how we can maintain it. But now we've come across a whole new issue: Pests. Our setup provided a great environment for our plants to grow. But it also created an environment which pests love and we even filled it with tons of healthy plants for them to eat. This would be fine if they provided some kind of service to our plants but all they want to do is snack on them and leave them wilted and yellowed.

We'll take a look at the most common pests that hydroponic growers encounter and we'll see how you can spot them in your own garden. Our number one defense against pests is to prevent them from making our gardens their home in the first place, so we will learn some of the techniques used to detect them early and prevent an infestation.

Pests aren't the only problem we face as hydroponic growers. Disease is also something we must be vigilant in spotting, identifying and handling. To this end, we'll look at some of the more common diseases and how we can prevent them.

Common Hydroponic Pests

While there are many pests that can try to make our gardens their home, there are certain pests that show up with more regularity than others. These pests fall into five key categories: spider mites, thrips, fungus gnats, whiteflies and aphids. If you find yourself with an infestation of pests, it is a safe bet that they'll fall into one of these five categories.

Spider Mites

Out of all five types of pest, spider mites are a particularly annoying one. While they are less than a millimeter long, these little guys are actually tiny spiders. Because they are so small, they have a tendency to start damaging your plants before you even notice that they have taken up in your garden. Spider mite damage will look like tiny brown and yellow spots on the leaves of your plants. While they don't look like anything serious when there are only a couple of bites, this damage adds up quickly to really wreak havoc on your garden.

To spot a spider mite infestation, there are two key signs to look out for. While the damage on your plants can be a telltale sign, it doesn't specifically tell you that spider mites are the problem. To spot a spider mite infestation you should check your plants to see if you can spot any spider-like webbing. Another way to check for spider mites is to use a tissue or clean rag to gently wipe the bottoms of your leaves. If you come away with streaks of blood, this will tell you that you have a spider mite problem.

One way of handling spider mites is to wash your plants down with a hose or powerful spray bottle. The force of the water can often knock the mites off of your plant and drown them in the growing medium. Spider mites also have some natural enemies ranging from ladybugs to lacewings and you may consider adding these beneficial insects to your garden to feed on the spider mite population.

Aphids

These little guys are also known as plant lice. And just like head lice, they aren't all that much fun. These tiny, soft-bodied pests are pretty much able to set up in any environment. They multiply quicker than rabbits, so you want to make sure to tackle an aphid infestation as soon as possible. These pests are typically a quarter of an inch in size and can come in green, yellow, pink, black or gray varieties.

Aphids like to feed on the juices of the plant and you can find them chewing on stems, leaves, buds, fruits or roots. They are particularly drawn to the newest parts of the plant. If you find that your leaves are misshapen or yellowing, checking the bottom can reveal aphids. They also leave behind a sticky substance referred to as honeydew. This sweet substance can actually attract other kinds of pests so aphids are particularly annoying little critters. This substance can also lead to the growth of fungus, like sooty mold which can cause your branches or leaves to turn an unpleasant black color. Aphids are also able to carry viruses from one plant to another so they can help nasty pathogens to spread quicker.

Like spider mites, spraying water on the leaves can dislodge them and leave them with a hard time finding their way back to your plants. If the infestation is large, dusting your plants with flour can constipate them and help convince them it is time to move on. Wiping down your plants with a mixture of soapy water can also help to kill and drive them off.

Thrips

Like spider mites and aphids, these little guys are also tiny. Often, they are only around 5 millimeters long. It can be hard to spot these little guys but they leave damage that is clear as day. If you start to see little metallic black specks on your leaves, you probably have some thrips snacking off your garden. Leaves that thrips attack will often turn brown and become super dry because the thrips like to suck out their juices.

Thrips are small and are either black or the color of straw. They have slender bodies and two pairs of wings. Because they are so small, they look like dark threads to the naked eye. They like to feed in large groups and will fly away if you disturb them. They stick their eggs into flowers and leaves and they only take a couple of days to hatch so a thrip infestation can feel like it just happened out of the blue.

Because thrips like to lay their eggs in plants, it is super important that you remove any dead or fallen plant matter. If you paid attentioN, you'll know you should be doing this anyway as it helps to prevent many issues that can assail our hydroponic gardens. Make sure that you inspect your plants for thrip damage and remove any that are infested. Hosing off the plants will also help to reduce their population. Ladybugs, lacewings and minute pirate bugs all feed on thrips and can be beneficial to your garden.

Fungus Gnats

Fungus gnats are an odd one. Adult fungus gnats have no interest in harming your garden. But their larvae enjoy chewing on the roots of your plants which slows growth and opens the plant up for infection. In extreme cases, fungus gnat larvae can actually cause the death of plants. They really like areas with a lot of moisture and a high humidity. You'll likely notice adult fungus gnats before you have any issue. As adults, these gnats are about three millimeters in length and kind of look like mosquitos. They tend to be a grayish-black color with a pair of long legs and clear wings. Their larvae have shiny black heads with a whitish-transparent body.

Adults typically live for a week and in that time lay up to 300 eggs. It takes half a week for the larvae to emerge but when they do, they start a two-week diet where their main dish is the roots of your plants. When they feed on your plants, they cause them to wilt, stunt their growth and cause a yellowing of their leaves. These nasty little things can have many generations living off the same plant.

If you suspect a fungus gnat infestation than you should inspect your plants by carefully turning up the soil around their stems and look for larvae. If you check a plant and it suddenly let's loose a bunch of adult gnats then you should dispose of that plant. They really like damp soils so make sure you aren't overwatering your plants. If you have a fungus gnat problem then letting your potting medium drain longer will help to kill off the larvae and mess up the development of fungus gnat eggs. You can also spray your plants with a combination of peppermint, cinnamon and sesame oils. This mixture is called flying insect killer and will help to get rid of gnats.

Whiteflies

About the same size as spider mites, whiteflies look like small white moths that take up residence on your plants. They are easier to spot but because they fly away when you bother them they can be hard to kill. Like aphids, they enjoy sucking the juices out of your plant and you see their damage as white spots and yellowing of the leaves.

They tend to lay 200-400 eggs in clusters on the underside of the higher leaves. These eggs hatch in about a week and unattractive little nymphs come out that crawl around on your leaves before they grow wings. These crawlers will spread out from the egg and find a place to start chewing on your leaves. They'll stay in that spot for the next week or so before growing into young adults which will repeat the cycle of movement-feasting.

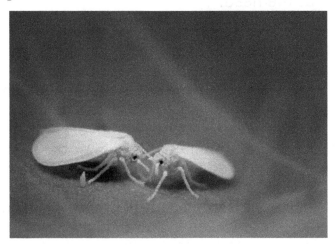

Ladybugs and lacewings enjoy eating whiteflies and so introducing them to your garden can help to kill off whitefly populations. Hosing off plants with a strong blast of water will help in reducing their numbers as well. There are a bunch of organic pesticides on the market which you can get to deal with whiteflies. These pesticides can also work for the other pests but pesticides should be a last resort option, one that you are careful with so as not to lead to undue stress on your plants.

Preventing Pests

Now that we have an idea of the pests that are most common to hydroponic gardens, let us turn our attention towards how we prevent these pests from getting into our gardens in the first place. Many of these techniques will help us to identify a possible infestation as it is trying to get started and so they offer us early warnings to prepare ourselves to battle pests. If we keep up our preventative measures and keep our eyes peeled for pests then we can save our plants a lot of damage and ourselves a lot of time by cutting off the problem at the head.

When it comes to pests it is also important to understand that not every pest is the same. This doesn't just mean that whiteflies are different from fungus gnats. What this means is that fungus gnats on the West coast are going to be different than fungus gnats on the East coast. Not every solution for prevention or extermination will work. A certain pesticide may be used to kill gnats on the East but the ones on the West might have grown an immunity to it. For this reason, it is important to check with your local hydroponics store to see if there is any region-specific information you need to tackle your pest problem.

One of the ways that we prevent pests is to make sure that we limit their ability to enter our garden in the first place. We can do this a few ways. Insect screens go a long way to keeping out pests. We also want to limit the amount of traffic in and around our setups. If at all possible, our setups will benefit greatly if they can be protected by airlock entrances as these offer the most secure protection against both pests and pathogens. Airlocks can be doubled up to create a space before the garden in which to wipe down dirt and any insects or eggs that are catching a free ride on your clothing.

In order to see if pests are starting to show up in your garden, use sticky traps around your plants. Yellow and blue sticky traps are both useful, as they attract different pests, so you want to make sure to use both kinds for the best results. Place traps near any entrances into your garden such as doors or ventilation systems. Also, make sure to place one or two near the stems of your plants to catch those pests that prefer snacking on the lower bits, such as aphids or fungus gnats. Get into the habit of checking these traps regularly as they can give you a great idea of what kind of life is calling your garden home.

While traps will help us to get a head start fighting any infections, they aren't a foolproof method when it comes to avoiding pests. Traps should be used together with personal spot checks. This means that you should be checking your plants for pests a couple of times a week. Take a clean cloth and check the bottom of your leaves. Check around the roots for any fungus gnat larvae. You can check the tops of leaves visually. Look for any signs of yellowing or bite marks as described above.

Make sure to remove any weeds that take up root in your garden as these plants are only going to sap your garden's resources and offer a breeding ground for pests. Also remove dead or fallen plant matter, of course. This includes leaves but also any fruit, buds or petals that have been dropped.

Finally, before you introduce any new plants to your garden, make sure to quarantine them first so that you can check them for pests. You can use a magnifying glass to get a closer look if you need to. Give the new plants a thorough inspection, making sure to check all parts of the plant and the potting soil before you transfer it over.

By creating a system and a schedule for inspecting your plants, you can prevent an infestation of pests from ruining your garden or causing you a lot of headaches. A vigilant eye will give you the upper hand in both preventing and dealing with any kind of problem you have with pests. Remember, a strong defense is the best offense when it comes to keeping your plants healthy and free from harm.

Chapter 10. Potential Problems and How to Overcome Them

It is very exciting to think you will soon have your own hydroponics garden, whether it is in a greenhouse, a room of your home, or outside. You are anxious to get started. You feel you have read dozens upon dozens of words about creating your system and how to grow the fruits, vegetables, and herbs. But, you are not quite ready to begin. You want hydroponics to be fun and rewarding, which means you need to effectively manage your garden and avoid these 11 common mistakes. These mistakes are in some ways related to the troubleshooting because there can be errors within your system that need correction; however, they are also things you, as a human might cause, which you have to fix before you can troubleshoot your gardening system.

Starting Your Garden without Proper Knowledge

Any hobby requires knowledge. Sometimes you can learn as you enjoy your hobby, but for hydroponic gardening, you will discover more fun and enjoyment if you arm yourself with the proper education first. A lot of novice gardeners start out without gathering all the information required to start, which can lead to issues with the system or proper nutrient dispersal. You have started out well by reading this book, but if there are fruits and vegetables not mentioned in the commonly grown plant section, then you will want to do more research.

Harvesting too Early

Each plant has its own harvesting time table. A few plants will go from seed to plant to full fruit or vegetable in as little as a month. Other plants can take 70 to 120 days from germination to harvest time. It would be nice if you can start picking fruits and vegetables off the plants as soon as they appear, but you risk an immature vegetable or fruit, which can mean a poor taste. Let the fruits and vegetables grow to full maturity before picking them.

Overwatering/Under Watering

Water is a crucial element to growing your plants; however, there is a fine line between not watering enough and watering too much. The reason hydroponic systems need to have a timer is so you can regulate the watering process with more accuracy. Continually saturating the plants with water will create drooping leaves, as well as hinder the growth of the plants. Some plants will start to rot due to too much water. You also cannot let the roots get too dry. Dry roots mean not enough nutrients, plus they will shrivel up and die. A good rule of thumb is to water your plants when you see the top layer of medium become dry. Stick your finger into the medium and test whether it is wet. If it is not, then you are not watering your plants enough. Other reasons to set up your hydroponic system with drainage is to ensure your plants are not over watered. The roots can soak up what they need and the rest of the water will go back into the reservoir.

Improper Lighting

Even the best gardeners know that sometimes daylight just is not enough because it can be infrequent. The sun might be behind a cloud or it might be raining, which takes away from the proper light required for your crops. For your crop to grow to its proper height and to keep the leaves a healthy green, you have to provide proper light. Reading lights and single bulbs are not the best lamps, which most novices tend to use. Fluorescent bulbs can be okay, but they are highly expensive to run and replace. This is why it is suggested to avoid the mistake of regular lights and fluorescent bulbs in favor of using high pressure sodium or LED lights, which are more cost effective. It does not mean plants need light 24/7, but consistent light without overheating the plant is necessary.

Ignoring pH

The hydroponic system works on pH regulation. New gardeners tend to do well at first with proper monitoring of pH, but once the novelty wears off, so does the time one pays to monitoring the pH. The nutrient solution needs to be monitored for a balanced pH, which may vary depending on the plants you are growing. You can buy equipment to help you adjust the pH. When growing different plants, it is easy to make mistakes on the pH because plants tend to need different degrees of acidic levels. For example, beans require a pH of 6 to 6.5, while cabbage is best grown in 6.5 to 7.5. Pineapple is on the other end of the scale at 5 to 5.5 pH. With hydroponic systems when the pH rises above 6.5, there are some nutrients and micronutrients that precipitate out of the nutrient solution. This means the nutrients remain in the reservoir or growing chambers, rather than reaching the plant roots. Iron is one mineral that will precipitate out at 7.3 and at 8 pH there is no more iron. A plant deficiency in nutrients means poor fruit or worse plant death.

Overfeeding the Plants

Like overwatering, anything can be done in excess. Providing fertilizer to your plants; particularly, in a hydroponic system, can be overdone. You could add too many salt deposits or create a fungus issue in the medium, which leads to stunted growth. Hydroponic fertilizer is the nutrient solution, which is combined with water, so if you are over watering, you may also be over fertilizing your plants. Hydroponic fertilizer is usually made with salts, such as potassium chloride. However, the chlorine can actually become harmful to your plants if you apply it for more than two or three days. Magnesium nitrate is another option, which is basically Epsom salts. The main ingredients of your hydroponic garden solution do need to be nitrogen, phosphorus and potassium, you also need trace amounts of iron, sulfur, zinc, manganese, boron, copper, magnesium, chlorine, calcium, and molybdenum. If you are not buying a premade nutrient solution, then study before you start to make your own to ensure you have the proper amount of all nutrients.

Insufficient Air Circulation

Another common mistake is not providing the proper ventilation your plants need to remain healthy. This does not mean you need to infuse the water with oxygen, but rather allow plenty of air into the grow room. Monitoring humidity and oxygen quality in the grow room will ensure you are providing proper air circulation for better plant health. You may need to have a blower or fan in the area. Make sure that none of your plants are directly in the path of the fan, blower, or air conditioning vent as this can make them cold and dormant.

Unhygienic Conditions

Hydroponic growing systems still need maintenance. Your reservoir tank might develop mold, algae, or a layer of dust film that interferes with proper health of your plant. You will need to keep things clean and dust free to keep your plants healthy.

Falling into the Cheap Trap

Anything labeled "plant food" might be something you think you need, but it rarely is. Hydroponic gardens are much different than soil gardens. You already learned about pH, proper nutrients, and air circulation, so you need to keep these things in mind when you visit a store. Going into a warehouse style store that sells anything and everything does not mean you need their plant food. Most people working in the gardening section have minimal training versus a plant dedicated store that specifically hires experts to work there. Asking for advice about the nutrients and fertilizers to purchase is good, but do not stop there. Ask why one brand is better than another or why they made that recommendation, so you can understand how it will work in your hydroponic garden. Purchasing seeds, plants, fertilizer, nutrients, and even hydroponic systems for cheap or through unauthorized dealers can lead to dead plants, foliage damage, and plant disease that kills your entire garden. To have a sustainable garden, you cannot make the mistake of starting off with ill or nearly dead plants. You will have a losing battle each time if you go cheap on the plants.

Pest Control via Plants

There is a common mistake many make when it comes to protecting their gardens from pests. They forget that there are natural methods that include actual plants. Garlic is one form of pest control. Adding this to an outdoor garden will help keep pests from coming to investigate the rest of your garden. Coffee grinds are another form of natural pest control. Dried coffee is a pesticide for most bugs that will eat your plants. You can sprinkle grinds around your buckets or the bottoms of the hydroponic system to prevent pests from crawling into the medium and up the plant. You do not want to use it on top of the medium as this would affect pH levels, which is also a common mistake for hydroponic newbies. Some already know coffee grinds are great for pests and put it in the medium like it is soil, thus contaminating their system.

Chapter 11. Hydroponic Tips and Tricks for Beginners

Gardening is a field that has developed gradually since the start of time. Since the early days until now, people have tried to develop better techniques to deliver a more effective and easy gardening technique. Different forms and new and better strategies have evolved over the years. Another such method is hydroponics.

Hydroponics helps you to cultivate your plants without any natural hazards throughout the year. Conventional gardening techniques require a number of external factors uncontrollable for plant cultivation.

Incontrollable variables such as different seasons, weather etc. play a key role in yield. Nevertheless, approaches that use water solution instead of soil minimize the risk associated with these variables.

These hydroponic systems can be made in your own home, if you are an experienced plant gardener. You can also go online for the kits made available by the company. Such kits are available in different sizes and can be chosen according to your particular needs.

Such kits include the necessary equipment and elements such as lamps, pumps, containers, nutrient systems, etc. In any case, you will need an in-depth understanding of plants and their different aspects.

There are many different aspects that make the Hydroponics device cycle a success. Lighting is such an important aspect. It is necessary that you give the plants sufficient light to grow.

At least a good eight hours of sunlight should be given to young plants for efficient growth. Remember always that too much is bad. Make sure that light is not too high, especially when using multiple lights.

Other very important factors in hydroponics are humidity and temperature. Each living organism has an ideal level of different environmental conditions, such as humidity, temperature, etc. If plants are grown indoors, it is very important for plants to survive in a good environment.

More carbon dioxide can also be introduced into the plant for better growth. In addition to external conditions, nutrition is equally important. You will be able to better understand their nutritional needs by studying the plants you want to produce.

When you have the necessary nutrient solution in Hydroponics, you must focus on the absorption rate. This ensures that the plant can absorb nutrients without any problems to the best of its ability. The aim of a controlled environment is to be able to change every factor in growing plants to maximize their efficiency.

Air pumps and sleeves can help to improve air circulation throughout the solution. For fact, the water used in the process can also be used over and over again. Whilst it's best to practice gardening before using the hydroponics, beginners can also grow their favorite plants and vegetables in a smaller size.

Hydroponic gardening is nothing other than soil-free planting. It is an economical way to supply plants with food and water. The soil's purpose is to provide plants with nutrients and to protect the roots of plants.

A plant uses food and water in the soil. The plant is supplied with a full nutrient solution and a growing medium in the hydroponic gardening to sustain the root plants.

It allows plants to access water and food more quickly. If you start your first hydroponic garden, a lot of resources and information can be found online. A good way to begin a hydroponic garden is to obey useful factors during gardening.

Some of them are listed below: Grow: you can grow hydroponically vegetables, flowers and medicinal plants. Many of them include tomatoes, peppers, cucumbers, orchids and medicinal plants. You can start a garden by buying seeds online or just buy it from garden centres.

System or method: There are six types of hydroponic systems that you can use for your greenhouse, including Ebb and Flow, Drip, Aeroponic, N.F.T and Wick System. Any device, lighting, and growing medium that suits your plants, garden size and budget can be selected.

Garden area: whether you need a small or large hydroponic garden, you have to decide. The flow of air and the ability to control moisture and temperature in the room depend on your area of cultivation.

Your garden always needs clean water and safe electricity. A continuous water supply with a good pH level is very critical. You need electric power supply for indoor gardening to operate water pumps, grow systems and fans.

Accessories: Depending on the complexity and size of your hydroponic garden, various accessories including light timers, fans, water pumps and meters for temperature and humidity measurement are required. Many hydroponic gardeners will help you to pick different garden needs.

Lighting system: Light is the key component if you plan to start an indoor garden. Understand your growing space and choose the perfect lighting for your garden.

You can choose high intensity growing lights that provide sunshine to your indoor garden.

Nutrients: You don't use soil in hydroponic gardening to grow plants. You must therefore provide the plants with full balanced nutrition. Plants require six types of micronutrients, Nitrogen, Phosphorus, Potassium, Calcium, Sulfur, Magnesium, in particular.

A plant needs some small traces of vitamins, iron, boron, zinc, manganese, cobalt and copper. Choose a perfect solution to provide sufficient macro and micro nutrients for your plants.

Growing medium: hydroponic means soilless gardening and therefore soil needs to be replaced by a perfect medium of production. This rising medium provides the plants with nutrients. There are enormous varieties of growing medium that cocoa, organic soil, mats, crushed stones and rock wool can be used.

Hydroponics is not a difficult planting strategy. In this process, the plant nutrients are liquefied during water. A rising medium substitutes the soil for oxygen, water and nutrients to the roots.

The first step in hydroponics is to buy your supplies. The seeds can be put in rock wool starter cubes that fit well into the typical nursery tray. The rock wool should be soaked overnight in a conditioning solution.

Place a seed in each cube.

In each cube. Place the tile under a fluorescent lamp with a semi-circular rim. Wait for the germination of the seeds and for the roots to come out of the cube base. This is the moment when the roots are transplanted into the hydroponic system.

A large yellow pail is required to serve as the external storage that contains the food and water for your plant. The plant actually sits in a small green pail with small pants. More products include fluorescent light bulb, root help marbles and plant food.

Punch small holes in the small holder to prevent too much water from flooding the roots.

Wash the ground from the roots until you see the root system's main part. Handle the roots with great care.

Place some marbles at the bottom of the little bowl. This can be from 1/2 inch to 1 inch to provide enough water and air for proper growth.

Enable the roots to settle at the base to access more water. Fill the bowl with more marbles once this is finished. Inside the larger container, position the small pot until it gets balanced.

You can illuminate the plant to speed up production. Water and feed the plant based on hydroponic gardening standards. Nutrient, salt and water measure. You need one Miracle Grow table spoon, another salt table spoon and one gallon of water.

Combine the solution and pour tenderly on the root until the waterline is almost one inch above the bottom of the small pot in the large container.

Make it a point for your plant to maintain. If the plant leaves turn into another color, a problem can occur. The water should also not be too low or too high. The PH balance is better known. To address this problem, change the water regularly. In any hydroponic supply store, PH level test tools can be purchased.

Chapter 12. Hydroponics as Business

It is indeed a fulfilling moment to harvest crops from your Hydroponic Gardens. Commercial hydroponics is not just about the hydroponic facilities being set up and managed. To be successful and perform a viable operation, you need to learn to do a number of other things:

- Choose the right crops to grow.//

- Have a feasible physical layout.

- Handle your staff and finances properly.

- Market your products correctly.

DECIDING WHAT PLANTS TO GROW

When deciding which plants to grow on a business hydroponics farm, consider the following:

- Facility for transplant propagation/cost. What will be the price (in time or money) to get your initial crops?

- How quick are the plants to reproduce if you intend to propagate themselves? Are the crops readily available? Is the proposed planting date the same as the year you expect to begin your operation?

- How easy is it to grow these plants? Do you have the skills to expand these varieties, or do your staff? Unless you have better than average expertise, challenging plants may be more expensive to produce, and more dangerous to get a benefit from.

- How long will it take for the plant to grow? Many plants produce a harvest that is ready for sale within months, and others take years.

- Adequate to your services. Do you have the proper buildings, equipment, and other facilities under consideration to grow the particular plants? Do you have space and money to provide those facilities?

- Climate suitability. What plants are best suited for growing in your climate?

- The environment. Operating with the atmosphere is always more effective than trying to recreate different environments

- Other competent growers are already growing the crop you'd instead grow? Could you bring in a fair market share?

- Distance from potential customers

- Transportation is expensive and can be hazardous. What are the other options available?

- Are the benefits (other than wages) likely to be a fair or sufficient return on your expenditure in terms of time and money

- Your staff skills. Don't pretend to do what you're incompetent to do. It's likely someone with better skills will do it better and cheaper.

RUNNING THE TRIAL- RECORDS AND REPORTING

Some measurements can give valuable data, including solution analysis, foliar mineral analysis, plant height, leaf area, and leaf area index (LAI), fruit quality assessment, plant dry weight versus fresh weight, water uptake, root dry weight, yields, marketable yields, taste quality assessment, shelf life, and photographs. There may be several features the grower wants to test.

EVALUATING THE TRIAL

Comparing the test plot against a cure or a set of treatment plots will assess the crop experiment. The trial assessment usually depends on statistical analysis that decides whether observable variations in control and trial plots are likely due to actual differences or incidence by chance. Plant and plots duplication is widely used to enhance statistical estimation. The higher the replication level, the lower the trial error margin.

Generic statistical analysis should be used for analyzing the trial to determine the actual outcome of the trial. It can be confusing to simply look at the species, and draw a conclusion from them. Quantifying the trial by counting plants and doing a comparative analysis of the data is much more useful in determining whether any observed effects are significant. For this to happen, the grower may need to hire a statistician or horticultural consultant's services.

STANDARDS

Like any business, a hydroponic farm must set and adhere to specific requirements if it is to be running lucratively. Those standards can be classified into three major groups:

1. Expenses for efficiency standards
2. Quality standards
3. Quantity standards

Expenses for efficiency standards

A stable relationship must be formed between production cost and selling price. Both of these numerical statistics need to be constantly monitored and held at an acceptable level in order to ensure market productivity. If production costs get too high, income will diminish. In such a case, the selling price must be raised, or the income percentage may become a negative-sum (i.e., you may lose money instead of earning it).

Cost of production

The following factors influence the cost of production:

- Site's costs (rent / lease)
- Cost of sites' facilities (power, natural gas, water, insurance, fees, etc.)
- Costs of products (soil, fertilizer, etc.)
- Unsold product's costs -certain amounts may be destroyed, die, or become invaluable. (Some horticultural companies spend as much as 30 percent of their stock.)
- Expenses on labor (your time, as well as your staff, should be included
- Promotion of marketing (printing, magazines advertising, etc.)

- Selling value (transport, invoicing, etc.)

- Tax (do not forget payroll tax, income tax, etc.)

Profit

This figure must be above and beyond the money you earn as wages. You would better put your money into some form of investment and work for someone else if you only work for wages (without profit). Profit should be higher than the rate you can get if you invest your money elsewhere. Typically, the income should be at least 15-20%. The profit margin in horticultural companies can vary greatly from crop to crop and year to year. You will note that some years, and other years, the income will be meager (perhaps nothing).

The income must be seen over several years on average. New operations should always have enough resources to support them if they have a few bad seasons before good seasons.

Price of Sales

The amount for which the products are sold will vary significantly. This can be because of factors such as overall economic circumstances, general market supply, and consumer demand.

Quality Standards

The following factors are to be taken note of when considering produce quality:

- The general appearance of vitality or health such as marking or lack of markings (e.g., disease, red, bruising, etc.)

- How it tastes or smell (e.g., how sweet or bitter)

- Freshness (i.e., the faster you can sell it after harvest, the better the quality will be).

Quantity Standards

Agricultural processing needs to meet such requirements in terms of the amount, weight, and size of each unit of the commodity being harvested (for instance, how many strawberries you select per square meter annually and how heavy each strawberry will be).

- Size is not critical for some plants, but the number is (for example, orchids are sold as flowers. A little smaller, or larger flower does not make a big difference in cost).

- Weight is important for other crops, but the size does not matter (for example, the beans are sold in kilograms regardless of whether they are small or large).

- Size and weight of other plants are important also (e.g., kilograms of strawberries are sold, but large plants are priced differently than small plants).

Marketing Your Product

Marketing involves everything involved in bringing the product to the end customer. If you want to sell your goods well, all aspects of the process must be identified, and each step must be performed as well as possible. Typical marketing moves are:

- Packaging and handling of the product–this impacts its quality and durability for a potential buyer.

- Transit of the goods.

- Promotion of products.

Selling

Considering Your Markets

In general, hydroponic goods, whether they are fruit, vegetables or flowers, are marketed through the following:

1. Direct selling to the public (for example, from your property's packing shed or a stand along the road). Several farmers have boosted their sales with tourism markets and catering for people visiting their land in other ways. In view of the establishing of hydroponic tours along with direct sales of products and perhaps a shop that sells souvenirs, refreshments, etc. It may be viable. Some of those activities can include' choosing your own' purchases, where the public pays a negotiated price for what they buy.

2. Sales through major markets Major cities thrive markets for fruit, vegetables, and flowers where farmers sell their products to business owners. You can hire a booth or sell on these markets via an agent (who usually takes a commission).

3. Direct selling to retail outlets It may be possible for you to market your products and if you are large enough to make it worthwhile. However, the distribution can be costly and time-consuming and should not be dealt with lightly. Many businesses project goods are produced in factories for manufacturing. Generally, the price paid for the commodity is fixed, restricting yet assured sales the amount of profit the grower can make.

Market Research

One key to success in any company is ' knowing the industry. ' When you know, there is desire for what you are going to grow, and if you can decide where that market is, the chance of success will greatly increase (not to mention sleepless nights). So one of the many crucial things you can do is research the market in depth before any new crop is developed. Successful marketing depends on knowing the people/groups you sell–what they want, how they can respond to your goods, and what they are going to spend money on, etc.

If you understand the market place you should take the following steps to successful marketing:

- Set realistic marketing targets.
- Have strategies for achieving those goals
- Evaluate marketing initiative outcomes and change the strategies accordingly.

- Market research includes all the practices that enable managers to make marketing decisions. It tries to make the secret known, and in most instances, it succeeds partially.

Market Research Steps

- What information is required? If a problem exists, interpret it.

- How can I increase sales by 10 percent, for example? Or should I change my way of distributing my products?

- Conduct an inquiry. Examine past records related to the problem, talk to people who know who can contribute to this problem. Try to find some relevant information released (for example, in trade magazines, statistical departments, etc.). - You can choose to monitor customers (or potential customers) if more information is required. Note: this entails far more prices.

- If the problem remains beyond you, a professional market research firm may be employed to manage the problem.

Conclusion

If you have read this far, I can conclude that you are really serious about starting your own hydroponic garden at home. Well done! You have taken the first and most important step; getting all the information you need. Now you can go ahead and make a list of the plants you want to start growing. Then make another little list of the few basics you need to purchase or assemble at home and you are ready.

I also want to congratulate you on making the right choice. The benefits of using hydroponics are many-fold. You are now making your contribution to keeping the environment healthy. In the first instance the use of pesticides, which is part and parcel of most traditional gardening methods, is eliminated. Because you grow your plants in a controlled space, you should not have any problems with pests. Your vegetables can be grown completely organically, so you are putting yours and your family's health first.

Secondly, a lot fewer resources are needed to grow your vegetables if you use hydroponic methods. The water used for the nutrient solution is recycled and re-used, which means that you use less. No spill-offs will occur which can damage the environment like in traditional gardening.

Lastly, hydroponic gardening is a lot less labor-intensive. You are working in a compact space and can arrange all your plants at waist-high level so that you do not need to go down on your knees or bend down all the time. You will also save lots of time.

With all these benefits in mind, I am sure you need no more convincing. So, go out and make a start. In no time you will be able to harvest your first crops and enjoy your wonderful healthy home-grown vegetables, filled with flavor and goodness. Not only will you impress your friends with your organic produce, but you may just convince them to start their own hydroponic gardens as well; especially if they see how easy, mess-free and space-saving it really is.

Hydroponics is not a hard method to grow with. In fact, it's so efficient you'll quickly see why people want to put in the extra effort to grow their plants this way. Don't be put off by all the science, in fact, if you head to your local hydroponics store they'll be happy to give you a basic arrangement and clear up anything you're not getting.

If you're starting out get a small system up and running first that way, once you have the hang of the monitoring you'll be less likely to kill an entire expensive crop.

Hopefully, you've learned a lot about the main components of hydroponics and how to get the best plants ever.

GREENHOUSE GARDENING

Introduction

Greenhouse gardening is the way to grow plants that don't suit your environment or just start your gardening. Inside your home, whatever shape or size you select, you create a separate small ecosystem. All that happens in the greenhouse affects all the plants because you're working in an enclosed space, so it's a more intense way to garden.

There are plenty of kits and full greenhouses from a wide range of suppliers. Gardening supply companies, lumber yards, hardware stores, and most large chain stores have stocks at their disposal. If you're so inclined to create your greenhouse, there's a lot to say. An idea to simplify the task of this do-it-yourself project is to purchase only the frame of a garden shed package, which saves all the angles involved in building your rafters and framing a doorway, speeding up the process. From there, you can use your materials such as collected windows and design your ventilation options according to your preferences.

The greenhouse ecosystem is developed with normal planting, soil, water, sunlight, and fresh air components. The soil must be rich in fiber so that seeds or seedlings can easily set roots. Well-rotted manure is a good starting point if it's available. Everything must be watered daily, whether it rains or not.

In the greenhouse, fresh air or air circulation is very important for your gardening and can be supplied in two ways. The air circulation may be adequate if you can locate the greenhouse to take advantage of natural winds and have adequate ventilation openings. By using one or more fans in the greenhouse, ventilation can increase. If the temperature and humidity are allowed to spike throughout the hot summer days, your gardening experience will not be very successful. We need to be tracked so that you know what's going on. Temperature and humidity can be tracked with a relatively inexpensive monitoring system that enables a greenhouse sensor to be transmitted to your household receiver. This device also helps you to know when the frost protection is required for your season gardening efforts. A small fan heater, or the fan you've already used with some type of heat source, will do the job.

Gardening has three aspects. The first is inside your home, where your garden is. The second is to use outdoor space for planting your garden. The third is under glass to do your gardening, which is called greenhouse gardening.

Greenhouse planting is very close to gardening outside. You must be able to control the temperature of the greenhouse. Keep in mind that plants do much better at temperatures that are slightly below house temperatures and need much more humidity. For your greenhouse plants, this will be the perfect environment.

You need to build your greenhouse in a location that maximizes the amount of sun it can get through the year. This is very important when the sun is at its lowest point for the spring and fall. Locate your greenhouse in a south-east to a south-west direction where the sun will be.

It will give better ventilation flow by spacing your plants around the greenhouse area on a regular basis. In the morning, open the greenhouse doors and then shut them in the late afternoon is a good idea for ventilation. In the winter you can even do this as long as you watch the weather not getting too cold.

Greenhouses contribute to any garden greatly. We encourage you to grow varieties of plants that are not appropriate for outdoor areas and expand the growing season to other crops. But it may seem daunting to know where to start for those first to consider setting up a greenhouse in their garden.

Heat: On sunny days, as the sun's rays are refracted through the window, the greenhouse will heat up beautifully. But for colder weather, you will also need other forms of heating. Electric heaters are the simplest to install, but you can also use gas (although this approach would allow you to wind the greenhouse for fumes. You will also need a way to prevent the temperature from becoming too high in the greenhouse. Do not add air conditioners for ventilation, as they will dry the air. Passive winds or exhaust fans will do the job or consider building the greenhouse instead. As such, you need soil that drains enough to prevent waterlogging, but also maintains moisture well so that the water can be absorbed by the plant roots. Ideally, the soil should be slightly acidic and contain a lot of organic material, which is essential. Only way to do this is to add compost.

Compost: Because the soil will not get organic matter-the rich topsoil full of nutrients and bacterial activity-from natural sources as the outside soil will, for example, from leaf litter, animal droppings, rotting plant material, you need to apply a good proportion of compost to your growing beds. Many guidelines suggest that you make everything from compost as much as a third of your beds. This will provide the plants with the best nutrient growing medium to survive in. If possible, choose an organic fertilizer or, even better, create your compost pile with scraps from the garden's kitchen and plant cuttings.

- **Types of Greenhouse**

The structure should face the right direction to obtain adequate sunlight exposure. It should mostly face the southern side and the roof should have the best covering material. a lean-to greenhouse is ideal for growing herbs and vegetables.

This structure was common during the Victorian period, and it is one of the traditional structures available. Building against the wall offers additional support to the structure, making it strong and wind resistant. The wall also absorbs heat during the day and releases that heat at night, which helps to maintain the temperature of the greenhouse during the cool nights.

If you're planning to use lean-to structure, you need to put the height of the structure into consideration together with any metal base. This ensures the ridges do not come in contact with any windows or drainage pipes in the principal building.

Advantages
- Cost-effective: This type of structure is less expensive compared to other greenhouse structures.
- Minimize building materials: The design is built against an existing wall, thus saving you on building material for four walls. It also minimizes roofing material requirements, since the design makes the best use of sunlight.
- The structure is constructed close to water, electricity, and heat.

Disadvantages
- Limited sunlight: Building lean-to structure against a house or garage limits the amount of sunlight to only the three walls. It will also

have limited light, ventilation, and minimum temperature control.

- Limited to the building orientation: The best structure should be on the southern exposure. The height of the building or the supporting wall affects the design and the size of the greenhouse.

- Temperature control: It is difficult to control the temperature of the structure because the wall absorbs a lot of heat during the day and distributes it for use in the cool nights. Some translucent covers lose heat more rapidly, making it difficult to control the heat.

- Foundation: You need to build a strong foundation for this greenhouse to last long, especially when using glass with the lean-to greenhouse.

Even Span Greenhouse Structure

Even span is another attached type of greenhouse, and it attaches more to promote plant growth. This standard structure is attached to a building, and its roof is made of two slopes of equal length and width. The structure can allow you to plant two to three rows, with two side benches and a wide bench at the center.

Even span design is more flexible and has curved eaves to boost their shape. Due to its great shape, there is plenty of air circulation in the greenhouse, thus making it easier to control temperatures. You also need to have an extra heating system especially when the structure is far away from a heated building. The heating system is especially important during the winter season.

even span greenhouse structure

photo credit: researchgate.net

Advantages
- It provides enough space for the growth of plants and vegetables.
- It is easier and more economic in construction, making it the most popular design for a greenhouse.
- You have easy access to water and electricity within the building.

Disadvantages
- High cost of construction and heating system compared to the lean-to structure.
- Reduced sunlight exposure due to the shadow from the house it is attached to.

Uneven Span Greenhouse Structure

In this structure, the roof is made of uneven or unequal width. The greenhouse is constructed such that one rooftop slope is longer than the other, making the design suitable for a hilly terrain or when you want to take advantage of solar energy.

Uneven slopes are laid so the steeper angles of the greenhouse face to the south. The transparent section should face south, whereas the opaque side of the greenhouse should face north to conserve energy.

Uneven greenhouses are no longer used because most farmers prefer setting up a greenhouse on a flat land.

Uneven-span greenhouse structure
Photo credit pinterest

Advantages
- As mentioned, this greenhouse is in a hilly areas.
- There is no obstruction of sunlight because the longer slope allows for more sunlight to enter the structure. The longer side also faces south, thus maximizing heat from the sun's rays.

Disadvantages
- It can be costly compared to even span greenhouses.
- They require more support on the slanted roof.

- Uneven span greenhouses usually need a lot of maintenance on the roof after some time.

- Too much solar can penetrate to the greenhouse if the uneven-span greenhouse is located in areas close to the equator.

A-Frame Greenhouse Structure

The A-frame greenhouse style is one of the most common designs. The structure is simple to set and it is ideal for a small backyard garden. To form the A-frame, you would attach the roof and sidewalls of greenhouse together, which forms a triangular-like shape.

Most of A-framed greenhouses use translucent, polycarbonate material, which helps to eliminate the cost from having to buy glass material. Most A-framed greenhouses are laid down in an open field or at the backyard facing the southern side.

Advantages
- It maximizes on the use of space along the side walls.

- Simple and straightforward to construct.
- Conservative structure style, using minimal material.

Disadvantages
- It has poor air circulation at the corners of the triangle.
- Its narrow side walls limit the overall use of the greenhouse.

Quonset Greenhouse Structure/ Hoop-House Structure

The quonset design has a curved roof or arched rafters, and its design is similar to military-hut style. The circular band in the structure's style is made of aluminum or PVC pipes, while the rooftop is made of plastic sheeting. The sidewalls of the design are set low, however, so there is not a whole lot of headroom. The hoops on the rooftop ensure there is no accumulation of snow and water on the top.

You would build this type of greenhouse in an open field or backyard with the structure facing the southern side.

Advantages
- Easy to build and one of the cheapest designs due to the use of plastic sheeting.

- Its design allows rain water and melted snow to run off.

- Suitable for a small plant growing space.

Disadvantages
- Limited storage space.

- Its frame design is not as sturdy as A-frame design.

- As stated, there is less headroom in the structure.

Gothic Arch Greenhouse Structure

Gothic arch has a nice aesthetic, and is one of the most visually pleasing designs available. The walls of the structure are bent over a frame, forming a pointed roof-like structure. The design requires less material to construct, as there is no need for trusses. Most of Gothic arch designs are made of plastic sheeting, and its design allows you to construct a large greenhouse where you can plant various products in rows.

Advantages

- The design has minimum heat exposure, thus making it easy to conserve heat.

- Plastic sheeting reduces the cost of construction.

- It has a simple and efficient design that allows rainwater and snow to flow away.

-

Disadvantages
- Not enough headroom and the design has a low sidewall height, which limits the storage of the greenhouse design.

Ridge and Furrow Greenhouse Structure

This type of design uses two or more A-framed design structures connected to one another along the roof eave length. The eaves offer more protection and act as a furrow to allow melted snow or rain water to flow away.

There are no side walls on the structure, which creates more ventilation in the greenhouse. It also reduces automation cost and fuel consumption, since only small wall area is exposed where the heat can escape.

Ridge and furrow greenhouse structure is ideal for growing vegetables, and they're mostly used in Europe, Canada, the Netherlands, and Scandinavian countries.

Advantages
- Ideal for large scale farming, and it's easy to expand this type of greenhouse.

- Provides more ventilation into the greenhouse.

- Requires few materials for construction because of its lack of side walls.

- Requires little energy to cool and heat.

Disadvantages

- Lack of proper water drainage system will damage your plants.

- Although the design has no side walls, shadows from the gutters can prevent sunlight from entering the greenhouse.

Sawtooth Greenhouse Structure

This type of greenhouse structure is similar to the ridge and furrow; however, sawtooth offers more natural ventilation. This is due to its natural ventilation flow path developed as a result of the sawtooth design. The roof provides 25% of the total ventilation to the greenhouse, and opening the sawtooth vents will ensure there is continuous airflow into the greenhouse. This makes it easy to control the temperatures and ensure the plants are in good climatic conditions for their growth.

Advantages

- Sawtooth arches provide excellent light transmission into the greenhouse.

- High rooftop allows for natural heat ventilation and airflow in the greenhouse.

- Excellent structure for both warm and cold climatic conditions.

- Simple and strong greenhouse structure.

- Has a large farming area.

Cold Frame Greenhouse Structure

Cold frame is ideal for greenhouse gardening in your backyard, and allows you to plant plants and vegetables at any time. It is one of the cheapest and simplest greenhouses you can set up. In cold frame gardening, you place a glass or plastic sheeting as the cover of the greenhouse structure, which will help in protecting your crops from frost, snow, rain, wind, or low temperatures.

Cold-frame greenhouse is suitable for planting cold-loving plants like broccoli, cauliflower, and cabbage among others.

Based on your budget, you can go for glass, polycarbonate, or plastic sheeting material to construct the greenhouse. The design requires a few openings to allow ventilation of heat into the greenhouse.

Advantages

- Simple design and easy to manage.

- Made from old windows or old wood pallets, which minimizes the cost of construction.

Disadvantages

- Overheating problem—a single day with a lot of sun and closed windows can do a lot of damage to the plants.

- Recycling of the old materials can affect the material quality of the greenhouse.

Hotbed Greenhouse

The hotbed structure acts as a miniature type of greenhouse that traps heat from solar radiation. This greenhouse can provide a favorable environment for plants that need a lot of heat like tomatoes, eggplants, and peppers.

If you want to extend the growing season, you can use hotbeds to provide the right weather conditions for your crops. Whether during winter, summer, or spring, there is always a family of vegetables, fruits, or herbs you can grow.

The hotbed structure provides a heat source to the crops through manure rather than using heat source from electricity, helping to speed up the growth of your plants.

When using a hotbed, you can set up the garden as wide as you want, provided the ratio of manure used and the growing medium is 3:1. The amount of time and money you invest in the garden will determine your farm produce success.

Advantages
- Simple to design.
- Inexpensive.

Disadvantages

- Hotbeds only lasts two months, so you will need to remove and replace the material with new ones around that time.

Window Farm

A window farm is an indoor farming garden for most vegetables. In a window farm, plants rely on the natural light from the window and temperature control from your living area to grow. This method is ideal for those who don't have a backyard or enough space to construct a standalone greenhouse.

You should set the structure in a window where it can receive a lot of light, facing toward the south.

Advantages

- Amazing for growing vegetables.

- Simple design and easy to construct.

Disadvantages

- Requires more components like nutrients, tubes, and pumps to grow your vegetables.

- It is difficult to maintain compared to a normal, soil-based greenhouse.

- **Constructing a Greenhouse**

Choosing Your Site

Determining where your greenhouse is located will be key to the success of your plants and the effectiveness of the structure. The more exposure to natural sunlight, the better off you'll be. You can pick an effective location by watching the shadows cast by tall structures like buildings, telephone poles, or trees. Track the sun's movement along the southern horizon by seeing how far the shadows around you extend on your site.

Position your greenhouse as far from the reach of shadows as possible – on the south side if it is feasible. This will allow light to enter the greenhouse even when the sun is lower in the sky during winter months. In the southern hemisphere, you would do the opposite. Pick an area that is flat and level, or that can be made flat and level by clearing foliage or moving dirt.

Local Codes and Ordinances

Some regions require special permitting or permissions to allow structures to be built on your property. It may depend on size, purpose, or any number of other factors. Before setting out on your greenhouse project, make sure to check with state, county, city, and local groups to make sure you can build the structure you have in mind.

Local codes may limit the design you use – both in the footprint and in scale. You may be limited to a specific size, or you might be required to meet certain engineering standards or construction codes. And in some cases, your greenhouse site may not be zoned for agriculture or commercial production. Most small-scale hobby greenhouses are small enough to dodge this type of regulation. But if your purpose requires more than the codes will allow in your area, you may need to find another site for your greenhouse.

Plumbing and Electrical

Utilities will take some of the work out of maintaining a greenhouse and the plants within. If you can incorporate electricity and plumbing, you can make sure plants are well lit and watered.

Plumbing may take the form of a water supply provided from a main water line, or it may be as simple as a garden hose, hand well or watering bucket. With any plumbing fed to your greenhouse, you'll want to consider frost protection and the potential for frozen pipes, fittings, and fixtures. If greenhouse vents are not functioning properly or left open during freezing temperatures, you could risk losing internal components to extreme cold.

Internal temperatures can be maintained with lighting, vans, or actuated vents. In order to keep these things running, you'll need to consider power. Providing electricity on a large scale will require adequate service panels installed by a licensed electrician. For backyard hobby greenhouses, you may be able to meet the needs of a small greenhouse with an extension cord and GFCI surge protectors.

Planning for both plumbing and electrical needs will allow you to provide the life-sustaining elements for plants when nature doesn't. However, you'll need to account for your water and electrical needs well in advance to make sure you install appropriately-sized systems.

Water Sources

Before determining the size of your greenhouse, make sure to consider your access to water. The source may be a municipal tower, a well, an aquifer, runoff, or natural bodies of water like rivers or lakes. Since water is a critical component to plant growth, you'll want to consider the source and test the water for quality and contamination. Water that looks clean may have significant deposits of toxic chemicals or heavy metals. Chemical additives in municipal water sources may also be harmful to plants. If your water sources are inadequate, you may need to look into alternatives.

Sourcing water can be simple or complex and may be limited in some cases. Depending on your region, you may be able to collect rain water – where in other areas it may be illegal. You may have unlimited water rights, or limited access due to drought restrictions. Natural water sources like creeks or streams may not be plentiful year-round and cold weather may hamper your ability to deliver water due to frozen pipes or pumps.

Make sure the location and scale of your greenhouse are within your ability to provide water. If you build a greenhouse that is too big for the amount of water you can supply, your plants will suffer. Be sure to check local restrictions on water use, water storage, and water sources before breaking ground on your greenhouse project.

Off-Grid Options

Since greenhouses afford a natural environment for plants in all types of weather, it may make sense to establish a greenhouse off the beaten path. In order to provide additional power and water needs for an off-grid greenhouse, you can look into power generation alternatives like wind or solar. You can also provide water by means of rainwater collection, cisterns, and gravity-fed systems.

Solar and wind power have potential to provide for your power needs but will likely limit the options for heat and lighting. In addition, you'll need to account for power storage and less sunlight in winter months. Still, you may be able to generate enough power for small-scale LED lighting systems if you have enough solar power, batteries, and sunlight to charge your system. To do this, you'll need to size an appropriate system based on average winter sunlight to make sure you can provide for your needs when the sun is at the lowest point of the year. Areas with high winds may be able to supplement solar power and add some wattage to the cause.

Hand watering can be adequate for your greenhouse and would eliminate the need for plumbing. This may take a bit of time and extra care on your part, but it does help to reduce the water consumption and waste caused by spray systems. It may be possible to reduce hand watering efforts by building a system designed around gravity-fed components. Things like water towers, cisterns, and even elevated rain barrels may be adequate forms of pressurized water delivery that won't require grid-tied plumbing. If you can provide pressurized water to your greenhouse, you can introduce drip-feed systems, or a simple water source for hand watering

Choosing the Correct Foundation

Your foundation is a critical component of the greenhouse. It must be able to serve a few specific functions, including a solid structural base, a stable and washable surface, and a material that can help to retain heat.

While greenhouses can incorporate dirt as the foundation, such as simple greenhouse tunnels or cold frames, most hold strong with the help of concrete or solid brick. Concrete and brick foundations allow heat to be absorbed and released slowly long after the sun goes down. It also provides a surface that can support tables, heavy potted plants, structural components, and can serve to protect other systems like electrical and plumbing.

Since water is a major component of successful plant growth, you can expect a few spills here and there. Dirt or other loose-fill substrates may contribute to muddy, sloppy surfaces that can become unstable or promote unwanted plant life in your greenhouse. Concrete and brick help to prevent these issues and provide an easy-to-clean surface. If you have a small space or pop-up greenhouse, you can position it on a concrete patio. If no concrete is available, you may be able to substitute with a similar product, like concrete masonry blocks (CMU), asphaltic roofing, or a similar impermeable barrier. Regardless of what you choose, keep in mind that you will want a water-resistant surface that is stable and helps to prevent unwanted plant growth at the ground level.

Preparing the Site for A Greenhouse

To prepare your site, you'll need a fairly level tract of land or pad to begin with. This will help to limit the amount of work when developing the greenhouse. The slope and grade will play a key role in water runoff, along with orientation and access.

All plants and vegetation will need to be cleared in advance of the initial work. If you are putting the greenhouse in a vacant lot, you'll need to make sure to provide access for vehicles or equipment and pay close attention to access limitations. You'll also want to consider damage that could be caused to existing landscaping as a result of tires, heavy equipment, and general traffic. Fences or obstructions may need to be removed.

When the site is cleared and ready for initial dirt work, you can begin with pulling sod and grading the earth to a level starting point. This will require that you call to mark out potential utilities that might be buried below ground. If you intend to frame up an above-ground pad that doesn't require digging, you may still want to confirm if utilities exist beneath the structure for future reference.

Once these initial elements are cleared out, you can start to stake out the ground and run a string level at all corners or the perimeter. This will help to determine the initial level surface so you can cut out or fill as needed. To find the level point, string a line between one stake and another and use a line level to adjust the height. Continue this process around the perimeter and make adjustments as you go. You may need to raise or lower your line to complete the task properly. Once your line is level, consider which direction you'll want water to flow off the surface of the floor, and off of the roof. Improper water drainage can erode surfaces and cause damage to the foundation. Pooling water inside the greenhouse can create slip hazards. Make sure your water has a path out of the structure, and away from the structure.

Top-Notch Materials for the Best Foundation

Once your base is level, you can choose what kind of materials to incorporate into the foundation. The best way to secure a solid, stable foundation is to start with a layer of aggregate (rock) of a type that tends to lock together when under pressure. River rock is rounded and moves easily compared to fractured rock that locks itself into place.

Once you have a solid base of aggregate, add a fine layer of sand and screet it into place. The sand will help to bind larger aggregate into place like mortar on a brick wall. It will also help to prevent weed growth.

At the surface of the rock and sand layer, you may want to include a vapor barrier. This will help to prevent moisture from wicking up from the soil below, and it can help to prevent destructive plant growth in your foundation. Keep in mind that a greenhouse will provide an ideal location for plants to thrive and if they find a way to grow, the roots may cause damage to your foundation.

Taking Steps to a Solid Foundation

The following step for your foundation will depend on what materials you choose. If your plan is to incorporate brick, you may be able to add another layer of finer sand and start mapping out your brick pattern right away. If you choose a concrete foundation, you'll want to set up rebar in the appropriate grid pattern required for the size of your pad. Concrete forms will be required around the perimeter to hold the concrete and rock substrate. This may require permitting and inspections before you can proceed to laying concrete.

Depending on the scale of your greenhouse, you might prefer to mix and spread your own concrete. However, it may be far more than you can accomplish on your on in a reasonable timeframe and skill level. You may want to consider contracting the concrete work out, or calling in a concrete delivery truck to reduce the amount of hand-mixing and spreading. Be sure to consider this in your budget and call to determine the costs of delivery and scheduling.

Your concrete forms and the grade of sand and rock will help to keep your concrete costs low. They'll also help to prevent cracks over time, and allow for proper curing. The concrete pour will need to be properly finished and sloped for water drainage. In addition, you'll want to make sure to allow the concrete to cure. This means it will need to harden as it dries, adding strength and integrity. Cold, wet environments can hinder proper curing, so schedule work during stable, dry periods.

Brick floors have no dry time, but will require special care with regard to cavities between bricks. Fine sand will help to prevent movement between bricks. Once you have your brick pattern laid out, you can sweep fine sand or powder between the cracks. This will help lock the bricks into place. A solid perimeter around all sides will also help keep brick contained.

- **Greenhouse Environment**

Considering Space and Climate

Your living situation may dictate the amount of space you can reserve for your greenhouse. If you don't have a large footprint to work with, you may be able to extend your greenhouse upward and make use of vertical gardening.

If you have all the space in the world but severe weather, you may be limited to the kinds of structures and systems you can use. The amount of space you have and the climate in your region play critical roles in what type of greenhouse you should build.

If you disregard your space limitations or your climate routines, you could waste significant amounts of time and money on a structure that doesn't perform as designed. For example, an American Even Span Greenhouse would likely fail from snow load or high winds in some regions of the world. And an A-Frame Greenhouse could potentially waste significant amounts of space and limit production. Be sure to select an appropriate structure for the space and climate in your region.

Ventilation Options

Ventilation is an important aspect of plant growth that is often neglected when it comes to greenhouses. Plants need some air movement to prevent stagnation, aid in reproduction, and provide cooling when needed.

Ventilation can be as simple as opening a zipper in a poly sheeted wall, or it can be a complex series of temperature-actuated closures that allow heat to escape and cool air to provide circulation within the greenhouse. Most commercially available greenhouses have ventilation in mind and include methods for allowing air to flow in or through them as needed.

If you build your own greenhouse, you'll want to consider installing fans, openings, vents, and manual or automatic controls to help keep the air circulating. Whether it's a box fan or a highly-sophisticated system, you'll want to provide the right level of ventilation for your building.

Testing for Level and Light

Most yards and landscapes that appear flat are rarely level. In order for a solid foundation, you'll need to test for level and make sure you can achieve this by either moving dirt or importing a leveling media like sand, fill dirt, or rock. To test for level, drive a series of stakes at the corners of your intended greenhouse. Then, use a laser level or a string line with a line level to find a level line around the staked perimeter. Measure down from the line to the ground and you'll be able to tell how much you'll need to do to get a level surface for your greenhouse foundation.

Before bringing in your fill material, make sure to test for light where your greenhouse stakes are. This will require that you watch the daily, weekly, monthly, and yearly shadow patterns and how they intersect with your greenhouse plot. Orient the broad side of your greenhouse toward the sun to get the most out of your greenhouse. Shadows from tall objects nearby will naturally encroach on the greenhouse. You can use marking paint to outline the reach of the shadows on a regular basis. Another method for testing light is to stake solar lights in the intended greenhouse footprint and watch to make sure they stay active year-round, or if any of them start to fall off during winter months.

Humidity Inside the Greenhouse

High levels of humidity will encourage growth of mold spores and other diseases, which will affect your plants. You need to know the humidity needs of your plants and control the humidity level in the greenhouse to favor your plants' growth. Plants that need the same humidity levels should be growth on the same part.

Place Growing Bags and Pots in a Garden Stand

Putting growing bags, pots, and other basic greenhouse tools on the floor can encourage the growth of pests beneath the pots and growing bags. Garden stands allow you to arrange your pots on a double or triple step stand, thus creating more space in your greenhouse. Using stands can help you maintain good hygiene within the greenhouse.

You should always adhere to proper hygiene in the greenhouse to discourage weeds and pest infections from growing and becoming issues.

Excess Watering

Avoid overwatering plants in the greenhouse, as the humidity inside is controlled and there will be less water evaporation from the greenhouse soil. The excess water on the plants will encourage fungal infections and other diseases in the greenhouse.

Follow proper watering schedules and create a set watering schedule for yourself, in which you water at the same time every day.

Poor Pollination or No Pollinators Inside the Greenhouse

You have to plant floral plants near your greenhouse to attract pollinators to the surrounding area and eventually to your garden. Pollinators are attracted to the color yellow, so planting plants like marigold will attract them.

In some cases, there may be few to no insect pollinators in the greenhouse, thus affecting the pollination process. In this situation, hand pollination is essential for pollinating vegetable plants.

Failure to Expose the Garden Soil to Direct Sunlight

You need to expose the soil and the potting mixture to direct sunlight; otherwise, it will attract pests and maggots into the greenhouse. Exposing the soil inside to direct sunlight will kill most of these pests and fungal diseases. Don't make the mistake of leaving your soil out of the sun, especially if you are in an urban area. Make sure there is direct sunlight to kill the pests in the soil.

- **Essentials for Your Greenhouse**

Greenhouse Equipment

Greenhouse equipment is built in the most accurate manner; this segment contains numerous brands that supply world-class goods. Such goods are checked several times before they are released on the market to give you a hint. What distinguishes them is the quality at hand; if you choose a premium brand, this can certainly give you the required performance. Now, coming to the selection portion, this is the first step towards the main building. You are advised to choose well and to suit your needs. One wrong move, and in the building process, everything can go wrong. You also need to work on small details that can deliver the best output for you. There may be information about the greenhouse's design and other safety features.

Greenhouse equipment is made up of watering, lighting, exhausts, windows, and other equipment for construction. Buying all of this in the right way will help to save time and costs. Digital shopping can be considered a good choice for your needs. There are times where buying online will certainly give you all the long-term benefits. Each brand that the equipment of the supplier has its website, you can search on their website for greenhouse equipment and then finalize your vision. Price comparison can be made online, online purchases, and quotations from the internet can be used for price comparison. In selecting the right products, this will give you an added advantage.

Just know the brand you want to buy through; it should have consumer credibility. One should not go ahead without testing the brand as you may not know the type of service provided. Check on the website for customer reviews, and this should give you an indication of the type of customer service offered.

Greenhouse equipment should be produced in compliance with international standards; if the product complies with local standards, then the reliability and overall stability factor are expected to decrease. It would also help to make the order easy and affordable by looking for free delivery options. You don't need to waste time arranging for the purchased products to be transported. When it comes to such goods, choose wisely.

Therefore, buying greenhouse equipment is proving beneficial in the long run. With such equipment and tools, your dream greenhouse can be installed in no time. Make sure you have full permission from your greenhouse building architect. Beautify your landscape with state-of-the-artist greenhouses.

Building Greenhouses Accessories worth Having

Greenhouses are typically a practical operation, but that doesn't mean that they just need to be functional. A lot of optional components can be added to a greenhouse to make it more comfortable and more functional. Read on and learn about the extras that can greatly improve your greenhouse. These are truly worth making greenhouse accessories.

An adjustable irrigation system is the first among the "key" greenhouse accessories. You can do this through overhead sprinklers or water feeds at the soil level. The main reason for this is to boost water distribution to all the plants, and the problem often requires a lot of effort. If you are able to swing an automated computer system, that's even better! So you can make the watering routine and just let it do its job.

Sturdy racks are highly recommended for those who want to grow plants in their greenhouse pots. Racks multiply the area on which you can grow plants, so you can add more plant biomass to your controlled system. It also makes things on your knees and back much easier, raising the need to pause or squat down to accomplish tasks. Make sure your racks are using rustproof and rot-proof materials, or you might face catastrophic failure.

It's nice to have a water pressurizer and a long nozzle-equipped pipeline. Not for plants to drink, although that can be done. Be patient, however, when doing so, as the pressure can crush or rip the plants apart. Cleaning is the key reason for having a mobile system with a pressurized water supply. It will make it much easier to clean your greenhouse, particularly for roof panels to be cleaned. Through climbing onto the roof, you will not have to take risks this way-just lean a ladder on the greenhouse side, ascend, and blast away.

It's a good idea to install a ventilation system in your greenhouse. Plants can wilt under excess heat, so you're going to need a way out into the greenhouse to cycle cool air. This is an emergency measure and can delete any discoveries you have made, but it can save the plants, which is better than starting from scratch. A chest or cabinet that is waterproof is a perfect place to store your equipment in the greenhouse. This will protect them against rust damage and moisture while reducing the need to move in and out of the greenhouse–behavior that will risk the greenhouse's temperature and health.

Have a few large sheets of plastic on hand to patch broken panes. Such temporary measures will keep the conditions of your greenhouse in check until you have a replacement stand. As you can see, a lot of things can be used to boost a greenhouse's functionality. There are things that we sometimes take for granted, which eventually give us a lot of support. You need to plan when constructing greenhouses to accommodate additional features, such as those shown above.

Building and running a greenhouse can be more than just a fun recreational activity you do in your spare time–it can help you financially (if you sell plants or produce) and safely (by eating healthy foods). Installing such main accessories will ensure that your greenhouse will provide you with maximum return and performance.

Vegetation thrives when the growth area, climate, and disease and pest protection factors are maintained at optimum rates. Accessories make it easier and quicker to know and manage these optimal conditions. These come at a high cost, but it may well be worth the returns.

Here are some useful greenhouse accessories to have:

Heaters: heaters are the first greenhouse equipment you need to install in your greenhouse. This is because plants need to thrive at a specific temperature. This is particularly important if your greenhouse for plastic or glass is located in a cold area that gets colder during winter. The heaters come in many types as per your specifications, such as gas heaters, paraffin heaters or electric heaters. It is important to avoid blowing air directly on plants, and however, as it can be harmful, it is always beneficial for the heat (or cool air) at the level of the soil.

Climate controls: Climate controls are also critical greenhouse devices, just like heaters. Depending on the season, a good climate control system can heat up or cool the greenhouse. It is recommended that you position your plants on benches so that even air circulation is provided. Heating and cooling thermostats, variable speed controls humidistat, cycle timers, and advanced controls are the various types of controls available on the market.

Ventilation equipment: As the name suggests, this device helps manage the air in your garden so you can grow plants that usually don't thrive in your area. Choose from any of the following greenhouse ventilation devices, such as evaporative coolers, exhaust fans & shutters, automatic vent openers, and circulation fans, for proper air circulation in your greenhouse environment.

Misting Systems: Effective misting systems are useful in any greenhouse construction process to maintain optimal humidity and temperature, ensuring plants grow at the desired rate. There is a wide range of options such as sprinkler system, misting systems, mist timers & valves as well as water filters that are commonly used in institutional greenhouse-style installations.

Watering supplies: as is obvious, water supplies are the most important part to take care of even during the design of the greenhouse. From a wide range of water supplies such as plant watering systems, drip systems, qualified water hoses, water timers, and overhead watering systems, you can choose according to your specific requirements.

Irrigation system: Without water, plants cannot grow. An irrigation system will make it easier to distribute water to the greenhouse plants quickly and evenly. Combining customizable nozzles, overhead sprinklers, and field drip feeders would be the perfect irrigation method.

Downpipe kits: You can save considerable watering costs by collecting the runoff of rainwater. Downpipe kits harness rainwater that will channel it to reservoirs that will then feed into the irrigation and/or cooling system of the greenhouse. The only catch is to ensure that the water is purified from soil or debris before being pumped into the irrigation or cooling system, as this may cause a blockage.

Greenhouse shelving: If you put in your backyard a greenhouse, space is likely to be a major constraint. Greenhouse shelves ensure that the vertical area is used as much as possible. Shelving comes in various heights, a number of shelves, and material for construction.

Growing racks: Growing racks ensure a mini greenhouse is used effectively and easily. The racks shield plants from extreme weather impacts, while the zippers allow access to the seedlings.

Shade cloth: Shades shield the plants from the harmful ultraviolet rays of the sun and also help regulate the greenhouse temperature. The shades can be manual or controlled by the sensor. For areas where sunlight and outside temperatures typically change rapidly, manual shades can be complicated.

Vent openers: Reduce heating and air conditioning cost by installing winds at suitable locations. You can choose between natural and automatic ventilation, which is costly but more efficient and can be built into central heating or air conditioning system.

- **Air flow, Cooling and Humidity**

Air flow is very important for healthy plant growth in a greenhouse, particularly in the heat of summer as temperatures (hopefully) soar. The air needs to keep moving which will prevent heat building up and damaging your plants.

Most greenhouses will come with vents and/or windows to help with the movement of air. A good quality greenhouse will have louver vents at ground level which draw in cold air (which is heavier than hot air) and then vents at the top which allows hot air to rise out of the greenhouse. This creates a very natural movement of air which your plants appreciate.

You are looking for a greenhouse with windows and vents that account for around a third of the entire roof area. They do not all need to be at roof level and, ideally, you will want vents at different levels.

If your greenhouse isn't suitably ventilated, then you are going to encourage all sorts of diseases such as fungal problems, powdery mildew, and botrytis. Worse still a greenhouse that is too hot will end up killing some of your plants.

You can leave the door open in the summer, but this can be a security problem depending on where your greenhouse is located.

The other disadvantage of leaving a door open is that pets, particularly cats, will decide to investigate your greenhouse. Dogs, cats, and chickens will cause havoc in your greenhouse from eating plants and fruits to sitting on plants. If you do have pets and want to leave the door open, then a wire panel will keep out most animals except cats.

Window or door screens can be used to keep out unwanted visitors, but the downside of these is that they can also keep out vital pollinating insects!

Mice and other rodents can find their way into your greenhouse through open windows or doors so it can be worth installing an ultrasonic device to keep them out. Of course, cats are excellent rodent deterrents but cause their own unique brand of chaos!

Shade Cloth and Paint

This is one of the simplest ways for you to provide shade for your plants.

Shade paint is applied to the outside of your glass, and it diffuses the sun and keeps some of the heat out. Modern shade paints are very clever and will react to the sunlight. When it is raining then the shade paint remains clear, but as the sun comes out, the paint turns white, reflects the sunlight.

Shade fabric is another way to cool your greenhouse, and this is put on the outside of your greenhouse to prevent the sunlight getting to your plants. It is best installed on the outside of your greenhouse, but you can put it inside, though it will not be as effective. When it is outside, it stops the sun's rays penetrating your greenhouse but when on the inside the sunlight is already in the greenhouse and generating heat.

Shading alone though is not going to protect your plants from heat damage. Combine this with good ventilation and humidity control to provide your plants with the best possible growing environment.

Shade cloth is a lightweight polyethylene knitted fabric available in densities from 30% to 90% to keep out less or more of the sun's rays. It is not only suitable for greenhouses but is used in cold frames and other applications. It is mildew and rot resistant, water permeable and does not become brittle over time.

It provides great ventilation and diffuses the light, keeping your greenhouse cooler. It can help reduce the need to run fans in the summer and is quick to install and remove.

A reflective shade is good because instead of absorbing the sun's rays it reflects it. This is better if you can get hold of it because it will be more efficient at keeping the greenhouse cool. The reflective shade cloth is more expensive than normal shade cloth, but it is worth the money for the additional benefits.

For most applications, you will want a shade cloth that is 50% or 60% density, but in hotter climates or with light sensitive plants higher densities such as 70% to 80% will be necessary. A lot of people use higher density shade cloth on the roof and a lower density cloth on the walls.

Shade cloth is typically sold by the foot or meter, depending on where you are located, though you can find it sold in pre-made sizes. These are usually hemmed and include grommets for attaching the cloth to the greenhouse.

A shade cloth with a density of 70% allows 30% of light to pass through it. For most vegetables, in that majority of climates, a shade cloth of 30% to 50% will be sufficient. If you are shading people, then you will want to go up to a density of 80% or 90%.

Air Flow

Keeping the air moving in your greenhouse during summer can be difficult, particularly in larger greenhouses. Many of the larger electrical greenhouse heaters will double up as air blowers in the summer just by using the fan without the heating element being turned on.

However, using a fan is down to whether or not you have electricity in your greenhouse, which not all of us will have. Although you can use solar energy to run your fan, you will find that it is hard to generate enough energy to keep it going all day.

Automatic Vents

These are an absolute godsend for any gardener and will help keep your plants alive and stop you having to get up early to open vents!

Automatic vents will open the windows as the temperature rises. This is usually by a cylinder of wax which expands in the heat, opening the window and then contracts as the temperature cools which closes the window. These do have a finite lifetime, typically lasting a few years but are easily replaced.

One technique which can help keep your greenhouse cool is to damp down the paths and the floor. As the water evaporates, it will help keep the greenhouse cool.

Remember too that some plants can be moved outside in the heat of the summer which will free up space in your greenhouse and help airflow.

An alternative to the wax openers is a solar powered automatic opener. These work in a similar manner, opening the vents as the temperatures increase. These are a little bit more expensive than the mechanical auto-openers though work well.

Choosing an Exhaust Fan

For larger greenhouses, you will want an exhaust fan. This is overkill for a smaller greenhouse, but anyone choosing a larger structure will benefit from installing one.

Your exhaust fan needs to be able to change the air in your greenhouse in between 60 and 90 seconds. Fans are rated by cubic feet per minute (CFM), for which you will need to calculate the volume of your greenhouse which is done simply by multiplying the length by the width by the average height.

To measure the average height, measure straight down to the floor from halfway up a roof rafter. It doesn't have to be precise as a few inches either way isn't going to make a significant difference.

To determine the cubic feet per minute rating, you need you simply multiply the volume by 3/4. Then you will need to find a fan that is near to or greater than this value.

Be careful and double check your calculations as a fan that is too small will not provide you with enough cooling. Together with a fan, shading cloth or paint and damping down it will help ensure the greenhouse is kept cool and your plants thrive.

As an example, if your greenhouse is 8' by 10' with an average height of 7' this will give you a calculation of 8x10x7 which is 560 cubic feet.

So, therefore, you will need a fan that is rated at least 560 CFM for sufficient cooling.

You will also need to calculate the shutter size. Do this by dividing your fan Cubic Feet per Minute by 250 which gives a shutter size in ft^2.

The fan needs to be positioned as high as possible, typically at the end opposite to the door. The motor needs to be on the inside of the greenhouse, and the fan can be mounted either on the inside or outside as convenient for you.

The shutters are installed at the opposite end to the exhaust fan. For those without a motor, they are installed with the vanes opening into your greenhouse. Motorized shutters are installed with the motor on the inside of the greenhouse and the vanes opening outwards.

Ventilating your greenhouse is extremely important and something many growers overlook. Plants need air flow to stay healthy. Poor airflow is a major contributing factor to fungal infections which plants such as cucumber and tomatoes are particularly susceptible too.

Ensuring your plants are not too crowded will also help a lot with air flow and preventing fungal infections.

Although your greenhouse may be too small for a fan or you may not have any electricity, at the very least you need windows though louver vents will help a lot. Making sure there is adequate ventilation in your greenhouse is vital so don't skip this step when setting up your greenhouse!

- **Greenhouse Irrigation Systems**

In hot weather, they can dry out very quickly, and this can cause problems such as leaf, flower or fruit drop which you obviously want to avoid.

If your greenhouse is in your garden then it is easy enough to pop down and water it, but if it is at an allotment or you are on holiday then watering becomes much trickier, putting your harvest at risk.

In the hottest weather, and more so in hotter climates, you will need to water your plants two or three times a day to keep them healthy no matter how good your cooling system is!

Although you can hand water the plants in your greenhouse, this can soon get boring and difficult to keep up. The best and most efficient way to water your plants is to invest in a greenhouse irrigation system. Which you choose will depend on the size of your greenhouse, what you are growing and whether or not you have electricity and water to hand.

If you are planning to irrigate your greenhouse, then the need to be sited near to water and/or electricity can heavily influence your choice of location.

There are a lot of different irrigation systems on the market with widely varying prices, so you do need to spend some time considering your requirements before rushing out to buy one.

Some plants require more water than others, so depending on what you are growing you may want to get an automatic irrigation system that can deliver differing quantities of water to different plants.

You also want a system that can grow with you as you put more plants in your greenhouse. At certain times within the season you will have more plants in your greenhouse than at others, so your irrigation system needs to be able to support this extra demand.

You do need to be careful because any irrigation system that is introducing too much water to your greenhouse could end up making it too damp, which will encourage the growth of diseases. This is one reason why you need to have your drainage and ventilation right to prevent damage to your greenhouse ecosystem.

You typically have two choices about how to deliver water to your plants, either through spray heads or a drip system. The former will spray water over everything in your greenhouse. The downside of this is that it can encourage powdery mildew on certain plants, but the spray can help damp down your greenhouse. It can also be a bit hit and miss as to how much ends up in the soil of your plants. If you are growing in containers, then a spray system may not deliver water precisely enough.

Drip systems though will deliver water precisely to containers and give each container exactly the right amount of water, so no plant goes thirsty!

The downside of most irrigation systems is that they require electricity, which can be difficult, expensive or even impossible for some greenhouse owners to install. You can purchase solar powered irrigation systems which will do the job, but they can struggle on duller days.

The water will come into the greenhouse with piping and correctly locating this is important. Hanging it from the ceiling and running it along the walls helps keep it out of the way and stops it getting damaged. Running the piping along the floor is a recipe for disaster as you are bound to end up putting a container on it and damaging it!

You will need a water supply and ideally mains water, but you can run some irrigation systems from water butts. You will have to check regularly that the water butt has enough water in it, but it is still much easier than manually watering your plants!

Drip Tubing

This is special tubing that you run throughout your greenhouse. It has tubes attached to it that run to the roots of each container to supply water directly to the soil. The big advantage of most drip systems is that you can control the amount of water dripped into your plants. This means that plants that need more water can get it and plants that need less don't get over-watered.

This is set to drip at a certain rate or to operate on a timer so it waters at regular intervals. It will depend on the type of system you buy as to whether it is constant or timed. Timed is by far the best as it allows greater control of the delivery of water, reducing the risks of over-watering.

This is a very water efficient method of watering your greenhouse with minimal wastage. It can also be set up to be completely automatic, which reduces the time you spend managing your greenhouse.

With some of the more advanced drip watering systems, you have sensors in the ground that monitor moisture levels and turn on the water when the soil becomes too dry.

If you are growing directly in the soil, then the type of soil will influence your drip rate. A heavy clay soil will take longer to absorb water, so it needs less water than a lighter soil because in clay it will puddle and pool, which you want to avoid.

When you are growing a variety of plants, this is by far the best irrigation method because you can control the amount of water each container receives.

Planning your drip watering system is relatively easy. You need to divide your greenhouse into an equal number of sections, and each area will hold plants with similar water requirements. Depending on the size of your greenhouse you may need multiple irrigation systems, but most are easy to expand with additional piping.

Drip irrigation piping comes in either black polyethylene (PE) or polyvinyl chloride (PVC). These are cheap, easy to handle and bendy when you need it to be.

PVC pipe is often used in supply and header lines as you can solvent bond connections and fittings. Polyethylene connections though need to be clamped. PVC pipe is also more durable, being less sensitive to temperature fluctuations and sunlight but it is more expensive to buy.

Polyethylene pipe is sensitive to high temperatures and will contract and expand. This means it can move out of position unless it is held in place.

Your main feeder piping may be 1" or 2" wide but for lateral, emitter lines ½" piping is sufficient. Each row of plants will have its own ½" line containing emitters. In smaller greenhouses, you can get away with one emitter line for every two rows when plants are spaced less than 18-20" apart.

There are some different types of emitter available. The perforated hose or porous pipe types are very common and are an emitter line with holes in it. The water then seeps out of these holes. Most will deliver water at a rate of anywhere from ½ to 3 gallons an hour. The rate of delivery is changed by adjusting the water pressure.

Alternatively, you can get emitter valves which allows you to control the drip rate for each pot.

Emitters are usually spaced between 24" and 36" along the main lateral lines.

One thing to remember is that you need to filter the water, particularly if it is coming out of a water butt. This will prevent any dirt getting into the system and clogging the emitters. This is vital as it will ensure your irrigation system works without any problems.

Some irrigation systems will allow you to install a fertilizer injector. This is useful as you can get your irrigation system to automatically feed your plants too! Depending on the system this can be set to deliver liquid fertilizer constantly or at specified intervals. This, though, is typically found in more expensive systems, and you need to be very careful in your choice of liquid feed to prevent clogging up the system.

The key with drip irrigation systems is to apply a little water frequently to maintain the soil moisture levels. This is a very water efficient system that is easy to expand and works no matter what size plants you are growing.

Most people who own a greenhouse and install an irrigation system will choose a drip watering system. They are easily available and very affordable though, as with anything, you can spend more money and get more advanced systems.

- **Heating Your Greenhouse**

For most people growing will end as temperatures start to drop, even though a greenhouse can extend the growing season by a few weeks.

To grow throughout the year or to keep frost tender plants alive over winter you will need to heat your greenhouse. Depending on what you are growing you may get away with just keeping the frost off, or you may need to heat the greenhouse to warmer temperatures. A heating mat may help you to germinate seeds, but plant growth is severely slowed in the colder months.

A greenhouse does help to keep your plants warmer, and it will help to keep frost from your plants. However, if temperatures plummet too far then no matter how well built your greenhouse, it will not keep out the frost.

Before you decide upon a heating solution for your greenhouse, you need to decide what you are growing. Different crops have different temperature requirements, and if you are growing plants which are frost hardy or tolerate cooler temperatures, then you do not need to heat your greenhouse as much.

Warmer weather crops such as tomatoes, chilies, and peppers are going to be extremely difficult to grow in a greenhouse in colder areas over winter as the heater simply will not be able to keep up. To heat your greenhouse enough, you would have to spend a fortune on heating which would simply not make the investment cost-effective.

A simple, eco-friendly way to keep your greenhouse warm is to dig out a trench down the middle of your greenhouse, cover it with palettes and then make compost in it. In smaller greenhouses, this isn't going to be a huge area, but it will help to raise the temperature in your greenhouse without investing in heating equipment.

Another free heating technique is to paint some barrels, buckets or sandbags black and leave them in your greenhouse. These will absorb heat during the day and radiate it back out at night. It isn't going to make more than a degree or two difference, but it could be enough to keep the frost off of your plants.

The easiest way to heat your greenhouse is with an electric heater, though this does require you to have electricity in your greenhouse. Running an extension cord out isn't safe so if you are installing electricity then get it done professionally and safely. It has to be waterproof if it is outside and there are likely rules and regulations in your country affecting how and where the cable can be run.

You need to ensure that your electric heat is stable and that it is away from flammable material. You also need to be cautious when watering your plants to ensure you do not damage your heater.

When using an electric heater, it is important that the air circulates properly. This will prevent hot spots as well as cold spots and also reduce condensation. Some heaters have fans built in but others will need additional air circulation.

As the price of propane has been increasing many greenhouse owners are turning to wood or pellet stoves. These are working out to be very cost effective even on a larger scale. You will need to check local codes and follow their requirements as well as follow common sense safety precautions. Pellet stoves are very easy to use, often come with temperature controls, and some even have blowers which will circulate the heat.

If your greenhouse is plastic, then a wood stove is not a good idea. The stove pipe gets very hot and will melt plastic. Ideally, your stove should be vented out through a masonry foundation or something similar rather than through glass.

Another alternative is to cover your greenhouse with plastic and line the inside with bubble wrap. This is a good solution in areas where the temperature doesn't drop too far in winter. However, in areas where there are months of freezing weather, this will not keep the frost out of your greenhouse.

You can buy specific insulation for your greenhouse which will help reduce heat loss and your heating bill. This is often put in place as the temperature drops and removed when spring has arrived.

There are propane, natural gas, petrol and other heaters available and these are effective. They are getting more expensive to buy, but they do a good job in a greenhouse which cannot have electricity. Many people with smaller, garden greenhouses will use a propane heater. The advantage of these heaters is you do not need to have electricity in your greenhouse, meaning your greenhouse can be sited anywhere.

Heaters are rated in British Thermal Units or BTU's. The higher the BTU, then the more heat it gives out. You can calculate the number of BTU's you need for your greenhouse using formulas found online or heater suppliers will help you. You will need to take into account a number of factors including the size of your greenhouse, how hot you want the greenhouse, the heat loss of the greenhouse and more. Getting this right means you do not waste energy heating your greenhouse or buying a heater that won't do the job.

Natural gas heaters require a gas line to be run to your greenhouse whereas propane heaters run on gas cylinders, making them the most popular heaters with home greenhouse owners.

Where to Put Your Heater

Where you locate your heater will depend on some factors such as the location of vents and shutters, where the doors are and more.

You need to be careful that where you site your heater isn't under a water leak or anything similar.

Depending on the floor in your greenhouse it may be necessary to build a plinth to mount your heater on. This will ensure the heater is level and safe.

Consider all the factors and if you are still unsure then speak to any supplier of heaters, and they will be able to advise you.

Types of Greenhouse Heaters

There are many different types of greenhouse heater on the market, and we touched on these already. Let's go into more detail now on these different heaters together with their advantages and disadvantages.

Paraffin Greenhouse Heaters

Paraffin heaters are one of the most popular ways to heat a greenhouse, being both affordable and readily available. For a home gardener with a smaller greenhouse these are ideal, but as the price of paraffin has increased in recent years, this has made these less popular.

You can buy paraffin cheaper online or in bulk, but the heaters are cheap to buy new. There is also a healthy market for used paraffin heaters, so it does make this a very affordable solution.

Paraffin heaters come in some different sizes and in most models the paraffin reservoir is large enough to last a day, or even two so are low maintenance. Being self-contained they have no requirement for electricity, and they also give off CO_2 which your plants will appreciate.

Paraffin has become less popular in recent years because of the cost of the fuel which has become harder to obtain. However, in our Internet age, it is easier now to source this fuel, though with the concerns about climate change and emissions this type of fuel is likely to wane in popularity still further.

This type of heat is always on and is manually controlled. You can end up with the heater burning when heat isn't needed and wasting fuel. There are no temperature controls on a paraffin heater as it just burns. You can often adjust the size of the flame, but there is usually no way to turn off the heat when the greenhouse reaches a set temperature.

One disadvantage of paraffin heaters is that they give off water vapor which can encourage mold if the greenhouse isn't suitably ventilated.

Electric Greenhouse Heaters

These are a great form of heating, but it does require your greenhouse to have an electricity supply. Electric heaters are controlled by a thermostat so you have greater control over the heat output and therefore over your running costs.

Because of the dangers of mixing water with electricity you have to make sure you get a heater that is designed to work in a greenhouse and that the electricity supply is safe and protected from water and damp.

Electric heaters are not for everyone because of the cost of running electric cable to a greenhouse. If you are on an allotment site, then you are very unlikely to have access to electricity. Depending on local regulations you may need to hire a professional to lay the cable and use armored cable.

The advantage of an electric fan heater is that it does circulate air around the greenhouse which avoids hot and cold spots. This also helps to reduce the risk of fungal problems from poor air circulation.

Propane Gas Heaters

Run from propane bottles these are relatively cheap to run, and propane can be refilled at many camping stores or gas stations. For a greenhouse without electricity, these are a viable solution.

You will need to ensure your greenhouse is well ventilated because propane gas heaters produce water vapor. They also produce CO_2 which your plants will appreciate.

Many propane heaters come with thermostatic controls which gives you a degree of control over your running costs.

Mains Gas Heating

This is an excellent method of heating larger greenhouses. The installation costs are high, but the running costs are reasonable.

You will need a natural gas pipe run to your greenhouse. Again this is not for everyone, and in most cases, natural gas is not going to be a cost effective form of heating your greenhouse.

This is most popular with commercial growers in large greenhouses and isn't something most home growers will install.

Greenhouse Heating Tips

Obviously, you want to keep your heating costs down during winter while keeping your plants warm and alive. Here are some of my favorite tips to effectively and efficiently heat your greenhouse.

- Bubble Wrap Is Your Friend – clip bubble wrap to the inside of your greenhouse frame to help reduce heat loss and block draughts. You can buy horticultural bubble wrap which is both toughened and UV stabilized. Remember that larger bubbles will let more light get into your greenhouse to your plants. This bubble wrap can also be used on tender outdoors plants and pots to protect them from frost.

- Don't Be Afraid of the Thermostat – if your heater has a thermostat then use it! You can set your heater only to come on when temperatures go below a certain point. You may need to experiment with the temperature a little so that the heat kicks in and heats your greenhouse before the plants get too cold.

- Choose The Right Temperature – most plants are not going to appreciate a tropical jungle temperature so if you are just preventing frost all you need to do is keep your greenhouse at 2C/36F. Some tender plants including citrus trees prefer a higher minimum temperature of 7C/45F as will many young plants. Delicate plants will require higher temperatures, depending on the plant.

- Buy A Thermometer – a good thermometer that can record maximum and minimum temperatures is going to help you a lot with your greenhouse. By knowing how low the temperature drops at night you will be able to use your heater more efficiently and save yourself some money. It also helps you understand how hot your greenhouse gets during the day, so you know whether or not you need to cool it down.

- Think About Heater Position – where you locate the heaters will influence how well your greenhouse is heated. Electric heaters are positioned away from water, and so it circulates the air around the greenhouse. With all heaters you need to be careful they don't point directly at plants and dry out the leaves.

- Heat What You Need to – heating a greenhouse can be expensive so if you only have a few delicate plants then put them in one place, surround them with a bubble wrap or Perspex curtain and then heat just that area. There is no point you spending money heating a greenhouse that is mostly empty when all you need to do is heat a small area.

- Use Horticultural Fleece – on the coldest nights a couple of layers of this will give your plants that extra bit of protection by raising their temperature a few vital degrees. Remember though to remove the fleece during the day, so the plants are well ventilated and don't overheat.

- Ventilate – heating your greenhouse increases humidity, so it is vital that you have good ventilation. This will keep your greenhouse healthy and prevent the build-up of fungal diseases.

- Water Early On – you can help reduce the humidity in your greenhouse by watering your plants early on in the day. Give the plants the water they need and try not to overwater or water the floor in your greenhouse unless you are damping down.

- Use Your Vents Wisely – open your greenhouse vents early in the morning on sunny days to clear condensation. Close them before the sun goes down, so you trap the warmth of the day in the greenhouse. This will help your heaters to be more efficient.

- Use a Heated Propagator – if you are germinating seeds in your greenhouse you do not need to heat the entire greenhouse unless you are starting off a lot of seeds. A heated propagation mat will help keep your seeds and seedlings warm without the expense of heating the whole greenhouse.

Depending on what you are growing and how much you want to extend your growing season you may want to heat your greenhouse. For many people though the cost is excessive and it isn't practical to do so. A small paraffin or propane heater though can be enough to keep the frost out of your greenhouse, extending the growing season enough so your tomatoes, peppers, and chilies have time to ripen fully!

- **Growing in Your Greenhouse**

Fruits

When you decide to grow a fruit, the most important factor that you should consider is choosing the right type of fruit for your garden. This choice is all it takes to ensure that you can grow the fruit well. I can understand the feeling of growing a specific type of fruit (which would typically be your favorite). However, before you decide that, try and perform a little research ahead of time.

Here is something you should know about fruit (thought I have a feeling some of you may already know this). Fruits do not appear immediately in a plant's life cycle. The flowers begin to boom first (which is a beautiful sight). Then, the petals of the flower begin to strip away. During this process, you will notice the fruit slowly swelling.

You can successfully grow the following fruits in your garden:

Avocado, plum, cherry, apricot, apple, pear, banana, plum, kumquat, loquat, guava, pineapple, fig, nectarine, crabapple, pomegranate, persimmon, strawberry, blackberry, blueberry, raspberry, kiwi, any citrus fruits, gooseberry, and grapes.

See? You do have a lot of options.

If you want to know what fruits are ideal for your particular climate, then you can take inspiration from the local stores and farms. What fruits are not in demand? What are the farmers producing in abundance? Which fruit can you easily find in the local supermarket?

Size

You must also think about the size of the fruit that you are planning to grow. Think of how each fruit you grow fits into your greenhouse. If you are growing melons, then they might require more space then blueberries. Will you be able to provide this space? If you can, then how many melons can you grow at one time? Is that better than growing grapes, where you can get a higher yield? Plus, remember that gardening is also about aesthetics. You can make different arrangements of your fruits to create a beautiful display when the fruits appear. If you have the space to arrange different fruits, then you should think of how to make that arrangement. Here are a few tips that you can follow:

You can use kiwi fruits to act as boundaries. Do note that the kiwi is a clambering fruit, so you might either require a surface to support it or you might need to plant stakes into the ground or container for growing the plant. Either way, kiwis make beautiful boundaries.

You can plant berries around your property, or against a particular wall.

If you have an archway or a pergola, then you could use kiwi or grapevine for that. Just watch them cover it beautifully!

You can plant a fruit tree near the entrance to your garden or greenhouse.

Citrus trees or berry bushes can adorn the corners of your garden, drawing the eye towards them.

As the focal point of your garden, you can plant either berry bushes or fruit trees. Both add diversity and color to your garden. Other alternatives to this can be pear or plum trees.

If you are growing strawberries, think about the fact that you can grow them in hanging containers. Wonder where you could place that?

If you want to add ground cover in your garden, then you can pick any berry bush.

These are just some of the ways in which you can use fruits to bring life into your garden. How would you decorate your garden?

Pollination

Decide on how you would like to arrange your fruits to allow for proper pollination. You might have to ask the salesperson or supplier about the pollination process of the fruits you are buying. Sometimes, you might need to plant many plants of the same variety. In other cases, you have to use different varieties of the same species. Make sure you are well informed before raising these fruits.

Buy Plants, Not Seeds

If you are planning to use seeds to grow your fruit-bearing plants, then I recommend against it. Unless you do not mind waiting. For a long time!

Instead, choose to get the plant itself and start from there. Even when you are purchasing plants, make sure to keep in mind the below tips.

Buy high-quality plants

Do not compromise on quality, because this might affect the yield. If you want to enjoy a delicious and healthy yield, go for plants that have a high grade. Seek the advice of your local supplier in this matter.

Certified and Tested

Always look for proof that the plant you are about to purchase is certified for quality and tested against viruses. You do not need to get a plant in your garden only to realize it has a disease.

Inspect

Make your own inspection into the plant. Remember how you can find out if a plant has pest or diseases? Make sure you take the time to provide a detailed examination of the plant. My tip would first be to ask the supplier about the quality. Get an assurance and then perform your own check. This might also clue you into the honesty of the supplier (in case you want to decide on whether you want to return to the same store).

Planting the Fruit

Once you have decided on what fruits you would like to use for your garden, checked the sizes, and purchased the plant, you can now focus on the process of planting itself.

You might have already guessed this, but your first step should be to prepare the soil for the fruits. You can perform a soil test with a special kit to determine the quality of the soil. This might require a little investment from your side, but I highly recommend getting the kit. This is because once you are sure of the quality of your soil, you can be confident about the growth of your plants. Otherwise, you might spend more in the future trying to solve one problem after another. Once you have completed the soil test, you can send across the sample to a lab for results. If you cannot perform the soil test, then reach out to a local farmer or expert to tell you about the soil. If you are using containers, however, you can get your own soil for the fruit.

Next, you need to know what soil conditions are required for the fruit you want to grow. This means balancing the pH value of the soil. Some fruits might require a slightly acidic soil, while others may prefer content that is more alkaline.

You can also make use of organic fertilizers to prepare your soil. Look for experts who can guide you in that area.

Depth of Soil

This goes without saying, but if you are using a container, then make sure that the depth of the soil is sufficient for the roots of the fruits you are planning to grow. Ensure you arrange for the right container for each fruit-bearer. Trees might need a lot more depth than bushes, so you are ideally looking for a tall raised bed or a large pot.

Select the Time

For fruit-bearing plants, there is one trick that you can use: ensure that you have grown the plant as much as possible before it has to face the climate that causes it stress. This means planting well ahead. For cool-season fruits, a good tactic is to plant them during spring so that they can enjoy a wonderful summer before facing off against the biting winds of the winter.

For warm-season crops, your best bet is during fall or early winter. That way, they can mature enough before the sun becomes the fruit plants' enemy.

Taking Care

Once you have planted your fruits, it is then time to make sure that you take care of them properly. This means that you have to check their water, make sure that the fertilizer has been added, and perform other important actions.

Let us examine each step in detail.

Watering

While you are watering your plants, it is important to remember that adding too much water can drown the plant or even encourage the spread of diseases. In some scenarios, you might have added the right amount of water, but poor drainage does not deplete the used water in time, causing it to accumulate in the soil.

For fruit plants that have shallow roots, you might have to provide more water than is usually necessary. If there is rainfall, then your plants might get more water. However, you should still keep an eye on how much water your plant receives, because with little rain, you might have to pitch in.

I have talked about drip irrigation before, which I feel is perfect for growing your fruits. Here are two reasons why:

1. You can manage the supply of water to the fruits.
2. You can ensure that the fruits receive all the water that you supply to them.

Fertilizing

The main thing to note here is that if you have worked on your soil prior to planting your fruits, then you do not have to worry too much about maintaining the soil. I recommend adding a little fertilizer. However, do make sure that the fertilizer has a balanced pH. This means that it is neither too acidic nor too alkaline.

Mulch

For fruit-bearers, you do not have to worry about mulching too much. This is because fruit bearing plants cast enough shadow to keep weeds at bay.

Pruning

For fruit-bearing plants, get your pruning tools ready; they might require you to attend to them regularly.

Here are two tips to keep in mind when pruning:

- Always make sure that the tools are cleaned properly. Dirty tools might spread diseases to the plants.

- Sharpness is important. Sharp tools cut through the plants in a clean manner. Blunt tools cause damage.

If at any time you feel that the work takes too much of your time, then stop planting more fruit-bearers. The entire process should be fun. While there are times when you might have to put in effort to make certain your plants are growing well, it should not feel like it is adding a lot of stress and difficulty to your life.

One way to approach this problem is to work on a small number of fruit-bearers. From there, you can decide if you would like to add more or add less to the entire arrangement. This helps you avoid a situation where you feel overwhelmed with all the work you are putting in (unless you don't mind, in which case, more is good!).

Herbs

If you look at the official definition for an herb, then it might mention that an herb is any plant that has leaves, flowers, or seeds used for a variety of purposes including flavouring, medicine, perfume or as ornamentals. However, what plants are herbs and which are not is sometimes too confusing to wrap your head around. Regardless, let us look at how we can grow these unique plants and add some spice to your garden!

Planting Herbs

One of the things you might notice about herbs is that there are no rules to follow with these plants. They can adapt to different conditions! Makes your job easier, doesn't it?

However, you do need to focus on the type of herb you are growing. Is it an annual herb or a perennial one? Does it require time to grow or can it grow quickly?

Planting Your Herbs

Unlike fruits, you might need to take special care when planting your herbs. Here are some tips for you to follow:

- Get your trowel ready. Find a nice spot that is covered by sufficient sunlight. Ideally, make sure you have well-drained soil. Once you find the spot, dig a hole into it. The size of the hole should be slightly bigger than the pot carrying the herb. Add compost and organic fertilizer. Seek out the help of local professionals to let you know which one you should use for the purpose.
- Now remove the plant from the pot. Remember never to pull the plant by its leaves. You have to get the plant intact, not with its leaves missing. If that happens, you

don't have a plant anymore. You just have a stem!

- Now examine the stem of the plant. Look for a soil line. This is a line that shows where the soil ends and where you can see the stem clearly. You need to make sure that you plant the herb in the same depth as it had while it was in the pot (using the soil line for reference.)

If you choose to plant the herb in a container, then make sure you follow the below steps:

- Choose a pot that has a big size. You might need it for the roots of the plant.

- Make sure the pot has a drainage hole at the bottom. If it does not have one, then you can create one for it. Be careful while doing so, because any work on the pot might shatter it.

- Finally, fill up the pot with potting soil mix. Make sure that the mix is damp.

- Remove the seedling from the herb you have with you and place it into the pot.

- Start watering it!

Caring for Your Herb

There is not much to do while taking care of herbs. You just have to make sure that you provide them with sufficient sunlight. They need a moderately fertile soil, so you should be good to go in that regard (provided you have utilized a good-quality organic matter). Drainage is important, because you need to make sure that they have enough water to survive but not too much to affect their growth.

Make sure that you do not utilize too much fertilizer. Use fertilizer sparingly. You could ask the supplier for assistance in this matter, as they know how to take care of the herb that you have bought from them.

Vegetables

Now we get to the good part - vegetables! There are so many to choose from. To get your vegetables in order, you must begin with the planning phase.

More Sunlight

When you are growing vegetables, then you need to make sure that you are working with the sun. There should not be obstacles nearby that block out sunlight. The sun not only helps the plant directly but also warms up the soil, keeping both plant and soil healthy. However, there are vegetables that require less sun. In such cases, you simply have to use a covering material such as a mesh or blind.

Planting Methods

You might be using the ground to plant your vegetables, or you might make use of a raised bed. You should approach both these surfaces differently when you are working with vegetables.

Natural Ground

When you are working on natural ground, make sure that the roots of the vegetables have sufficient space to grow. You might encounter sod, which is essentially grass and the soil that it holds. You can remove this layer effectively by using a spade.

If you encounter weeds as well, then make sure you have the right tools to get rid of them. You can always make use of a weeder to rip out weeds that are stubborn.

Raised Beds

With raised beds, you avoid all the work you put into the ground. You already have good drainage inside a raised bed and if you encounter weeds, you can remove them easily. Similar to using natural ground, make sure that you provide enough depth for the roots of the vegetables, depending on the vegetable of course. Use high-quality soil to fill up the raised bed. This is necessary because you might encounter less problems as you work with your vegetables.

Soil Tactics

Whether you prefer to use a natural bed or a raised bed, you need to make sure that the soil is in good condition for the plant.

Here are a couple of tips for you to use:

- When you dig to make space for the roots, you can dig a depth between 8 to 12 inches. This is sufficient for most vegetables. However, you should check again before planting the vegetable to ensure that you are making the right measurements.
- Make sure you add in as much organic fertilizer or matter as possible. You need to make the soil appropriate for the crop, or the vegetable might not even survive a couple of months!

Using Seeds

Gardeners often prefer to get their vegetables as seeds. When you are acquiring your vegetables, think of the time you want to spend on growing the plants, when you would like to harvest the vegetables, how much you are willing to spend, and how much effort you are willing to put into growing your vegetable. Seeds allow you to grow high-quality vegetables, since you will be providing the right growing conditions from the beginning of their life. However, they require more attention and time. Alternatively, you could get starter plants, which require less time to work on. The only drawback is that you have to be content with the quality they come in. You could make sure that you only purchase high-quality plants to ensure that you have a good crop growing in your garden.

Fertilizing Your Vegetable Garden

If you have been working on your garden for a while and it already has sufficient compost and fertilizers, then it is not required for you to add more. However, I still recommend that you add them just so you do not deprive your vegetables of essential nutrients.

When you are working with fertilizers, you typically get instructions on how to use them. Follow those instructions so that you do not use an excessive amount of those fertilizers.

Now all you need to do is take care of your vegetable patch and you will soon be the proud owner of your own collection of vegetables.

- **Scheduling in your Greenhouse**

Greenhouses are great for your summer crops and extending your growing season, but if they are heated, you can grow all year long. However, this isn't particularly cost effective as the cost of heating your greenhouse far outweighs the cost of buying the vegetables you can grow.

Saying that though, even an unheated greenhouse helps you to grow throughout the year and can be very cost effective indeed.

In late winter and early spring, you can start off hardy plants such as cabbage, leeks, lettuce, peas, onions, broad beans, Brussels sprouts and so on. These are then planted out once the weather warms up.

If you do heat your greenhouse, then plants such as tomatoes and peppers can be started off early too.

In mid-spring, your more tender plants are started off, such as pumpkins, zucchini (courgettes), squashes, sweetcorn, French beans and so on. This means that towards late spring they are ready to be planted outside or under glass. At this time of year, you can also buy ready grown pepper and tomato plants for your unheated greenhouse.

As spring progresses and summer begins you can plant your summer plants in their final locations in your greenhouse. Your outdoor crops are hardened off and planted out once the risk of frost has passed, which frees up space in your greenhouse.

If you have space in your greenhouse then towards the end of summer you can sow lettuces, salad leaves, and even baby carrots under glass for a future crop. You can also plant your Christmas potatoes in bags.

In winter time you can sow your broad beans and peas to overwinter before being planted out in spring. Calabrese and French beans can be planted and will mature in the greenhouse. Hardy lettuces will also grow happily in your greenhouse. You can also start any over-winter onions too.

Hardy plants such as kale and chard typically grow well outside during the colder months, but in some areas, they may benefit from being under glass during the extreme cold to ensure you get a good crop.

What you can grow throughout the year in your greenhouse will depend greatly on where in the world you live and how cold it gets. In colder areas with heavy snowfall plants which would be left outside over winter (kale, Brussels sprouts, etc.) will benefit from the protection of the greenhouse. If nothing else this will prevent the snow from damaging the plants.

In warmer areas, the greenhouse will let you start your plants off much early so you can make the most of the growing season.

Unless you are going to heat your greenhouse, you will not be able to get crops such as tomatoes, cucumbers, peppers and chilies during the winter months. Unfortunately, the cost of heating tends to be prohibitive.

Most greenhouse owners will usually only heat their greenhouse enough to prevent frost, which will damage their tender plants. If you grow rare or unusual plants that cannot tolerate colder temperatures, then heating becomes much more expensive but necessary.

The location of your greenhouse plays a big part in how much you need to heat your greenhouse and what you can grow over the winter months.

A greenhouse positioned in a sunny, sheltered area will obviously remain warmer than one, such as mine, which is located in the open. A lean-to greenhouse will be warmer because it benefits from the heat coming through the wall from the house behind.

When it comes to growing all year long, you can be creative. But with so many variables there are no hard and fast rules, so you will have to experiment, seeing what works best in your greenhouse in your area.

- **Greenhouse Environmental Control Systems**

Technology advancement has made owning and running greenhouses simpler than ever before. Options of environmental control help the professional horticulturist or home gardener by automatically adjusting light intensity, humidity, and temperature from a remote location or within the greenhouse. A system of environmental control would enhance plant life within the structure by offering a continually monitored atmosphere, producing a more consistent yield.

You can automate your greenhouse environmental control systems according to your requirements. Greenhouse accessories are pre-set in phases in line with the plant's needs and gardener's choice. These systems present the most significant advantage by providing the facility to control light intensity, adjust humility, adjust the temperature, and monitor the atmosphere, to mention some of the operations.

Accessories Controlled

Cooling systems, heating systems, fogging, systems, misting systems, vents, and fans are all controlled by control systems. The operations could be very straightforward and offer an immense benefit to keeping your greenhouses in ideal shape.

The first phase of execution could be as simple as on/off switch to control fans circulation. By semi-automating a control system using a timing device, a thermostat, or a humidistat, the accessories will run only when necessary; this saves energy and reduces the operating costs. A fully automated system can be controlled through a cell phone, by remote programming system on a PC, or semaphore, saving a considerable amount of time. The fully automated system could be programmed to keep a particular set of conditions for stable plant comfort, putting into consideration the circumstances outside the structure, which might affect the growth of plants.

Advantages of Automated System

Improve Vegetation Quality: Mimicking a colder night temperature, boosts the quality of vegetation as it more directly simulates the natural environment.

Precise humidity and temperature control offer consistent growing conditions to improve production and quality.

Reduce costs of fuel: Lowering the temperature of a greenhouse at night when eighty percent of the heating takes place, lessens the consumption of energy. Centralizing temperature sensors, controlling them with a single unit, prevents cooling and heating systems from running concurrently.

Increase Production: An automated system permits you to focus on growing the plants, not adjusting settings.

Advanced Accessories

Additionally to regular greenhouses accessories, environmental control systems could be programmed to contain advanced elements like remote programming, semaphore, soil sensors, photo and light sensors, drip systems, foggers, and coolers. Your time can now be spent tending to plants instead of messing with their growing environment. Asides the time and cost-effectiveness of the greenhouse control system, Mother Nature will also benefit. Control systems lessen the use of chemicals to aid the growth of plants as the environment is more closely adjusted to produce the perfect condition and reduce energy costs and waste. Here are some of the greenhouses advance accessories:

Greenhouse Benches
These benches will make performing gardening functions stress-free. Whether you're transplanting, pruning, potting, or washing farm produce, benches provide alternatives in space and height utilization. The greenhouse benches are built to complement any existing or new structure. The polyethylene grid-top and galvanized mesh offer both good drainage and air

circulation while giving room for light to pass through to the plants underneath.

Raised Seedling Beds

Seeding beds are another fantastic accessory for greenhouses. Unlike conventional greenhouse benches, they extend growing beyond only pots. A seedling bed is about six inches deep and is supported on four legs. It is often filled with soil for growing plants. Seedling beds are the ideal way to bring a vegetable garden or flower bed straight into the greenhouse. With this, you don't have to get on your knees to plant and tend the garden as the bed is raised.

Gravel Bench

This is specially used to produce moisture. This type of bench is tailored for use in greenhouses or with plants such as orchids. You can use a fixed bench built with a metal top rather than a conventional mesh top. To apply, fill the top of the bench with gravel and water to create a source of moisture for the flowers.

Grow Lights

A greenhouse such as a lean-to with low light and conventional side walls or ceiling wouldn't generate the amount of natural heat needed by specific plants. The addition of grow light is a simple solution. There are also conversion lighting kits. The grow light permits high-pressure sodium light bulb and metal halide to be interchanged. You can rotate the bulbs as the greenhouse advances and plant selections change. These lightings promote new growth and keep plants healthy. There are several forms of grow light in the market nowadays; for example, compact fluorescent produces light and incandescent light. Most of these models may not last long and are dangerous if water comes in contact with their bulbs. I recommend lights featuring high-pressure sodium or metal halide bulbs:

I. High-Pressure Sodium

A high-pressure sodium (HPS) bulb has a yellow glow that isn't as visually pleasing as the blue light metal halide produce. The bulbs can last for twenty-four thousand hours (about five years). HPS bulbs are suggested for greenhouses with enough lighting but want to produce more flowering plants, fruits, or vegetables.

II. Metal Halide

Metal halide bulbs emit a blue tint that mimics real sunlight and can last for twenty thousand hours. Plants become fuller when placed under a metal halide bulb. If you want to elongate daytime growing hours, the ideal option is the metal halide system as you can turn the light on before sunset and again a few hours after sunset.

Heat Mats

When propagating plants or starting seeds, a heat mat will be a useful propagation tool. Plug the waterproof rubber mat into an outlet to generate heat. The heat will produce warm seedling trays that will help to grow plants faster.

Plant Hangers

For you to take advantage of all the available space within your greenhouse, plant hangers will help just in achieving that. You can hang orchid boxes along with hanging flower baskets. You can also hang tomatoes pot if you wish. You can as well install multiple rods in your greenhouse to offer ample space, and hang many baskets from it for an ever-growing plant assortment.

Advanced Ventilation

Eave vents and ridge vents are a crucial part of any functioning greenhouse with a serviceable passive system of ventilation. When the air is not vented, it turns out to be stale, stagnant, and gives room for diseases to breed. To avoid this scenario, you need to install eave vents and ridge vents in your greenhouse. Both systems work similarly but on different parts of the greenhouse. The two units are operable panels of glass-enclosed within a frame separate from the structural framework of the greenhouse. The vent will open by a motor that is dampness-resistance, or manually with the help of a rod operator. It will open to a specific direction and give room for air into the building. Both systems have screens that prevent debris and insects from gaining entrance to the greenhouse.

Ridge Vent

The ridge vent is essential for a greenhouse. Warm air upsurges and builds up at the top of the greenhouse. When you open the ridge vents, the warm air breaks out, and fresh, cold air breaks in. The ridge vents will also enable air circulation. If there is light wind outside, it will get into the structure and help in circulating the air; this will lessen the spread of diseases. If your greenhouse is in use of exhaust fan/intake louvers, the ridge vents will help in getting rid of hot air, so fresh air can go into the building.

Eave Vents

The eave vents are situated on the walls of the structure and would also open. And this allows fresh, cold air into the building. The air would spread through the room and reduce the temperature. It makes the house calmer and helps lessen the emergence of disease in greenhouse plants. You can also add rain sensors to the units so the when rain or snow hits the vents, they close automatically. If you operate an environmental control system in your greenhouse, you can program the ridge vents into your specified system. Without aeration, your greenhouse would become a glass box filled with stagnant air.

Advance Watering Systems

The perfect methods of providing your plants with essential sustenance are watering systems. Watering with the hand can become time-consuming and tedious as your plant collection grows. An automated system of watering is well-suited for plants that require high humid environments. There are several available watering systems. For example, a misting system that sprays a mist and makes the air to be saturated. The water drips are larger than the ones provided by a fogging system.

You can fit all the systems with different nozzle heads and utilize them within the same greenhouse. There are various flow rates for different nozzles so that you can create poles-apart zones. You can use a larger fluid nozzle to make sure seedlings don't dry out, while a small amount of water might be perfect for mature plants. You can program all the systems to work on a timer to control the amount of water that reaches the plants

Drip Misting System
You can use a drip misting system for a slow release of water. This system is perfect if you travel frequently or you have busy schedules. This system is run in such a way that it provides constant water supply to individual plants. You can fill the tubes and rearrange the holes.

Riser Misting System
This system is programmed for the utmost flexibility, and it's mobile. Therefore if you regularly change the layout of your greenhouse, riser misting system will be your best option. You can place this system anywhere

on the bench and move to a different area whenever you like.

Suspended Misting System

These misting systems are lifted above the benches of the greenhouse to give room for unhindered bench space. In the suspended misting system, you will directly insert the nozzles into the water source. The building runs the benches length, and it's suspended from a jack chain that you can position at any height you prefer.

Retractable Hose Reels

Water is unavoidable in any greenhouse. If you don't use a system or watering can, then the probable option is hose. Most gardeners are aware that hose can be bulky and occupy valuable space. When it uses a hose holder, and the unit usually twists and folds under the hose weight. To prevent these, a retractable hose reel that is mounted to a wall or rafter will help. A simple tow of the entire length of the hose retracts unit will provide a neat appearance and prevent tripping hazards. The reel turns left and right, giving maneuverability all through the greenhouse. You can also mount these units outside a greenhouse by attaching them to a garage or home.

Greenhouse Shelving

Shelving options offer additional growing and storage space for any greenhouse type. You can attach a shelf to the rafters in front of glass windows or add it to a solid wall. If there is enough space, you stack shelving on a wall. You can use this shelving for any conventional or glazed building, as they are designed to go with the aesthetics of the environment. You can turn a bay window into a miniature greenhouse by adding shelving. Garden windows usually contain several shelves for growing plants.

Best materials for shelving:

Glass
Glass is conventionally used in garden windows since it gives room for the sun to get to the shelves, and provided that you use saucers under the plants; it requires a minimal level of glass cleaning. The glass shelves would be the perfect artistic match to the façade of the window.

Wood
Wood is another aesthetically attractive option for shelving. I recommend cedar or mahogany since they can endure humidity and moisture. Once you have stained the wood, it will look like a conventional English greenhouse. Using wooden shelves will reduce sun to lower shelves, which is best for shade-loving plants like orchids.

Metal
Metal is solid and allows for the flow of air into the plant's bottom. The aluminum mesh is an excellent option for bonsai that usually demands the movement of air to thrive. Metal won't warp or rust and is a handy option for any greenhouse.

Polyethylene: Polyethylene is almost the same with metal shelving in form and benefits. The main variation is that the former is plastic with reprocessed substance. The polyethylene is black and covers dirt quickly, while metal shelving is silver.

Bench Shelving
The lower bench shelves for greenhouses are handy for plants that flourish in the shade or minimal sun conditions. These benches can be about eighteen

inches deep and position beneath the existing greenhouse benches. Addition of the lower shelf increases the available growing space and provides added storage space for equipment and supplies.

Shelf Supports

The shelving supports could be either a decorative corner or a simple metal bar. Decorative corners are an ideal option when aesthetics matters. You can attach a metal bar from the above or beneath the shelf to create a hanging shelf. They are available in different forms that mimic the traditional structural design and English greenhouse.

- **Greenhouse Cleaning and Maintenance**

Cleaning Your Greenhouse

You will need some routine maintenance to keep it in good condition to grow healthy plants in your greenhouse. You will also prolong your life by looking after your greenhouse and ensuring that it stays beautiful in your garden or allotment.

To help control pests and diseases, you can maintain a weekly cleaning routine and conduct an annual deep cleaning. Sadly, while a greenhouse offers optimal growing conditions for many plants, it is also the perfect environment for many plant-damaging diseases. Greenhouses can fall into disrepair if not held in good condition, and you may be at risk from broken glass, trip hazards, and defective electrical equipment.

Inspect your greenhouse periodically for any broken or damaged glass panes to make sure there is no damage to the frames. Greenhouses in aluminum will need less care than greenhouses in wood that should be treated with a preservative or non-toxic paint. Check for any signs of humidity or rot and flat any rough edges down.

You will need to clean the glass to ensure maximum sunlight can enter your greenhouse. You can use a seal of hot water and wipe it to dry naturally with a sponge. When you find a lot of dirt gathered in the joints, then it should be dislodged by a pressure washer or jet-wash attached to your garden hose, and you can clean it away.

To keep weeds and diseases from spreading that flourish in dry, humid conditions, make sure that you prune and pinch your plants regularly and keep an eye out for fungi, aphids, and mildew. Use an organic pesticide if necessary to remove any unwelcome infestations from your greenhouse.

Turn off any electrical equipment like heaters or irrigation systems until you start a comprehensive cleaner and cover the plug sockets. Unless it is very cold, remove all plants and place them in a protective fleece wrapped outside. Take this opportunity to check for dying leaves from each plant and any other signs that might indicate pests.

Throw out and compost any old growing bags and sweep the river. Wipe the shelf surfaces and spray them with a mild disinfectant. Until planting the plants, wash the windows inside and the brickworks and board.

If you're worried about any electrical equipment, don't try to repair it yourself, but call a qualified professional.

Your greenhouse will be the ideal place for your plants with a little care, as well as making your garden an attractive feature.

Maintaining Your Greenhouse

To keep a greenhouse, the first thing you need to consider is the cost which will depend on several factors. Like I have mentioned before, greenhouses are available in a variety of shapes and sizes. So its maintenance will vary from one garden to another. The information I'm about to discuss will be based on the most economical ways of maintaining your greenhouse to be sure you don't end up emptying your wallet.

Another question to ask is how hard is it to maintain a greenhouse? The same is applicable to every hobby; being a beginner can be a determinant of whether you will find something hard or not. But I can assure you that mastering and following the below tips will make it easy for you to maintain your greenhouse.

Maintain a Constant Temperature in Your Greenhouse

Keeping a steady temperature is one of the most crucial factors in ensuring proper maintenance of your greenhouse. To accomplish this, you can:

- Purchase and make use of readily available monitoring systems. The work of some operations is not limited to monitoring the internal temperature of the greenhouse, but also checks the moisture and acidity of your soil, which are also very important.

- Consider using an evaporative cooling system as this is very popular as it cools the air inside with water. It is evident that most plants grow well in a moist and humid environment; this makes it an ideal choice if you want to maintain a constant temperature. Having a proper cooling system is one of the best and affordable ways of maintaining a greenhouse.

- Ventilation is another crucial factor to consider. Given that greenhouses naturally trap heat from sunlight, the temperature may be drastically increased. And this can be avoided by having proper aeration. You might need to consider installing an air conditioning unit if opening windows and doors proved insufficient. Also, installing airflow fans will help improve circulation. Another good idea is having lots of vents in your greenhouse surroundings.

- Lighting is also an essential factor in maintaining a stable temperature inside the greenhouse. It is necessary when you're growing plants that aren't in season. Apart from light, you may also buy heaters. Some heaters are very easy to use as they are automatically regulated.

Maintaining humidity in a greenhouse

Do not apply excessive water on your plants. If you have puddles of water, the moisture tends to increase. Applying water directly to the soil (not to the leaves) will also help to reduce evaporation.

Maintaining a greenhouse in winter

If you don't buy the idea of high-end heating systems, then the following budget-friendly tips will be of help:

Use bubble wraps. You can purchase horticulture bubble wraps at a nursery. Just remember that the larger bubble holds more light than the smaller one. Also, remember to use thermostat. If your heater already has a thermostat, then that's a plus, since the heater can be set only when needed. By always checking, a good thermostat will help, you will be able to know when a heater is needed and when not. Therefore, it will save you money and resources.

Be sure to place your heater in the right spot, where it would work most effectively. As part of the greenhouse maintenance budget rules, it's best to put electric fan heaters in an open area of the structure. Most preferably, place them in the centre. If your greenhouse is larger, heating the entire area may be costly. In this case, you may divide the structure into smaller spaces so you can decide what area to be heated.

- **Hydroponics in a Greenhouse**

Growers, especially new growers, tend to wonder how true the possibility of growing plants effectively without soil is. Well, it is not only true that it is possible but it is also more popularly practiced than one would usually assume. Growing without soil, which is also called Hydroponics, is a technique of cultivating plants using a prepared nutrient solution.

The idea is based on the fact that all plants generally need only light, air, water, and nutrient to grow healthily. And while the plants grown on soil would struggle to get all these necessities from the soil and the environment, they can be easily provided to them by the grower especially in an enclosed environment such as a greenhouse. The plants can grow anywhere as long as they are supplied with the necessities for their healthy growth.

Hydroponics (growing without soil) is a creative technique that offers people with non-arable lands although interested in gardening the chance to finally have their own garden without having to worry about the poor soil condition in their area because they won't even need to use soil at all.

If you are new to this, you might want to ask how this system works, it is quite simple and we will get right to it now:

How does Hydroponics work?

In this system of gardening, the roots of the plants are dipped inside a nutrient solution contained in a reservoir. The nutrient solution is pre-mixed with all the needed nutrients by the particular plant being cultivated. Using this system makes it easy to plant more in a seemingly limited space in a greenhouse. It also improves the yield at the end of the day, producing healthier products that are free from any form of diseases and pests. There are generally 6 major methods of hydroponic system, these are Aeroponics, Wick Irrigation system, Flood and Drain, Water culture, Nutrient film technique, and Drip system.

Drip system

This is a method of hydroponics which employs the use of drip lines to transfer the nutrient solution directly to the base of the plants regularly. While soil is not used, a growing medium is essential in this method of hydroponics to support the plants. This method is usually used in a large-scale production garden but for it to work effectively, it requires that each plant has its own container and invariably its own drip line. A pump system can be used (with an attached timer for automation) to take water into the drip manifold when needed. The timer is important to avoid flooding the plants and causing more harm than good in the process. A drip system can also be either a recovery system where the excess nutrient solution is recycled or a non-recovery system where the excess nutrient solution is drained off as waste instead.

Nutrient Film Technique

This method of hydroponics is usually used to grow small and quickly growing plants. The growing tray is set at an angle that enables a constant flow of the nutrient solution. The interesting thing about this method of hydroponics is that it doesn't even require a growing medium as the roots of the plants are suspended in the air. The NFT method requires the use of a pump which pumps the nutrient solution into the growing tray and also another pump connected to an air stone to ensure aeration in the nutrient solution.

Water Culture

his method of hydroponics is considered suitable for commercial growers interested in large-scale production because it is cheap. It is a very simple method, if not the simplest of all methods, as the plants are placed in hanging baskets while their roots are suspended in the nutrient solution. Because the roots of the plants are always in the nutrient solution, an air pump is important to supply oxygen for aeration in the reservoir holding the nutrient solution.

Flood and Drain

This method is also called ebb and flow. In this method, the root system of the plants is flooded with nutrient solution intermittently and the supply is usually controlled by a timer. When the timer is off and the pump stops, the nutrient solution flows back down into the reservoir through the overflow tube set as a draining system. A bigger tube should be used as the overflow tube and the grower should also keep in mind that a growing medium is needed to support the roots of the plants in this method of hydroponics.

Wick Irrigation System

The hydroponic wick system is the easiest system to set up because there is no need for electricity or the use of a pump in the system. It's a good choice for growers just starting out with hydroponics although it's not a suitable system for larger plants. The container which holds the plants in this method is placed on the reservoir containing the nutrient solution and a wick is used to suck up the nutrient solution into the growing medium in the container holding the plants.

Aeroponics

This is said to be the most advanced method of hydroponics; it does not require a growing medium as the roots of the plants are merely suspended in the air. The suspended roots are fed by a sprinkling system set up in the nutrient solution and the attached nozzles should be specially designed to deliver the nutrient solution in mist form. It is said that aeroponics gives more yield than other methods of hydroponics, this is probably because aeroponics allows the grower to grow more in a limited space and also because the exposed root system of the plants gives them access to more oxygen and thereby aerates faster and better.

It is important to note that the roots of the plants in aeroponics tend to dry out faster and therefore must be fed with a nutrient solution as often as needed. A timer can be set accordingly to ease up the stress while the grower ensures that there is no power outage or provides a backup power supply in case there is a power failure.

Growing without using soil is best carried out in a greenhouse and while it requires a bit of 'technical know-how', the quality of the result that will be obtained cannot be overemphasized when things are done right.

The right method of hydroponics should be chosen based on the purpose of gardening and the right nutrient solution should be used for the right plant not forgetting the use the right growing medium when the method chosen requires one. All these are important so as to achieve successful soilless cultivation in a greenhouse.

Top Ten Reasons to Grow a Hydroponic Garden

1. Grow indoors all year round–hydroponic gardening is one of the best ways to produce fresh food throughout the year. It is also a great alternative for the cultivation of a number of plants in smaller areas, such as indoors. Electricity costs indoors are typically less than $3 a month, depending on the size of your device. You can also install your hydroponic installation outdoors. (I do that because I have a small house) But you can avoid various environmental problems, such as insects and other pests, like squirrels and birds, which are looking for your delicious veggies too! Heavy rain, strong wind, or excessively hot weather damaging your plants are also not of concern when indoor growing.

2. Grow even more in fewer space-nutrients are directly injected into the plants in the hydroponic garden so that plants can grow closer together. The roots of plants must not fight for water and nutrients. This is possible. For instance, if you wanted to grow plants in the traditional way, you would space the plants in the ground to take enough water and nutrients for them to grow properly. If you wanted to grow 20 lettuce plants in the soil, the area would take around 20 square feet. In a hydroponic setup, 20 plants in an area of only 8 square meters could be grown.

3. Monitor all the growth factors— All the factors, including light, water, and nutrients, can be regulated with a hydroponic system by simply turning a switch on or setting a timer. The PH of the nutrient solution is also controlled. This is much harder with a conventional garden rooted in the dirt. You can not regulate soil quality, for example, without adding expensive back-fill fertilizers with potting soil. You can't control the lighting because it could be cloudy some days. Watering your garden is easy to control, but if you do not have a water well stored, then you may have to water more than

your bill of water, especially if you live in a dry climate. Watering in your garden is easy. The ability to control these factors enables you to make your plants grow faster, healthier, and more bountiful.

4. No weeding-In a hydroponic system, nuisance weeds do not flourish (unless they are planted there) 5. No back-breaking work-because there is no soil, you don't have to work the soil in a hydroponic system. Ideally, a hydroponic system is built up a few feet so that you don't have to get trapped in the garden.

6. Freshwater scarcity–Ocean water can cover more than 70 percent of the surface of the Earth, but thirsting humans rely on limited hydration and agricultural supplies of freshwater. Just 3 percent of all water supplies are projected to be freshwater, mainly found in the Arctic. And these finite supplies are rapidly spoken for, with explosive population growth, especially in poor countries. Hydroponics can help mitigate this issue because many processes recover the solution of nutrients. Hydroponic systems, according to experts, use ten times less water than conventional farming. The use of vapor condensers in greenhouses where hydroponics are used can further reduce this.

7. Poor soil quality-soil is the most widely used plant medium that not only helps provides nutrients and oxygen; it also transmits water and other beneficial microorganisms to its roots. This tried and true development is still commonly used in all large parts of the planet. This same soil, on the other hand, often carries risks for your plant, such as bug infestation, pH, poor drainage, poor water retention, and wear due to soil erosion. Soil infertility causes lower yields and low-quality products due to constant cultivation. Hydroponic cultivation is an attractive option for many producers for these reasons.

8. Hydroponics is an option for people living in an urban environment. In general, residents of apartment buildings have no access to an open area where vegetables can be grown. Often they have a balcony or patio, but due to limited space, only a small number of plants can grow in containers. Hydroponics solves this problem by allowing more plants to be grown in a smaller climate.

9. Less reliance on foreign oil— 60% of all oil imported into the US is used for food production. Whether the oil is used by farmers to grow or truckers to sell it. Our desire to eat demands considerable amounts of oil. Growing food locally through hydroponics would decrease those food miles, maintain more nutrients in the crop, help the environment, minimize the country's dependence on foreign petroleum and build a less central food chain, with a lower risk of widespread disease or terrorism. More and more incidents have occurred nationally. For example, the reminder of fresh spinach cultivated in California due to an E threat. Contamination of bacteria. When one of these food accidents occurs, people who want to know the origin of their food seem to have heightened curiosity. People want local fruits and produce. Seasonal consumption and purchases locally establish a stable local economy and enable everyone to eat better.

10. It's fun–Another reason to grow a hydroponic garden is it is enjoyable and fun. If you like to tinker with things, it could be for you.

- **Potential Problems and How to Overcome Them**

We have already covered everything that you need to know about building a greenhouse, growing plants in your greenhouse, and finding success in doing so. We've talked about all the different ways of planting and all the different tips and tricks that we have for you. Now that we've reached the end, let's look back and talk about some common greenhouse problems that you might face. Problems can pop up in greenhouses no matter how well you treat your plants. Do you not feel bad if any of these problems pop up? Simply look back at this information and figure out how you can solve the issue quickly and effectively. We are going to go over every common greenhouse problem that you might come up against you in your journey of growing a garden inside of a greenhouse. We will look into the problem in detail, who learn why it occurs, and learn how to fix it. Let's get started.

First, let's look into what to do if you get bugs in your greenhouse. Is there something that you would think of dealing with outside? Obviously, you do not want to need to deal with them inside of your greenhouse. The first reason is that you are already in a structure—you should not have to deal with something like bugs. The second reason is if bugs are in your greenhouse, it is not like they're simply going to be like when they are outside. If bugs are in your greenhouse, they probably think that they are there to stay. You will need to do something to get them out of your greenhouse. They are not going to fly away like they were outside.

Let's start by looking into why bugs get into greenhouses. If there is any space that allows bugs to get into your greenhouse—like a crack or hole or even vent or door that was open for a few seconds—bugs can get in. Bugs go inside greenhouses because they know they're filled with plants and because they want to pollinate them. Bugs can also go to clean houses just to simply explore. Other bugs are looking for plants to eat. Obviously, you really do not want these latter bugs in your greenhouse. You definitely do not want your plants getting eaten by anyone except for you.

Next, let's look into some ways that you can prevent bugs from getting into your greenhouse. One of the easiest ways to prevent getting bumped into your greenhouses is to look at the things that you are bringing inside. If you are bringing inside a plant, make sure there are no bugs in it. If you are bringing in new soil, make sure you do the same. Anything that you bring in should be checked to ensure that there are no bugs that could hurt your plants on them.

Another thing that you can do to avoid getting bugs in your greenhouses to make sure that they do not have a way in. Make sure that all cracks and holes are filled. Also, if you have a fence, you could consider putting a screen on them. You can put screens on the windows as well. You can also make sure that when you come in and out of the greenhouse, you do so quickly and you do not leave the door open.

It is also a good idea to not plant anything around the outside of your greenhouse. If you put plants around the outside of your greenhouse, these plants can attract bugs. If you attract bugs to your greenhouse, they will likely know that there are plants inside and they will likely find a way in. You want to keep all of your outdoor plants far away from the greenhouse to avoid this happening.

Now, let's look into what to do if you already have bugs inside of your greenhouse. In an outdoor garden, you might reach for the pesticides. This is not a great idea inside of a greenhouse not only because they are toxic chemicals but because in such a small space they can be a hazard. One helpful way to catch bugs inside of your greenhouse is to use bug traps like tape. You can hang out tape all around in your greenhouse, and it will not affect your plants. It will, however, catch the bugs that you do not want to be there. You could also consider making sure to get rid of anything that will attract bugs. For example, make sure that there is no standing water available in your greenhouse. If your bugs are not attracted to anything inside of your greenhouse, they may leave. If you are really having a hard time with bugs in your greenhouse, you could always ask a professional exterminator for help.

Something that can be problematic is your greenhouses diseases. There are many different things that can cause diseases in your plants. These diseases can come from mold, bacteria, and viruses. Greenhouse diseases can be some things that are hard to beat. Let's look into some ways that you can prevent these diseases from occurring in your greenhouse.

What is the most important thing that you can do to prevent disease in your greenhouses? It is to sanitize. You want to make sure that you sanitize everything after you use it. You will need to sanitize 2, trays, and even shelves. If you do not sanitize your tools, it increases your risk of spreading disease inside of your greenhouse from plant to plant. This is because if one plant had a disease and you used a shovel to scoop it out and throw it away, and then use the same shovel in another plant, the new plant would probably get the disease as well just from being touched with the same shovel. The spread of disease in plants inside of greenhouses is really similar to the spread of disease in humans. If you stay clean, you will have a much better chance of not spreading diseases.

You allow someone to watch your humidity and make sure that you are greenhouse does not get overly humid. If your greenhouse is too humid, mold and fungus are likely to grow on your soil. If these grow in your soil, your plants will get the disease because of them. Mold and fungus can also spread very quickly and easily. It is something that you really want to avoid having in your greenhouse.

When watering your plants, you will want to make sure that the tool does not touch your plant's insurgencies, and you will also want to make sure that the water does not splash while you are watering. If water splashes from one plant to another, it can spread disease. Because of this, you will want to use a tool for watering that does not allow water to splash. You will want to use the tool that has a light spray that soaks into the soil and does not splash at all.

One last thing that you can do to protect your plants from disease is to look at them every day. Walk around your greenhouse and look for signs of disease. Look for things that look out of the ordinary. If you see a plant that does not look healthy, consider taking it out of the greenhouse and quarantining it for a while. This will allow you to tell if the plant is infected with the disease as well as keep it away from other healthy plants to make sure that they do not catch a disease if it has one. With this process, it is helpful to know what plants look like when they are diseased. If the plant has mold or fungus, you will probably be able to tell right away. If it has mold growing in the soil or mushrooms growing in the soil, it means that it has mold or fungus. This is one of the easiest diseases to tell if your plant has. Another sign that your plant has a disease is that it has large, raised brown lumps on its leaves. These lumps typically mean the plant is sick. Plants that seem to be dying even though you are taking great care of them can be diseased as well. Any plant that is showing signs that are not normal should be taken away from your healthy plants just in case a disease is present.

Next, let's look into what to do if a plant is serious. If you see that a plant is diseased, make sure you take it out for greenhouse right away. This will help to make it not infect other pants. Also, you should look at helping it right away—especially if you are able to save your plant when all signs of the disease are gone and bring it back to the greenhouse. If not, at least, you only lost one plant and not your entire greenhouse to a disease.

Diseases in greenhouses are not fun to deal with, you should be able to handle them with success. If you take the necessary precautions to make sure that diseases do not enter your plants and take it seriously when a plant is looking unhealthy, you should have good success in keeping this problem away.

We are going to look into what to do if you look at some plants in your greenhouse and see that their leaves are turning yellow. Yellow leaves are a common occurrence and plants, but they are not a good sign. There's something that you want to deal with and help right away. If you do not help a plant that has yellow leaves, it is very likely that it will die from the cause of the discoloration. There are many different things that can cause yellow leaves in plants, so let's get started in figuring out what they are.

The first thing that can cause yellow leaves in plants is something called moisture stress. Moisture stress is when a plant gets either too little water or too much water. If a plant is not watered often enough, it will have both dry soil and yellow leaves. If a plant is watered too much, it will have wet soil as well as possible mold or fungus growing in it and yellow leaves. It should be pretty easy to tell the difference between these two problems. You will know if you have been watering your plant a lot or if you have forgotten many days in a row. Even if you do not know this information, you will be able to tell by the moisture level in the soil. If your plant has yellow leaves that have too much water or too little water, it is very easy to fix. Simply make sure that you give your plant the accurate amount of water starting at the moment that you notice the yellow leaves. If your plant is under-watered, you can consider giving it a water soak. To do this, you can soak the plant in water in assessing or in a tub for anywhere from a few minutes to a few hours. If your plant is overwatered, consider giving it some period without water. Once it is dry again, however, make sure you water it normally. Do not wait too long to water it again because then it could turn yellow from not being watered enough.

If you find yellow leaves on a plant and you know that you have been giving it the correct amount of water, think about how much light it is getting. If a plant does not get enough light, its leaves can turn yellow. If you have a plant with yellow leaves and you know that it has not gotten enough lately, considering moving it to a location that it will get more sun in. If you do not have a space in your greenhouse available where this plant and get more sun, you will need to give the plant adequate artificial lighting in order to help it survive. This again is an easy fix. If you find a plant with yellow leaves and it needs like, once you give it light its leaves should correct themselves, and it should go back to being a healthy plant.

Another reason why a plant can have yellow leaves is that the temperature for the plant is wrong in the environment that it is in. If your greenhouse is too hot or too cold, the leaves of plants can turn yellow. Most likely, if this is the cause, many plants in your greenhouse will have yellow leaves and not just one. This is because all of the plants are experiencing the same temperature, not just one. That is one good way to tell if yellow leaves are caused by temperature. If a plant in your greenhouse is too hot or too cold, you simply need to fix the temperature in the greenhouse to allow it to go back to normal. Once the plant reaches the temperature that it wants to have, it should fix itself, and its leaves should start growing green instead of yellow. This again is an easy fix if you notice it while the plant is still able to be healthy.

If you believe that the environment for your plant is completely perfect and that you have been wondering it well, the yellow leaves may be caused by something else. The last cause for yellow leaves that we will look into is plant nutrition. If you have been treating your plant perfectly and it still has yellow leaves, this could be the cost. Typically, you will be able to tell when plants are turning yellow from a nutrition problem because the yellow will appear in strange patterns. It will not just be a yellow leaf for half of the yellow leaf. The yellow may come in lines, or it may appear only in the veins of the plant. Usually, when a plant has a nutrition problem, it is either caused by having too much fertilizer in the soil or by the plant having a disease. If you have been treating your plant and have not put too much fertilizer in it, consider separating the plant from the others to make sure that you are not allowing it to spread disease.

Overall, there are a lot of causes that can cause a plant to have yellow leaves. Luckily, most of them are very solvable and very easy to figure out. When you look at your plants and consider what it means and what it is not getting, you will be able to figure out why it is yellow, and you will be able to fix it quickly.

The last issue that we are going to look at is the occurrence of dying plants. Dying plants are typically caused by one of the greenhouse problems that we have already mentioned. They are typically caused by greenhouse problems that go on seeing, however. Because of this, if you keep a good eye on your plans and watch their symptoms, you should not have to deal with dying plants.

If you have plants that have bugs in them, for example, you should be able to notice the bugs right away. Every time you go into the greenhouse, you should see bugs flying around, or you should see bugs crawling on your plants when you inspect them closely. You may even notice that your plants are being eaten by these bugs. These signs are hard to miss. However, if you miss them, you will start to see dying plants in your greenhouse.

Once again, the same holds true the yellow leaves. Yellow leaves usually have easy fixes as we read about just now. However, if you do not notice yellow leaves and you let the plants continue to suffer and not get what they need to survive, you will eventually have dying plants instead. You need to notice your yellow leaves when they are only on a few leaves of the plant. If you notice that your plant is covered in completely yellow leaves, it is probably too late to save.

If you start to have many dying plants in your greenhouse, make sure that you are spending enough time outside with them. Then, look at the common problems that we have already talked about such as bugs, diseases, and yellow leaves, and look at your plants with these in mind. Try to figure out if any of these issues are taking over your greenhouse. If they are, you will know exactly how to solve your dying plant problem. Most likely, the problem will be easy to solve. You just need to see what it is in order to bring it to an end.

Overall, we can see that there are a lot of problems that can go around your greenhouses. Luckily, common greenhouse problems are easy to solve. If you follow the information that you have learned and if you spend enough time in your greenhouse with your plants, you should never have a problem with losing a lot of plants. You should be able to see a problem right away and know how to fix it using the right, appropriate, and efficient methods. We know that this information will help you and that you will be able to have success every time you come upon a problem if you use these tips and tricks.

- **Making Money From Your Greenhouse**

If you have a successful greenhouse that grows beautiful plants and flowers, why not consider making some money from your hobby? You might not have ever thought about your hobby as a profitable business, but if you have at least a little bit of extra time and patience, you can actually make quite a nice income from your greenhouse.

Becoming a Business

One of the first things you should do before you actually start conducting business is become a business. This means getting a business name, typically done through your county clerk's office. Most who start a small business use a Doing Business As or Assumed Name; this means that income from your business is the same as income from any other place. You simply add up your income and subtract your expenses and report the final amount on your tax return at the end of the year.

Unless you plan on opening a retail flower store you probably don't need to collect taxes from your customers as you would be considered a wholesaler. However, if your business grows and you're concerned about your need to collect taxes, you can probably quickly speak to a CPA over the phone and ask. Usually applying for a tax ID is very easy and probably done at your county clerk's office as well.

These certificates - your Assumed Name and tax ID - are typically very affordable, usually less than twenty dollars each. Don't hesitate to call your county clerk's office first if you want to be sure your chosen business name isn't already taken or aren't sure which certificate is right for you. You can probably also check online as many counties have their own website where you can run off the forms you need and can find out the charge.

Once you have your business certificates you can open a commercial checking account at just about any bank and may also want to check to see if you can reserve a website name that is at least close to your business name.

Important: When coming up with a business name you can of course have it a bit whimsical; people often assume a greenhouse or flower shop has a bit of whimsy or creativity. Just make sure that it still sounds professional and is easy to remember and spell so that potential customers can remember it and find it again very easily. For instance, you might want to avoid "Debbie's Total Supply of Flowers and Plants From Her Own Greenhouse to Your Table" since it's incredibly long and wordy, but "Deb's Greenhouse and Flower Supply" is much easier to remember!

Finding Customers

So how to find customers and what type of items should you sell? Here are some things you want to consider.

First, make sure your gardening is reliable and that you can grow enough of an inventory on a regular basis so that your customers won't be disappointed. Being able to produce one flowering lily plant is all well and good, but if you want to actually make money from your business you're going to need to produce beautiful flowers on a regular basis.

This will of course mean being very attentive to your greenhouse and your plants. No one wants to buy their flowers from someone who comes through with deliveries only when they can. Yes, you'll lose some flowers here and there and of course can't always count on how many flowers you can actually grow, but to be successful with your business you're going to need to have a pretty reliable idea of what you can and cannot deliver.

Then you'll need to consider what type of customers you can support with your inventory. Flower shops sometimes have their own greenhouse for their supply and supermarkets may have a floral shop but because of how many flowers they need, they may want to deal only with a large commercial greenhouse facility. However there are many other possibilities when it comes to customers that you can support. For example:

- Do you have any mini markets or corner stores near your home that sell a small quantity of flowers? Even if you don't see them selling flowers now, if you were to talk to the manager or owner of the store you might be able to convince them to carry a small inventory.

- Restaurants sometimes want fresh flowers for their tables. You may be able to speak to a manager about providing carnations or other colorful blooms for their dining area or décor.

- Retirement communities also sometimes have fresh flowers on their dining tables; you may be able to provide these for them on a regular basis.

- Businesses often give flowers to their employees on secretary's day or when someone has had a baby or other occasions. If you're priced cheaper than large, national florists you may be able to provide for local businesses when the occasion calls for it.

- Weddings of course are a big business for many florists. While you may not be ready to supply to very large weddings on a moment's notice, if you spread the word among your friends and relatives you might find that someone you know is interested in working with you, especially if your costs are lower than national florists. Many brides today are looking to save money in any way they can so they may be happy to simply choose from the flowers you have available.

- Your friends and family too may want to see what flowers you have available on special days and occasions. They may check with you for anniversaries, birthdays, and holidays.

Very often getting the word out there among your friends and family and local businesses is all that's needed to get your first order, which in turn can lead to so many other orders down the road!

Some Important Considerations

Before you just run out and start talking to those retirement home managers and restaurant owners, consider some of the following points.

- Consider getting a website even if you don't plan on selling online. A website is actually a great marketing tool because potential customers will often bookmark your site and visit again when they're ready to purchase. A website address is often easier to remember than a phone number, so customers might visit your site looking for your actual contact information. Websites are usually very affordable if you just need a few pages with your contact info and a few photos of your product.

- Most places that purchase flowers from you may expect some type of special packaging. For example, that corner market might be interested in purchasing single blooms that they keep by the cash register for one-at-a-time purchases. However these blooms are usually wrapped in cellophane and may have additional ferns or baby's breath inside. Be prepared with these extra materials and for the wrapping involved; don't just show up with an armful of single blossoms.

- Stores may also expect you to provide the large vase that these flowers are kept in near the register. View this as a marketing opportunity; put a card with your business name and phone number or website address on the front of it.

- Get to know the accessories you need for many of your products. If you're going to provide bridal bouquets, you'll need the little handles they fit into. Boutonnieres for groomsmen usually are attached with a pin. That retirement community may also ask you to provide vases. Shop for wholesale items online so you can purchase these things very cheaply.

- If you're very dedicated about making this greenhouse into a successful business, take a flower arranging class. Putting together bouquets and arrangements is usually part art but part science. Sometimes certain colors or sizes of flowers are just too busy or may look overdone when used together. At the very least, study bouquets you see online and practice some on your own before trying to sell them to a customer.

Another thing you might want to consider about getting customers and selling is to have some marketing material available. At the very least you should have professional business cards made up so that when you call upon potential customers you have something you can leave with them so they have your contact info handy.

You might also be able to make up a flyer or brochure with some featured products. If you can't do this on your own you can easily hire someone with a marketing degree to do this for you; chances are you might even have a friend with some talent that can easily design some business cards or marketing material. Any nearby office supply center can probably print these things out for a very affordable price.

How to set your own prices?

Setting your own price might be a difficult prospect; don't worry, most first-time business owners struggle with the question of what to charge their own customers.

There is no right or wrong answer when it comes to the price you should charge others, just some things to consider to come up with your own answer:

- Remember that when you sell flowers to a store for them to sell to their customer, they're going to expect to mark up the price they pay by at least half over again, and usually twice the amount they've paid. This means that if they charge a customer $1.50 for a single bloom, they expect to pay their supplier (that's you) about 75 cents for that bloom. If you think a customer at a store is going to pay $1.50 for that bloom of course you don't charge your customer that much or otherwise they wouldn't make a profit and won't have any reason to sell your item. Consider the price they need to charge and make sure you're being reasonable as their supplier or wholesaler.

- If you don't incur a lot of costs with your own greenhouse you can pass this savings along to your potential customers and gain more business. Larger greenhouses employ a lot of people and have those labor costs as part of their overhead. If you are working alone or it's just you and your spouse, and don't incur a lot of costs for your greenhouse, then you can sell for a much cheaper price than most.

Another thing to consider is just how much of a profit you really want to earn. If you're working with friends and relatives for a wedding or other occasion then of course it's only right that you be compensated for your work but do you need to make as much of a profit as those larger greenhouses and commercial growers? If you're reasonable about your pricing and what you can provide you may get many more customers in the long run.

Remember too that you'll probably make a few mistakes in the first months of your business and may need to raise your prices down the road; don't worry too much about your decision in this regard since many first-time business owners need to make adjustments to these things as they learn more about running their business.

Conclusion

In the greenhouse, fresh air or air circulation is essential for your gardening and can be supplied in two ways. The air circulation may be adequate if you can locate the greenhouse to take advantage of natural winds and have adequate ventilation openings. By using one or more fans in the greenhouse, ventilation can increase. If the temperature and humidity are allowed to spike throughout the hot summer days, your gardening experience will not be very successful. We need to be tracked so that you know what's going on.

It's a good idea to install a ventilation system in your greenhouse. Plants can wilt under excess heat, so you're going to need a way out into the greenhouse to cycle cool air. This is an emergency measure and can delete any discoveries you have made, but it can save the plants, which is better than starting from scratch. A chest or cabinet that is waterproof is a perfect place to store your equipment in the greenhouse. This will protect them against rust damage and moisture while reducing the need to move in and out of the greenhouse–behavior that will risk the greenhouse's temperature and health.

If you are up to the greenhouse challenge, it is highly recommended that you adopt some kind of reliable strategy. This greenhouse design should be sufficiently detailed to direct the construction phase step-by-step and help make your greenhouse construction project a success. This plan should outline the order you need to build your greenhouse to avoid wasting your time.

CPSIA information can be obtained
at www.ICGtesting.com
Printed in the USA
BVHW061014220321
603175BV00003B/211